PLAYS FROM WOOLLY MAMMOTH

BROADWAY PLAY PUBLISHING INC
56 E 81st St., NY NY 10028-0202
212 772-8334 fax: 212 772-8358
http://www.BroadwayPlayPubl.com

First printing: September 1999
ISBN: 0-88145-159-2

Book design: Marie Donovan
Word processing: Microsoft Word for Windows
Typographic controls: Xerox Ventura Publisher 2.0 PE
Typeface: Palatino
Copy editing: Liam Brosnahan
Printed on recycled acid-free paper and bound in the U S A

CONTENTS

PLAYS FROM WOOLLY MAMMOTH

Edited by Robert Alexander
and Michael Kyrioglou

Howard Shalwitz, Artistic Director
Kevin Moore, Managing Director

Honorary Publishers:

Kenneth W Crow
Jeffrey Cunard
John Mendonca
Sheldon Repp
Karen Schneiderman
Sunny Jung Scully

for Broadway Play Publishing Inc
Christopher Gould

FOREWORD

At the very outset in 1980, I admit I had problems with the name. The Woolly Mammoth Theatre Company! Come on!

For one thing, it raised notions of extinction and that's never a particularly wise tactic when you're starting a theater. The name also seemed to evoke some late-night, drug-fueled gathering in the 1970s. I could just imagine someone glassy-eyed, piping up between puffs on a joint, "Man, do I have a great name for a theater troupe!"

My reservations were unnecessary. In no time flat, Woolly Mammoth proved itself to be the most unusual, daring and all-around unpredictable theater company in Washington. And, believe me, in the 1980s, the city needed it.

If the company's name has long since entered into the local vocabulary (people now talk affectionately of "the Woollies"), it is because the company's vision has prevailed. The plays it has always championed— and done best—are dark, scratchy, outspoken and eager to buck both the status quo and theatrical convention. In Washington, where compromise and double-talk are endemic, the Woollies' theatrical candor was, and is, refreshing. Over the years I covered the theater, I got accustomed to seeing spectators who were angry, indignant, flummoxed and outraged. Bored, I never saw.

Initially, it was customary to say that Woolly Mammoth was Washington's equivalent of Off-Broadway, and then, as Off-Broadway became more and more mainstream, the equivalent of Off-Off-Broadway. But that's too facile. What helps make the company so unique is its proximity to the White House, the Capitol and all those other enduring national symbols. Geographically and physically, it is particularly well situated to probe the myths, realities and delusions of this democracy of ours.

In a way, I suppose, that bizarre name was prophetic in that it signaled a one-of-a-kind theater, determined to shun fashion and go its own way, shaking up the landscape and disrupting the foliage as it went. Washington, a city of consensus, was bound to sit up and take note. It still does.

Read these plays and I think you'll understand why.

David Richards

David Richards, former drama critic of The New York Times *and* The Washington Post, *now writes mystery fiction.*

INTRODUCTION

So what is a "Woolly" play? We started with an anti-realism bias inspired by Brooks and Grotowski, some highfalutin notions about the need to be theatrical (i.e., not like film or T V), and a cranky determination to take risks. And while our rhetoric may have evolved, the basic tenets have remained essentially the same for twenty seasons. In picking plays, we go first and foremost for stylistic invention and edginess, so long as there's a good story in there somewhere. We tend to focus on characters from the margins of the culture rather than the center. We keep asking what we can do on stage that other theaters don't. And we perversely ignore most playwrights that our audience has actually heard of.

It's little wonder that Woolly Mammoth has been described as a suicide mission that we somehow keep surviving. I give credit to Washington's open-minded audiences for embracing our off-center vision and giving us a surprisingly lasting place in the theatrical landscape.

Principles aside, the actual source of Woolly scripts has changed significantly over the years. In the early eighties, the core of our repertoire came from European absurdists like Slawomir Mrozek and Boris Vian, as well as their English-speaking counterparts like N F Simpson, Harold Pinter and Jean Claude van Itallie. In the mid- and late-eighties, the focus shifted toward edgy American writers, with the tone set by Wallace Shawn and Harry Kondoleon. Shawn's MARIE AND BRUCE in 1984 and Kondoleon's CHRISTMAS ON MARS in 1986 established our reputation for neurotic comedy, which has remained an important part of the mix to this day. This accounts for our association with a certain over-the-top acting style— we keep picking plays that won't work any other way.

Despite a smattering of world premieres in our first ten seasons (notably T J Edwards' NEW YORK METS and NATIONAL DEFENSE), it wasn't until 1990 that our focus shifted toward new work. Unquestionably it was three plays by Nicky Silver that put Woolly Mammoth on the new play map. FAT MEN IN SKIRTS (1990), FREE WILL AND WANTON LUST (1993), and THE FOOD CHAIN (1994) have by now had dozens of productions around the globe, and would certainly be included in this volume if they hadn't already been published many times over. But we've had several successes among playwrights premiering more than one work at Woolly, including Drury Pifer, Stanley Rutherford, Amy Freed, and Regina Porter. Their writings go in a wide variety of directions, but never down the middle. In fact, the late nineties have been marked by a certain eclecticism at Woolly Mammoth, as we've shifted away from strictly neurotic plays and sought a greater range of approaches toward off-centeredness.

In selecting plays for this volume, we decided to avoid the greatest hits approach and simply include Woolly's most recent premieres, i.e., the plays that are representative of what we're doing today and most likely to be of current interest to readers and potential producers. The one exception is Amy Freed's THE PSYCHIC LIFE OF SAVAGES, dating back to 1995, which is included because Amy is still one of our core writers, and her more recent Woolly play, FREEDOMLAND, was already published in the South Coast Rep volume in this series.

THE PSYCHIC LIFE OF SAVAGES, Ms Freed's parodic take on the lives of four mid-century poets, is a work of dazzling language and big vision. Like many Woolly scripts, it can be challenging on the printed page, but with the right actors and the right sense of humor, it plays like gangbusters. Surprisingly, the brilliantly original copy-cat poems in the text, which one might think would stop the action, provide tremendous propulsion on stage.

Stanley Rutherford's THE CHINESE ART OF PLACEMENT and Billy Aronson's THE ART ROOM are the newest Woolly scripts, and they sustain our tradition of nutty comedy. THE CHINESE ART OF PLACEMENT may be the best and most fully-rounded play for one actor I've ever come across, both very funny and very moving. It provides a good education on several important topics, including feng shui, party-planning and espionage, and should prove an ideal vehicle for some loopy middle-aged actors. THE ART ROOM is inspired by a neglected Feydeau farce, but transforms and enriches its story through a mental ward setting and some wild flights of linguistic fancy. Fueled by mistaken identities and in-and-out-of-doors shenanigans, it also manages to be incredibly endearing.

The weightier dramas in this volume are Regina Porter's MAN, WOMAN, DINOSAUR and Robert Alexander's THE LAST ORBIT OF BILLY MARS, both of which take place in black family settings with ailing mothers and deceased fathers. Beyond these similarities, however, the two plays are vastly different in style and intent. Ms Porter's graceful, redemptive script unfolds in a mythic rural landscape surrounded on every side by the spirit world. A classic coming-of-age tale, its hero Toochie is trapped in a stultifying existence and finds his way out through courage and love. In Mr Alexander's urban tragedy, on the other hand, the hero Billy Mars is an outsider drawn by his open heart into a web of lies and destructiveness from which there is no escape. Positively Greek in its dramatic compression, this disturbing play represents the darker side of Woolly Mammoth. Both of these impressive dramas have a powerful impact on stage, fueled by soaring language, rich characters, and indelible images.

Christi Stewart-Brown's THE GENE POOL appears to be the most straight-forward play in this collection, but slyly makes its point as much by what it doesn't address as by what it does. Its unspoken intent, and the source of its inspiration and hilarity, is to make a family with two moms seem as utterly natural as a family with a mom and a dad. THE GENE POOL may count as the very first "functional family" play ever produced at Woolly Mammoth.

Most of these plays have already begun to find a life at theaters across America, and we hope the trend will continue. Our most passionate goal at Woolly Mammoth is to develop and promote plays that shove the center of the American theater toward the wild and free side. Sometimes we take this goal real seriously. Mostly we try to have a good time.

Howard Shalwitz, *Artistic Director*

ABOUT WOOLLY MAMMOTH THEATRE COMPANY

Woolly Mammoth Theatre Company is dedicated to developing and producing unconventional new plays that are highly charged emotionally, verbally and intellectually; nurturing superb Washington theater artists; and sponsoring community arts projects that meet pressing needs in the Theatre's metropolitan neighborhood. Through its programs, Woolly Mammoth engages audiences in an energetic exchange of ideas, promotes education and dialogue among diverse people, and acts as a constructive citizen of Washington, DC.

The theater was founded in Washington, DC in 1980 by Howard Shalwitz, Roger M Brady and Linda Reinisch. Mr Shalwitz continues to serve as Artistic Director, with Kevin Moore as Managing Director. The theater is governed by a twenty-two member Board of Directors, run by a full-time staff of nine and employs a fifteen-member acting company and dozens of other theaters artists largely from the Washington area. Since 1987, Woolly Mammoth has been located at 1401 Church Street, NW, in a 132-seat facility along Washington's historic 14th Street corridor. A search for a new, larger home is currently underway.

Woolly Mammoth's programs include a five-play subscription season of new works, second productions, solo performances and avant garde classics; the FOREPLAY developmental reading series; the Woolly Mammoth Theater School, featuring classes for beginning and advanced actors; and the OUTSIDE WOOLLY outreach program providing neighborhood theater workshops for children and adults in partnership with a range of front-line service organizations.

Woolly Mammoth has received nearly a hundred Helen Hayes Award nominations for its productions and sixteen Helen Hayes Awards, including five Charles MacArthur Awards for Outstanding New Play. The OUTSIDE WOOLLY program has been honored with the Washington Post Award for Outstanding Community Service, and Mr Shalwitz has been honored by *Washingtonian* magazine as a "Washingtonian of the Year" in recognition of the theater's contributions to the community.

Woolly Mammoth is a member of the National New Play Network, Theater Communications Group, The League of Washington Theaters and the Cultural Alliance of Greater Washington. The theater's programs are supported by the National Endowment for the Arts and the DC Commission on the Arts and Humanities, and Woolly Mammoth is a participant in the National Theater Artist Residency Program funded by the Pew Charitable Trusts and administered by the Theater Communications Group.

We express our deepest gratitude to Woolly Mammoth's thousands of subscribers, institutional funders, individual donors and board members, whose exceptional generosity makes our work possible.

ACKNOWLEDGMENTS

Robert Alexander's participation as Editor was made possible by the National Theatre Artist Residency Program, funded by the Pew Charitable Trusts and administered by the Theater Communications Group—to whom we are deeply grateful. Thanks also to our Honorary Publishers, all of them past-Presidents of Woolly Mammoth's Board of Directors, without whose support this volume would not have been possible. Special thanks to David Richards for generously providing the Foreword. Thanks to Kip Gould for his leap of faith, and for the edgy new ripple he's brought to play publishing over the past decade. Thanks to all of the Woolly's artists, staff members and others whose dedication helped bring these works to life on stage. Last but not least, thanks to the participating playwrights, and to all Woolly playwrights over the past nineteen seasons.

THE ART ROOM

Billy Aronson

THE ART ROOM
© Copyright 1999 by Billy Aronson

ABOUT THE AUTHOR

Billy Aronson's plays have been honored with publication in *Best American Short Plays 92-93* and a New York Foundation for the Arts grant, and are performed frequently at Ensemble Studio Theater. His play THE ART ROOM premiered at Woolly Mammoth and is published in this volume! His writing for the musical theater includes the original concept and additional lyrics for RENT, and the librettos for a pair of operas commissioned by American Opera Projects, with music by Rusty Magee and Kitty Brazelton. His T V writing includes shows for P B S, Comedy Central, Nickelodeon, M T V, A & E, and Children's Television Workshop. A Yale Drama School graduate and member of Ensemble Studio Theater and the Dramatists Guild, Billy lives in Brooklyn with his wife Lisa Vogel and their children Jake and Anna.

ORIGINAL PRODUCTION

THE ART ROOM premiered at Woolly Mammoth on 24 May 1999. The cast and creative contributors were:

NORMA .... Donise Stevens*
JACKIE .... Jennifer Mendenhall
JON .... Oliver Wadsworth
THOMAS .... Delaney Williams
MADELINE .... Maia DeSanti
ART .... Hugh Nees

Director .... Sara Chazen
Set design .... Robin Stapley
Costume design .... Lynn Steinmetz
Lighting design .... Jay Herzog
Sound design .... Dan Schrader
Properties .... Susan Senita Bradshaw
Stage manager .... Annica Graham

*The role of NORMA was later played by Lynn Steinmetz

THE ART ROOM *Show Sponsors*
Alan Gilburg and Martha Spice
Laurie Kauffman and Hal Rogoff
Sheldon and Barbara Repp

CHARACTERS

NORMA
JACKIE
JON
THOMAS
MADELINE
ART

THE ART ROOM was inspired by Georges Feydeau's TAILLEUR POUR
DAMES.

Thanks to the following people for their help with the development
of THE ART ROOM: Sara Chazen and the cast, designers, and crew of
Woolly's world premiere production; the actors and directors who took
part in readings at M C C, Primary Stages, and in Woolly's ForePlay series;
and Melinda Page Hamilton, William Hill, Thomas Lyons, Dan Maher,
Ellen Mareneck, Sheri Matteo, Jamie Richards, and Chris Smith, who took
part in numerous staged readings at E S T. Thanks also to Beth Blickers,
Carol MacVey, and Howard Shalwitz for their guidance and support,
and to Lisa Vogel for everything.

ACT ONE

(The common room in a mental ward)

(A door leads to the hall. Doors on either side lead to bedrooms. Another door leads to a closet.)

(Chairs are overturned, magazines are scattered.)

(NORMA, in hospital-worker uniform, carrying a tray of medications, sits in a trance.)

NORMA: What the hell was I thinking. I wanted to get out of my depression. So I came to work in a hospital. That's like trying to get rid of your fever by crawling into an oven. Excruciating pain everywhere you look. Cheers you right up. I thought graduate school was depressing. Borrowing twenty thousand dollars to spend your life in a library. No classes. No friends. Nothing to look forward to but going to sleep. I started going to sleep earlier and earlier at night. Then I started going to sleep in the afternoon. Then one morning I just woke up and lay there. Howling. Best years of my life. But this place has made me miss lying in bed howling. I began in the emergency room. Severed limbs. Blood gushing. Internal organs hanging out. That got to be too much of a good thing, so they put me in the geriatric ward. Old men with tubes in their noses kicking and hissing at me and biting at me 'til their toothless gums bled. When the other workers took coffee breaks, I'd take howling breaks. So they moved me here, the one place in the hospital where nobody's in excruciating physical pain: the mental ward. Maybe there's no severed limbs or gushing blood. But compared to this place, the emergency room is a picnic. These people spend their days kicking and hissing at their own thoughts. They fill up their lives with little art projects and inane chores the doctors assign them. Jon checks the other patients for head lice. There hasn't been an outbreak of head lice in a mental ward since the middle ages. But it gives him a reason to get out of bed. Jackie buffs the floor with a sock. All day, every day. But the most pathetic thing is, Jackie and Jon got this idea they're married. They can hardly have a ten-second conversation without one of them going into convulsions. And now it looks like Jon's sleeping around. He's not in his bed, or hers. When Jackie finds out what he's up to, they'll need to bring out the restraints and give her a half-dozen injections. Too bad I won't be in on the fun. After this shift I'm out of here. Freedom. My life has been transformed by a toothpaste commercial. This lady in the ad is invincible because of her smile. All around her cars crash, paints spill, walls fall, but she just walks right through, blue silk scarf fluttering in the breeze, toothy smile sparkling in the sun. In my desperate state the image seemed profound. So I did like the toothpaste lady. Put a bounce in my step. Bought a dozen blue silk scarves. And no matter what, kept smiling. When people asked how I was, instead of telling about my last nightmare, I smiled. Then they smiled. Then they invited their smiling friends to join the fun. Soon the smiling people were piling on. But when the smilers asked about my work, then what. Didn't want to say I provide pathetically inadequate assistance to people in excruciating agony for a degrading salary. So I said I'm applying for a fancy bank job. And I applied for a fancy bank job. And I got a fancy bank job. I'll have clients. Assistants who treat me like a grown-up. A salary. And: A love life. Guy saw me in a bookstore, smiling like an idiot. How could he resist. Totally different from other guys I've been with: He's sane. It's a stretch for me, I know. But it's been such a long dry spell, I'm willing to overlook the fact that he's reliable and fun to be with. He's picking me up this afternoon—it's only our second date—but he's taking me to his house in the country for the weekend. Would have been nice to have made a dent here. Cured people. Ended human suffering as the glorious strains of Tchaikovsky poured down from the firmament. But hey. I'm getting myself out of bed in the morning without howling. A miracle in its own right.

(*During the above, the door on the right opens. Out crawls* JACKIE, *in hospital pajamas, buffing the floor with a sock.*)

NORMA: Morning, Jackie. Chilly out today. Salisbury steak on the dinner menu. Pill time.

(JACKIE *stops moving, starts again.*)

NORMA: Mashed potatoes too. You like mashed potatoes, right? I know I do. Come get your pills.

(JACKIE *stops moving.*)

NORMA: I like that sculpture you made out of all those things you collected. I saw it under your bed. You've got a real eye. A real talent. Me, forget it. Couldn't draw my own face. Jackie.

(JACKIE *says something faintly.*)

NORMA: What's that?

(JACKIE *says something only slightly louder.*)

NORMA: Volume.

JACKIE: D'yuh give Jon his pills?

NORMA: I always give Jon his pills.

JACKIE: Yuh always give Jon pills before yuh give me pills.

NORMA: It's time to take *your* pills.

JACKIE: He take his?

NORMA: Jon gets medication every morning, you know that.

JACKIE: His door's closed.

NORMA: That it is.

JACKIE: Every morning yuh knock on Jon's door. Give Jon pills. Leave door open. Sometimes wide open. Sometimes just a crack. Always open.

NORMA: Well, no one always does everything in the exact same order, Jackie. The important thing is—

(JACKIE lobs her sock at NORMA.)

(NORMA sits there.)

(JACKIE doesn't move. Then she leaps up and embraces NORMA.)

JACKIE: I'm so so sorry.

NORMA: It's one of those days, huh.

(JACKIE takes her pills.)

NORMA: There you go. *(She starts to leave.)* I'll make my rounds.

JACKIE: The thing about Buck was his thumbs.

NORMA: Buck?

JACKIE: Buck.

NORMA: Okay.

JACKIE: Didn't like his thumbs. So I didn't marry'm.

(NORMA waits. JACKIE's silent.)

NORMA: Sounds like you made the right choice. With thumbs like that.

JACKIE: I tried to call him later. But he wouldn't be there.

NORMA: Men.

JACKIE: But the thing is—and, yeah, I do like mashed potatoes—all the parts of somebody's body are with my Jonny's body. The pores. The hairs. The lips, yuh know. And I'm here. This is my body. My body needs to be with what's going on, but it just can't be because I don't got the, the stuff inside me, the ingredients.

NORMA: Jackie.

JACKIE: There's nothing inside me. But it takes up so much space.

(JACKIE holds her chest, gasps for air, crawls into her room, slams the door.)

NORMA: Always nice to be of help.

(There's a banging on the door to the hall. NORMA *lets in* JON, *who is dressed in pajamas, but also wears a necktie. He darts all around the room in a frenzy, taking his medication a little at a time.)*

JON: Everything's a lock. You want to go somewhere, you try the door, but does it open? No. It's a lock. Lock lock lock. Good lock everybody. You got something, lock it up, that's right. Lock lock lock lock lock lock. What is this, the lockazoic era?

NORMA: We lock the doors because—

JON: Norma. Look at me. Norma. I'm cruising now. My feet can just go. Know why, Norma? No locks. This is my feet with no locks. This is my feet with locks. Which is more democratic, huh? Which of the two leading options provides me with the greater possibility to realize my potential as a human citizen? No locks, right?—

NORMA: Better slow down, at this dosage, or your shaking might recur.

JON: Well, we're just going to have to write to somebody about these locks alright. We'll write and write and make them like it. Somebody's going to be very highly written to, oh yes. Intensely written to, that's what they'll be. And if they don't like being written to, having their lockish deeds wiped in their filthy faces, well then, just let them tear down these locks, Mister Gorbachev.

NORMA: The locks are only a problem for patients who go wandering at night.

JON: Did Jackie notice?

NORMA: She noticed.

JON: Noticed what. There was nothing to notice. What the hell was she doing noticing things.

NORMA: She knows you were out.

JON: I wasn't. I was in there the whole time. I'm in there now. Dead asleep. You tried to wake me. Gave up. Felt ashamed. Feared you were losing your wake-up-ability. So you shut the door on this blemish on your record. Slammed it tight. Walked away. Hush hush. But now I'm up and I'm talking, so it's time to come clean.

NORMA: If you leave the room during the night again, they're going to have to start locking you in.

JON: Then how can I see Madeline?

NORMA: Who's Madeline?

JON: New patient in "B" ward. Had a breakdown. Luckily for her.

NORMA: So you're—

JON: Craving this once-in-a-lifetime fantasy human with splendor screaming from her flesh.

NORMA: Ah.

JON: An actress, she is. Smile that makes you float, weep, smash your skull. This thespian has the potential to make me one profoundly contented Jonny.

NORMA: You don't look contented.

JON: Of course I don't look contented now, do I, because I spent the night in a closet, didn't I, because at midnight she was supposed to unlock the door to the ward, but it was locked at midnight and it was locked at twelve thirty-seven and twelve fifty-two and twelve fifty-nine and one and two and three and four and stop thinking what you're thinking you can just shut up, she does want me. She lets me tell her things. Lets me touch her elbow. Lets me give her gum. She's not a good rememberer, that's all. But she's a good wanter, and she wants me to get her, and when I get her I'll be good. So good that she'll feel good. So good that she'll smell good. So good that she'll thrust her trembling fists through the giddy vault of heaven.

NORMA: What about Jackie?

JON: That's not forever. Everybody knows that's not forever. It was never meant to be forever.

NORMA: I think you said it was forever.

JON: It was never forever.

NORMA: Fine.

JON: Jackie's fine. She's great. But she'll always be, you know, just what she is. But I've got that certain, you know, so I could never be contented just— I mean, look at me. I've got all this burning...stuff, to share, to build...with someone else who has the stuff to share to build.

NORMA: Before you get building with the actress, you better explain to Jackie.

JON: Of course of course I'll explain to Jackie, what d'you think I'd creep around like a weasely weasel? No no, I'll sit her down, tell her plain, spell it out.

NORMA: Uh-huh.

JON: "These are my needs, those are your needs, I need to be there, you need to be here, I'm going in this direction, you're going in that direction—"

(JACKIE crawls out. JON freezes up. Pause)

NORMA: I'm going in this direction. (She exits.)

JON: Hey there. Morning. Want a Coke? Coke is life. I saw something on
T V. No, the papers. Big headline. Something about a dog. Smells funny
in here. Oh, I was thinking of the time I threw up. Smelly season, spring.
Used to love kickball. Never liked electricity. Makes your hair stand.
Policeman stood on my hand once. Thumbnail fell off. East-west relations
fell off in the fifties. Eisenhower, my god, that guy was bald. Khrushchev
too. Such power. And such baldness.

(JACKIE *speaks softly*.)

JON: Huh?

(JACKIE *speaks softly*.)

JON: Cat got your tongue? Oh, there's this gigantic—

JACKIE: Where were yuh last night?

JON: There's this gigantic. Thing.

JACKIE: I just lay there. Whole night. Staring at the insides of my eyelids.

JON: Oh, I was going to tell you about this huge platter of—I was in "C"
ward. With Thomas.

(JACKIE *shakes her head*.)

JON: Head lice. Awful case.

JACKIE: Wearing a tie?

JON: I am, thank you, yes. Granddad's. He passed away. We miss him
dearly.

JACKIE: Yuh put on a tie to see Thomas?

JON: I did, because the knot protects my Adam's apple from stray lice, no,
but seriously, when I lean forward the tie hangs out due to gravity, so it
serves to keep me aware of not leaning in too close to the patient, really
though, the tie lends a nice appearance, which tends to elevate the patient's
overall mood.

JACKIE: So why didn't yuh come to bed after?

JON: How the hell could I, what am I, a magician? I got the call, world's
loudest knocking, can't believe you didn't hear it, grabbed my stuff, ran
over, ran back, grabbed my tie, ran back over, and thank God I did, because
by the time I got to "C" ward the nits had blanketed Thomas's scalp. Sticky
eggs on every strand. Tried to coax them with the comb, but they clung. So
I went for my glop. Glopped every follicle. Prayed the glop would take, but
no luck. Thomas reached up to scratch, right through the glop, so I feared
the worst, washed out the glop, scanned the scalp, and that's when I saw it:
live, hatched, gnawing lice. Grabbed my poison pen, rammed the pellets
into the fat face of each lousy louse. Thomas squealed like a pig. Clawed like

a hawk. When he begged me to stop I had half a mind to head out, let nature do its worst, come crawling back to you. But let's not fool ourselves. If those lice took Thomas, they wouldn't stop there. They'd sweep through the ward in a day, the floor in one more, the wing in a week. Soon: not an itchless head in the house. Ever-mindful of the masses, I summoned my last full measure of devotion, wrestled Thomas to the turf, gripped the poison pen in my throbbing palm, and crushed every last one of the wee wiggly bastards. Round about dawn the scalp was still. Groggy but gratified, I hobbled on home. If Thomas gets up before tomorrow, I'll be shocked.

(THOMAS *enters.* JON's *body begins shaking.*)

THOMAS: Hi hi, everybody.

JON: Thomas. Get back in bed. You're exhausted.

THOMAS: I feel really really good, because—

JON: You look disgusting, and no wonder.

THOMAS: Oh no no, I—

JON: You're wiped out. Dead.

THOMAS: He just makes me laugh and laugh.

JON: You weren't laughing last night.

THOMAS: Oh yes I was, because, oh I can't wait to tell you—

JON: You came to thank me.

THOMAS: No no, I want to—

JON: Oh I remember now, I told you to come back for the follow-up.

(JON *checks* THOMAS's *head.*)

THOMAS: I really really can't wait to tell you about this dream.

JON: This won't hurt as much as last night, when I rushed over in the middle of the night—

THOMAS: You shouldn't wink at people if they're not winking at you. Ouch.

JON: Sorry, but I've got to crush and crush the corpses, crush, crush.

THOMAS: You didn't see me last night, silly. Jon is a silly person.

(JACKIE *throws herself against a wall, goes out the door to the hall.* JON's *body stops shaking.*)

JON: She's going to call her mother. Why the fuck did you have to show up.

THOMAS: Because I really really need to tell you—

JON: Wipe your face.

THOMAS: —about this dream I had.

JON: I've got to sleep.

THOMAS: Oh, but what I have to say will be really really good for you, because the dream made me so so happy that I woke up and thought how can I help all my friends and you're my best friend in the world, because I really like you.

JON: Please go far away?

THOMAS: So I thought the best way I could help was, since I get to be in charge of all the keys to the whole sixth floor—

JON: The extra copies of the spare keys, that no human has ever actually needed.

THOMAS: I thought, since some of the times nobody uses those rooms, I could lend the keys to my friends.

JON: Why.

THOMAS: So, like, if you didn't want to check people's heads in their rooms or right here, you could use a room on the sixth floor like a real office. And Jackie could buff up there too, just like a real cleaning lady, she could buff the ladies' room, the men's room—no, she couldn't do that—

JON: Your idea is moronic, which is a big step up for you since you're an idiot.

THOMAS: You like it?

JON: If by like you mean hate, yes. Now that you've told me what you came here to tell me—

THOMAS: Oh no no, I came here mainly to tell you about my dream.

JON: I said—

THOMAS: I was sinking into the mud—

JON: I'm tired.

THOMAS: There was mud all around me—

JON: Shut up.

THOMAS: I was sinking down.

JON: Shut up.

THOMAS: I was stuck there.

JON: Shut. The.

THOMAS: I was sinking in the mud, when all of a sudden—

JON: Can't you understand? I do not want to hear your voice.

THOMAS: (Whispers) I was sinking in the mud—

JON: Oh God, look at the time. I just realized there's a guy coming down to get checked.

THOMAS: Who?

JON: A new patient.

THOMAS: I really like new patients.

JON: Nobody likes this guy. He's unlikable.

THOMAS: What's his name?

JON: Boring. That's what they call him, and is he ever. Goes on and on.

THOMAS: Like me?

JON: Worse. He'd bore even you. So run.

THOMAS: But I really really want to tell you my dream now.

JON: And I really really wanted to hear it too. Oh well.

THOMAS: Oh well.

JON: Oh well.

THOMAS: Hey, you want to hear a really good idea?

JON: No.

THOMAS: I'll stay in your bedroom for five minutes while you're checking Boring's head, and then I'll come out and you can tell Boring, "Oh look, it's this really boring guy, I just remembered I have to check his head," and then you'll be all free so you can hear my dream. Have fun with Boring. Tee-hee.

(THOMAS *goes into* JON's *bedroom.*)

JON: My room has been occupied by an idiot.

(JON *lies down on a table and closes his eyes.* JACKIE *returns.*)

JACKIE: I'm not the problem, you're the problem.

JON: Your mother's coaching is the problem.

JACKIE: I do not have to be remained in the presence of by someone who is stepping on me viciously at all times.

JON: Jackie.

JACKIE: I would like you to dis-inhabit this area. That's just it. This chair, those chairs, the magazines, and all other property in this half. That's just what I'm saying.

JON: Jack.

JACKIE: Please remove your entire body from the air that is touching me. I do not wish to be in an atmosphere that contains you, things you see, the sight of you, or the sound.

JON: You're not going to trust Thomas's memory against my word—

JACKIE: *(Silent scream)*

JON: You really didn't hear the knocking?

JACKIE: *(Silent scream)*

JON: You're obviously upset.

JACKIE: I do not wish to have a liar so near my teeth. Stop from touching me now. Stop. Get.

JON: What's this really about.

JACKIE: These.

(She takes pieces of wrapped chewing gum from her pajamas and throws them at him. JON's body starts shaking.)

JACKIE: You don't chew gum.

JON: Great. You go through my things. They're not my things. Yes, they are. But not in the way—that does it. Day after day I go out, touching heads that might be crawling, and you're going to tell me I can't even test options, for protecting my fingers, new methods, such as gum wrappers. *(His body stops shaking.)*

(JACKIE shakes her head.)

JON: Look at these fingers. What are they covered with? Hairs. What do lice get into? Hairs.

(JACKIE shakes her head.)

JON: What would you suggest I use? Dish gloves? Bulky, sopping—

JACKIE: Yuh could use hospital gloves.

JON: And deprive my patients of the minty scent?

(JACKIE hisses at him, covers her face.)

JON: Your mother did this to you. She hated me before she met me. You're trying to reason. Right? What's reasonable about hating someone first, then knowing them second?

JACKIE: I'm scared.

JON: Yes, you're scared, your mother knows you're scared, and she uses that to make you more scared. Don't be scared.

JACKIE: I will.

JON: Isn't it better not to be scared?

JACKIE: No.

JON: You know it's better not to be scared.

JACKIE: No.

JON: You know it's better not to be scared.

JACKIE: Yeah.

JON: Then listen to me, don't be scared. Because you know how I feel.

JACKIE: No.

JON: You don't know how I feel?

JACKIE: No.

JON: You don't know how I feel? After all this time? Look at me. You really don't know how I feel? Should I scream? Should I run around? This is me. You know me. You know how I feel. I'll jump. Do you want me to jump, because I will. My whole body is about to jump. Look at me.

(JON embraces JACKIE. THOMAS comes out.)

THOMAS: That's Jackie. That's not Boring. Jon said you were Boring, Jackie, but you're not.

JON: I need to be alone with my Jackie.

(JACKIE hugs JON then freezes up.)

JACKIE: Too much people. Got to hibernate.

(JACKIE goes into her room, closes the door.)

JON: She's the best. But I've found someone who's more best, so I need one of those rooms you were talking about on the sixth floor.

THOMAS: Oh good—oh, you can use the art room, because it's just like a real doctor's office, because it's got pretty paintings everywhere.

JON: Art...will keep my... *(Weird laugh)* ...patient...loose *(Weird laugh)* ...as I...operate *(Weird laugh)*.

THOMAS: See how really happy you are? And it's all because of this dream I had that—

JON: Tell me as I inspect my new office.

(They start out the door but hurry right back in. JON's body shakes.)

JON: Madeline's coming. Get into my room.

THOMAS: I just was in your room.

JON: Get there. Get somewhere. Get here.

(JON *shoves* THOMAS *into the closet, sits, picks up magazines, pretends to read, stops shaking.)*

(MADELINE *enters.)*

THOMAS: *(From inside closet)* Can I tell you my dream from here?

JON: If you shut up until she goes, you can tell me your entire dream eleven times.

THOMAS: *(From inside closet)* I really really can't wait.

MAD: I had the nicest walk over. The hall was open. The walls were still. The echoes steered clear of the shadows. But best of all was the light. It didn't buzz. Didn't pinch. Just washed right off my skin.

JON: It's great light for magazine reading, I can tell you that. Read read read, that's me. Suck the words right off the page.

MAD: I didn't know my husband was going to stay over last night.

(JON *doesn't look up.)*

MAD: He kept saying he was about to go home.

(JON *doesn't look up.)*

MAD: He's still in the building, so I told him I was coming to have my head checked for lice.

JON: Spearmint?

(He offers gum, she takes.)

(She chews, he paces. She dozes, he creeps close. She jerks awake, he resumes pacing. She spits, he sits.)

JON: There's more where that came from.

MAD: I'm sorry if you waited for me last night—

JON: No, I'm sorry, because I'm the one who couldn't make it. Up all night with my magazines. Got way behind. *(Reads)* "Frequent Death. Massive Slide. President Pushes Congress." The nerve.

MAD: But doesn't it make you dizzy?

JON: Sure. What.

MAD: The magazines have a story. It comes to life. It's about your world. But you're not in it.

JON: Oh yeah.

MAD: And then suddenly you show up in there. Your face is in that world. But you're not controlling it. It's your innermost soul, but it's all an act. Then your phone starts ringing.

JON: Oh yeah.

MAD: Everybody's got comments.

JON: Exactly.

MAD: It's all out of control.

JON: You got that right.

MAD: Everybody thinks something about you. Feels something about you. But you don't know what.

JON: Yup.

MAD: Your life is an image. That you never meant. And you're dead.

(Pause)

JON: If I had a nickel for every time that happened to me.

MAD: Are you mocking me?

JON: No no oh no no, if you think, let me tell you, the reason I started, what first drew me to magazines, was just that kind of baloney. These eyes are trained weapons. They don't just brush the surface. They plunge the depths. Filter the bad. Grope for the good. When they find it, they yank it out. Into the air. Into the light where it can sizzle and bulge.

MAD: I don't think we have the same idea of a nice day.

JON: Try me.

MAD: Soft light. Soft breeze. Everybody just moves. Everybody just lives. Everybody just looks straight ahead.

JON: I'm there.

MAD: The exact opposite of a sideshow. You know sideshows, right? Clowns poking. Beasts sniffing. Crowds shrieking. Dads yelling.

JON: Sideshows suck.

MAD: You won't...tell anyone...the things I say?

JON: Never.

MAD: You're very supportive.

JON: I like supporting you.

MAD: Being supported lets me get closer to opening up.

JON: I want you to open up.

MAD: I'd like to open, sometime.

JON: You can't open here.

MAD: Why?

JON: Too open. So I've secured a key to the art room.

MAD: Oh.

JON: Meet me there after lunch.

MAD: What's there?

JON: Art. Me. Space for supporting.

MAD: After lunch...

JON: Tons of support. Tons of gum. You'll open and open and chew and chew and—

(MADELINE *collapses into sleep.*)

JON: Uhh...

(*He touches her shoulder, she wakes.*)

MAD: Sorry. New dosage. Mind if I doze?

(*She leans on him and closes her eyes.*)

ART: (*From down the hall*) Maddy?

MAD: (*Eyes closed*) My husband.

(JON's *body shakes.*)

JON: No meet husband. (*Shaking* MADELINE) Make husband go.

(JACKIE *opens her door, sees* JON *shaking* MADELINE, *closes her door.*)

(JON *darts around, looking for a hiding place.*)

MAD: (*Jerking awake*) If he comes and you're not here, what will I say?

ART: (*Getting nearer*) Maddy?

JON: Can't think. Must flee.

(JON *crawls around in circles.*)

(MADELINE *looks for a hiding place, opens the closet.*)

THOMAS: I was sinking into the mud, when—

(*She closes the closet door and hides behind a table.*)

(ART *enters speaking alternately into a cell phone and a small tape recorder.*)

ART: (*To phone*) We're very shaky. Unload debt. Downsize dead weight. Scoop up a silent partner. (*To tape*) Press Bob for a merger. (*To phone*) Rear end the raiders before they screw us. Right. Right. Right. Right.

(JON *crawls out the door into the hall.* MADELINE *comes out from behind a table.*)

ART: I thought you were getting your head checked.

MAD: All done. He had to step out.

ART: Will you be okay?

MAD: Will you be okay.

ART: Drowsy?

MAD: No.

ART: Dizzy? Ringing? How your bones.

MAD: The dosage is fine.

ART: *(To tape)* The window in the basement.

MAD: Don't forget the heater.

ART: How do I get open the thing?

MAD: The heater doesn't have a thing.

ART: The shiny thing. Near the tube. In the box.

MAD: You. Don't. Hear. My. Words.

ART: With the rusty edges. The little flame.

MAD: God.

ART: Hanging open. Covered with cobwebs. Gushing with sickening fumes, it's a thing.

MAD: There is no thing.

ART: *(To tape)* Cat food. *(To* MAD*)* I took care of the forms.

MAD: Drain the plants.

ART: *(To tape)* Plant closings. *(To* MAD*)* You'll be okay?

MAD: The people like me.

ART: Of course they like you. Everybody likes you.

MAD: Are you mocking me?

(They stand there.)

ART: I'll be here Tuesday. First thing. What kind of flowers do you want? *(To tape)* Have Elaine check the deductible.

MAD: Everything's ugly falling out of me.

*(*ART *hugs her. She doesn't respond.)*

ART: *(To tape)* Frozen holdings.

MAD: What time's your plane?

ART: My plane. What a weekend. Wall to wall meetings right through Monday.

MAD: You don't want to have a baby.

ART: I'm trying to build a life worth sharing with another life so you won't have to give up your life.

MAD: What life?

ART: *(To tape)* Have a baby.

MAD: Remember the plumber.

ART: I'll be out but I'll leave the keys with the Smiths.

MAD: That's not fair. The Smiths will have to stay in so you can go out. It's our plumbing that's messed up. There's nothing wrong with the Smiths' plumbing. So you should be the one to stay in. Is the world your colony?

ART: No the world is not my colony. *(To tape)* Invest in the islands.

MAD: What if...I don't know.

ART: What? What?

MAD: I. Don't. Know.

(ART spies gum wrapper.)

ART: Has someone been buying you gum?

MAD: You don't believe I can buy my own gum?

ART: Anything is possible.

MAD: I'll walk you to the lobby.

ART: I was going to have my scalp checked.

MAD: I told you he stepped out. People don't just appear because you want them.

ART: I'll give him a minute.

MAD: I need to get back.

(MADELINE moves to hug ART, but when ART moves to hug her she goes.)

ART: *(To tape)* Sitting ducks have sore butts.

(THOMAS comes out of the closet.)

ART: Oh, there you are.

THOMAS: Oh, here I really am.

ART: I wonder if you'd do me a favor and take a look at my scalp.

THOMAS: Only if I can tell you my dream.

ART: You're like my dentist.

(THOMAS rubs ART's head.)

THOMAS: I was sinking into the mud.

ART: *(To phone)* Cancel my eleven and tell my one o'clock I'm running behind.

THOMAS: I was sinking into the mud.

ART: *(To phone)* Have her meet me where my eleven was supposed to be. I'll call her myself.

THOMAS: I was sinking into the mud and—

ART: *(To* THOMAS*)* The problem started last night when I fell asleep in the chair in my wife's room. The back of my head was resting on the chair, there was no protective cover.

THOMAS: I was sinking into the mud.

ART: When I woke in the middle of the night I felt a little ping. Figured I was dreaming. But then I woke up scratching, both hands, full force. The more I scratched the more it itched, 'til I was on fire, infested—The back of my head was a foreign object that scared the shit out of me. I tried to rip the whole thing off. Hurl it out the window.

THOMAS: I was sinking into the mud, when all of a sudden, down from the sky came a sparkling—

ART: *(To phone)* It's me. You're not there. I can't wait to see you. Call my office for directions. *(To tape)* What am I doing. *(To* THOMAS*)* What am I doing.

THOMAS: I was sinking into the mud. I couldn't breathe. Then down from the sky came a great big—

ART: Maddy. *(He runs out.)*

THOMAS: *(To nobody)* I was sinking into the. When down from the. *(He sits.)* Telling a dream to yourself just isn't good. You've just got to tell it to somebody who's really not you.

*(*NORMA *enters with a suitcase.)*

NORMA: Are you going to have a nice weekend for me, Thomas?

THOMAS: Oh, I had this really really good dream I just can't wait to tell you.

NORMA: I have to head out now.

THOMAS: O K, O K, but then I get to tell you Monday, promise?

NORMA: Actually, I won't be here Monday. I'm going...on a vacation.

THOMAS: But I don't want you to go on a vacation.

NORMA: Well, I need to.

THOMAS: But who will take care of me?

NORMA: Other people take care of you all the time.

THOMAS: But not like you.

NORMA: Better than me.

THOMAS: But everybody else wipes me in a hurry, and it really hurts.

NORMA: You should tell them to wipe you more slowly.

THOMAS: I do, but they just keep wiping in a hurry. When it comes to wiping, you're just the better one.

NORMA: You can tell me your dream.

THOMAS: Well, I was sinking into the mud. It was sucking me down. I could hardly breathe. I was stuck there. Then down from the sky there came this sparkling bubble. And then the bubble popped and it turned right into a princess. And she was really really pretty. And she had a really pretty face. And she waved her wand. And it touched my nose. And the sky got all pretty colors. And white birds flew out. And all the mud disappeared. And I was standing there. And I was looking really clean. And I could do all these things with my arms. And so she said let's get married. And we got married and I was really really happy.

NORMA: I like your dream.

THOMAS: I liked it too, so when I woke up I drew a picture of my beautiful princess and just stared and stared. And this is really weird: I kind of knew the face, even though I never saw it before. Do you think I ever really will find someone to marry me?

NORMA: Well, it's never easy.

THOMAS: I would be really really nice to her. All she would have to do is cook me meals two times a day or just one time and wipe my face really slowly. She wouldn't have to stay with me every minute. She could go out every night. She could gossip with her friends. I wouldn't care if she was a great big gossip. I would just want someone to be mine and that would be so nice. Why are you crying?

(NORMA *covers her face.*)

(*Unseen by these two,* JACKIE *crawls out from her bedroom, holding her sculpture made of found objects.*)

(*She reaches into the sculpture, pulls out a knife, rises to her feet, moves towards the door, knife drawn.*)

END OF ACT ONE

ACT TWO

Scene One

(We're in the art room.)

(Door leads to hall. Doors on sides lead to supply closets.)

(The room is cluttered with easels that display patients' paintings, the creations of tormented minds. There are also sculptures, some of which are covered.)

(JON charges in circles.)

JON: I'll be going and going, the earth will shake, 'til my head rips the skies and the gods flood the trees and all faces sprout wings and to breathe is to scream is to fly. *(He checks his pocket for gum.)* Spearmint. *(He smooths the shirt of his pajamas.)* Dressed to kill. *(He checks the lock, jiggles it furiously.)* Doesn't lock. Of course. Why else would they give Thomas the keys. *(He rages at the door.)* Muh duh buh guh. *(He paces, stops.)* *(Pointing to his hand)* You: Assume her shoulder. Win its trust. Clear a path straight across her back. You: *(Pointing to his leg)* Inch over. Make contact. But subtle. Subtle, you hear me? Don't make me pull you aside. You: *(Pointing to his tongue)* Luhl luhl luhl. You: *(Pointing to his crotch)* Clean slate. Just be yourself. Feel the music, gain momentum, think big. *(Pointing to his head)* You: You're going to see some things. On her body. But just let them stand for what they are. Don't start comparing them to things that have nothing to do with the matter at hand. Just stay right in there with the action, unless something itches, then back off, just enough to get perspective, and if anything starts to twitch just leave it be, and if anything starts to run just let it go. *(To a sculpture)* Shut up. *(He paces.)* Dry run. *(He mimes opening the door, speaking to someone, seating her, putting his arm around her, licking her.)*

(MADELINE comes in. JON jerks around, begins shaking.)

JON: I was just fuxing up. Fixing up. *(He pretends to straighten up, props an easel against the door, then another, and another, and another, forming a barricade.)*

MAD: Why are you propping easels against the door?

JON: Tax purposes.

MAD: On the tenth and eleventh stairs my head was bunching up, but on the top step the shadows let go and my last three years didn't matter.

JON: Spearmint?

(She chews. He watches.)

MAD: An art room. Like high school...

(As MADELINE *speaks* JON *tries to touch her shoulder, but his hand shakes so violently he has to keep pulling it back.)*

MAD: Your heart is so open. Every song seeps into your soul. Saving seats. Sharing sodas. Passing notes. Screaming it's over. Sobbing you're sorry. Strolling through snow as the world slips from one majestic masterpiece to the next. Why are you nervous?

JON: Ozone layer.

MAD: Your arm is shaking.

JON: Right, because I lift weights, so the massive engines of ligamentation tend to shift into overdrive and vibratitillate.

MAD: My husband's still around.

*(*JON *springs up and runs in circles.)*

MAD: I told him I had art therapy, but he might peek in.

JON: Muh duh...

MAD: You have no right to be angry at me.

JON: Not angry. Feel great.

MAD: Are you nervous because you care....

JON: ...buh guh...

MAD: ...for me? You've got a soft spot.

JON: ...It sure is.

MAD: I think...I'm ready to open up.

JON: With your husband down the hall?

MAD: Sit.

*(*JON *sits, shakes.)*

MAD: I'm not here now. I've been dislodged. What happened was, I did a toothpaste commercial. Let them borrow my being and that was it. One wrong turn, you know? You're not careful and they divvy you right up. Bits of me are scattered all over the airwaves. How can I act, share my voice, present myself honestly, when there's nothing quite left of me, except this residue with an odor, and a kind of um, what's it called, "loneliness-that-you-can-taste?"

*(*JON *shrugs.)*

MAD: When your mouth is moving but your words are coming from outside the room?

(JON *shrugs.*)

MAD: You know, "Dizziness strikes between syllables"?

(JON *shrugs.*)

MAD: Particles of me still gather near this flesh, but I can't make them settle. See? *(Exposing her skin)* Do you see any of Madeline?

JON: Uh, yes?

MAD: I think you're wrong. I think I'm something in that painting. Do you see me there?

JON: No?

MAD: You really see *me* here?

JON: Oh yeah.

MAD: I think you're right, my self is settling in. Then grab it, quick, before it slips away. I said: Take me by the skin.

JON: Uhh.

MAD: Is Madeline in your hands?

JON: *(Choked with horror)* It would seem so.

MAD: Hold tight, it's a balancing act, she can't settle, the flesh is on crooked. If I could just slide the face into place on my skull, I'd have Madeline for you. *(She tugs the flesh on her face.)*

JON: Oh, don't bother.

ART: *(Outside)* Maddy?

MAD: Keep grabbing me by the skin.

JON: Can I take a rain check?

MAD: Don't let go, I'll fly apart.

JON: Rain check. Rain check.

(The door flies open, knocking easels over, as ART enters.)

(JON leaps to his feet, drags along MAD—who holds his hand on her flesh—to the easel, where he pretends to be an art therapist.)

JON: *(To ART)* Jacques I am Jacques the art therapist, yes I am dressed like patient, yes I maintain close bond with patient, for your wife she must heal, she must paint, she must take brush, take aim, and then attack attack attack attack.

ART: *(To* MADELINE*)* This guy— *(To phone)* Hold on *(To* MAD*)* —is helping you?

*(*JON *guides* MADELINE'*s brush-holding hand so that she keeps painting.)*

MAD: People in the arts are human.

ART: *(To* MAD*)* Why do you think I don't think people in the arts are human? *(To phone)* One sec.

JON: *(Re* MAD'*s painting)* No no.

MAD: Because you're looking at him like you looked at my brother.

JON: No no no no.

ART: *(To* MAD*)* I like your brother.

JON: No, that is not you that is not true.

MAD: When my brother wanted to major in film, you said he needed a vacation.

JON: You must dig deeper, deeper, deeeeeeeep.

ART: *(To phone)* I'm all yours. *(To* MAD*)* I don't need a vacation.

JON: That is shit.

MAD: Who said you need a vacation?

ART: *(To phone)* Not you. *(To* MAD*)* I'm not taking a vacation.

JON: Shit. Shit.

MAD: You're taking a vacation?

JON: Shit shit shit shit shit.

ART: *(To* MAD*)* I'm not taking a vacation. *(To phone)* Hold on. *(To* MAD*)* I'm all yours.

JON:
(Moving MAD'*s hand and brush furiously across the easel)*
There. There it is.
Yes. That is you.
True you. True
beauty. True truth.
True youth. Yes.
Yes. Yes. Yes Yes
Yes yes *oui oui oui*
oui oui oui yes yes
yes yes yes.

MAD:
You *are* taking a vacation.
ART:
(To phone) I'm not taking a vacation. *(To* MAD*)* I'm not having this conversation. I'm heading out to catch my plane, and I'm not stopping for anything—

ART: —except to ask your doctor about this art teacher. *(He exits.)*

JON: I'm a dead man.

MAD: Could he be?...leaving me behind?

(JON darts around, stacks easels against the door.)

MAD: I should ask him. Or not. I should grab him. Or not. I should check if the locks have been changed. Am I homeless? *(She tugs the flesh on her face violently then starts to drift into sleep.)*

JON: *(Stops stacking)* What am I doing. I've got to get you out of here.

MAD: I need you to hold me. And watch over me. As I sleep. *(She tumbles onto JON, asleep.)*

JON: No sleep. *(Shaking her)* As long as you're here, he'll come back again and again and a—

(THOMAS enters, knocking over easels.)

THOMAS: It's your landy-lord.

JON: Idiot.

THOMAS: How's my really best tenant?

JON: You gave me a room that doesn't lock, you drooling moron.

THOMAS: Since I've been a landy-lord filling up my castle, I really think my princess with the white birdies is on her way...

JON: I'm going to hell and he's going to kindergarten.

THOMAS: ...so I'm going to paint the halls all happy colors.

JON: First help me get Madeline out—No, go keep Jackie downstairs.

THOMAS: But I told Jackie to come *upstairs* to give your new office a scrubby.

JON: You retard. With Madeline asleep on my lap I can't be seen by—

(JACKIE enters. JON pretends to be checking MADELINE's scalp.)

JON: Jackie. Sedate, huh—Not "it's a date"—She's sedate, it's not a date, just wrapping up—gum wrappers? *(Stuffing his fingers into gum wrappers)* Better late than never.

THOMAS: He's so silly. *(He exits, painting walls.)*

JACKIE: I got the means, Jonny.

JON: What means?

JACKIE: The means to make an end, because I saw yuh with somebody, who put me in the mind of a sparkly smile and a sky-color scarf, yuh were clinging to your scarf lady, lifting into her world, leaving my world gone. I don't want to know, Jonny, but I'm just gone to know, and when I know it'll bust open, Jonny, ripping right from the root of my mind, and once it's sprung then who knows what, Jonny, so stop, *(Losing volume)* Jonny, stop, Jonny, stop stop stop.

JON: You're accusing me of—with her? Her husband's been walking the halls all day, right, Thomas?

*(*THOMAS *reenters, painting walls.)*

THOMAS: Yup, and if you don't believe me see for yourself, because he's standing two doors down talking to his little bitty box.

JON: He's back? Toss me a paint brush.

JACKIE: Why?

JON: Because...

JACKIE: Cause yuh been lying.

JON: No no no, I said brush because we've got to give him the brush off and rush off, because he's a pathetic, disgusting sight.

THOMAS: I think he's so cute, 'cause he really likes it when you pet him on the head.

JON: But you shouldn't, he's from incurables. Internal organs about to burst. Eking his last words onto a tape, it rips your heart out. His own wife can hardly endure the sight of him. So everybody into the supply closet.

THOMAS: Oh goody, we'll be hiding.

ART: *(Out the door, on phone)* If he tries to screw us...

JON: *(Lifting* MAD*)* Help me lift her up.

THOMAS: I can lift up my bedpan, but a person is a whole lot heavier than a poopy.

*(*JON *drags* MADELINE *around by himself.)*

ART: *(Outside the door, on phone)* ...we'll squeeze him 'til he bleeds.

JON: Never mind.

*(*JON *leaves* MADELINE *on a chair, removes a cover from a sculpture, drapes it over her.)*

JON: *Voilà.* Let's go, Jack.

JACKIE: I won't go in there.

JON: Then go away.

JACKIE: Don't want to go away.

JON: Then stay here.

JACKIE: Don't want to stay here.

JON: Then do what you want.

JACKIE: Don't know what I want.

JON: Jackie.

(JACKIE *follows* JON *into a supply closet.*)

THOMAS: Can't I hide too?

JON: *(Peeking out)* You stay out and get rid of him. Tell him Jacques is at a cafe, having wine with a famous performance artist. *(He enters the supply closet, closes the door.)*

THOMAS: *(Practices)* Jacques is at a cafe, having wine with a famous performance artist. Jacques is at a cafe, having wine with a famous performance artist....

(ART *enters.*)

ART: *(To phone, furious)* I said send my one o'clock where my eleven was supposed to be—not where I actually was at eleven. *(Losing control)* So she really is coming to meet me here, in the hospital? *(Takes a deep breath, regains control)* I'll deal with it. *(To* THOMAS*)* Oh, it's you. Where's—

THOMAS: In the closet.

ART: What's he doing there?

THOMAS: *(Thinks)* Whining with a famous performance artist.

ART: While I'm waiting for him, could you check me again? *(Tape)* Cancel check, cancel tennis. *(To* THOMAS*)* I'm about to meet someone very special, and those little pings are spreading all over my body.

THOMAS: I'll check your whole body, but then I have to straighten up for my princess.

ART: *(To phone)* Bob. I'm about to become unreachable through the weekend, but here's what you've got to do while I'm gone.

(THOMAS *checks* ART's *entire body, removing clothes as necessary.* ART *talks business,* THOMAS *misinterprets.*)

ART:	THOMAS:
(To phone) It's time to go for it. Take a good look. Closer. Really close. If you see any rough spots smooth them out now. Smooth them out or they'll rise up against you. They'll rise up, I'm telling you. Bob. Bob. Don't let them push you. You push them. Don't	My magical princess is on her way. I really really can't wait. *(Examines* ART's *skin)* When she gets here I'll be really really happy. *(Rubs)* I'm going to really tidy up, and it's going to be really nice and really tidy. *(Bobs, tweaks, gropes)* There are

be afraid to press hard.
Fiddle with 'em, you know? See
if they jiggle a little. Let
things get prickly. Make them
sting. Keep looking for a
break. Check out the terrain.
If they give you an opening,
take it. There's bound to be a
crack. Bob. Bob. Don't be
afraid to get your hands
dirty. Dig in. Pick away. Make
your move before it gets
messy. What? Go lower. Lower.
Bob. I want you so low they're
shaking. Let them shake. If
they shake, lick them. Sure
you can lick them. I'm not
asking, I'm demanding: Lick
them now. I want you to
swallow those guys right up.
Chew them up and swallow them
down. What are you waiting
for? Are you afraid to use
your goddamn teeth? Devour
them now. They're not going
anywhere. If they hang in
there, cut them off. Cut them
right off—but no, don't touch
those. Back off completely. Do
a dance. That's right. Keep
our butt covered. I don't want
anything left hanging in the
wind. Keep dancing. That's it.
Yeah. Dance. Right. Later.

going to be pretty colors, and
she'll be really pretty and
you should have seen her in my
dream, she had a really pretty
face and hands and pretty eyes
and she was so pretty that I'm
going to be so happy, think
how happy, with those pretty
hands and face, that's why
everything's just got to be so
bright and really pretty just
for her. And since she's so
really pretty *(Goes lower,*
bobs) she gets really pretty
things all around her every
single day. Anyway I saw her
in a dream and I'm going to be
so happy every little day now,
every single little day,
(Licks) because she'll be oh
so really nice to me all the
time she'll be really nice. I
can just feel her on the way,
(Chews) I can tell she's
really coming because can't
you just sometimes tell when
something's about to happen,
(Considers cutting) you know
you can sometimes tell?
(Dances, puts ART's *clothes*
back on) so I have to get
everything really neat and
really pretty so I really have
to go now, bye bye bye.

(THOMAS *goes.*)

ART: *(To phone)* I'm checking about flowers I ordered. "I'm crazy for you my
Melody". *(Losing control)* I said I need them on the sixth floor by one, not the
first floor by six. *(Takes a deep breath, regains control)* Then cancel the order.

(JACKIE *crawls out of the supply closet, struggling free from Jon.*)

JACKIE: *(To* JON) Got to hibernate.

ART: *(To himself)* The famous performance artist who was whining with
Jacques. I hate weird theater.

(The supply closet door shuts. JACKIE *moves around the room, toward the door to the hall.)*

JACKIE: *(Observing* ART, *to herself)* Internal organs about to burst, just like Jonny said. Incurable. Doomed.

ART: *(To tape)* It's like she sees stuff nobody else can see....

JACKIE: Those shoes tomorrow: empty? Body: rotting? Weeds on his face.

ART: *(To tape, moved)* ...and she really feels what she's saying...so I feel it too.

*(*JACKIE *grunts.)*

ART: *(To tape, even more moved)* Messy, but true.

JACKIE: Talking to nobody.

ART: *(To tape, verge of tears)* Aren't we all.

JACKIE: *(Moved)* So pointless. So gross.

ART: *(Weeps aloud)* Yes. Yes.

JACKIE: *(Verge of tears)* I'm looking at a guy who's gone. *(She howls, embraces* ART.*)*

ART: Bravo.

*(*JON *peeks out, as* JACKIE *tears herself away and exits.)*

JON: Jackie?

ART: *(To* JON*)* Hey, get out here.

JON: Too busy.

ART: I didn't come to hassle you. The doctor explained that you art therapists really do touch the patients.

JON: No we don't. Never never.

ART: I came to ask where my wife is.

JON: I would try the other end of the building.

ART: Oh, I don't want to find her. I just want to make sure she's not here, since there was a mix-up and my new girlfriend's coming to meet me here. *(To tape)* Meat. Freezer.

*(*JON *darts around.)*

ART: *(To* JON*)* Maddy and me have been arguing constantly. That's not a life. *(To tape)* Cereal. *(To* JON*)* You okay?

JON: Huh?

ART: You're jumping around like you've got to go to the bathroom.

JON: I'm part Indonesian.

ART: I'm not saying anything about the affair to Maddy, in case it doesn't pan out. *(To tape)* Bacon. *(To* JON*)* I'm just testing the waters. You've been in this situation before, I'm sure, being an artist.

JON: We artists, always testing each other's waters.

ART: *(Joking)* Just so you don't test Maddy's waters.

JON: *(Laughing)* Right right right.

ART: Oh, if I found her with another guy I'd be fine.

JON: *(Laughing)* Sure sure sure.

ART: At first I might fly off the handle, bust his chops.

JON: *(Holding his jaw)* Ow.

ART: But after a while I'd be fine. *(Laughs)* He wouldn't.

*(*JON *laughs, hysterically, 'til he can hardly breathe.)*

*(*THOMAS *enters with a glob of wax, laughs along.)*

THOMAS: *(To* JON*)* I told you he was fun. *(To* ART*)* He said you were "a pathetic disgusting sight". Tee hee.

ART: *(To* JON*)* The guy who checks heads is really out to lunch, isn't he?

JON: He sure am. Is.

THOMAS: *(Leaving off wax)* So here's Jackie's cleaning wax, I'll be downstairs bringing my princess's picture upstairs. *(Sees* MADELINE*)* What a heavy sleeper—

*(*JON *pushes* THOMAS *out.)*

JON: —sculpture, yes, very heavy sculpture.

ART: You can get back to whatever, Melody'll be here any minute.

*(*MADELINE *stirs under the cover.)*

JON: Here?

ART: I told you.

JON: Girlfriend coming here...

ART: You said Maddy's on the other end of the building.

JON: Yes yes, but wouldn't it be nicer to meet your Melody someplace more *(Surrounding* MADELINE *with paintings)* spacious, scenic, ambient, ramified—

ART: It's too late to change plans now.

JON: Then I'll get a box for Maddy's body. Of work. *(He goes into the other supply closet.)*

ART: Real life. *(Beats his chest. To tape: squeals, pants)*

(ART *hides the tape recorder as he sees* NORMA *approaching, dressed in street clothes and blue silk scarf, carrying suitcase, smiling.*)

ART: There's the smile that sends me soaring. Melody. *(He embraces* NORMA.*)*

NORMA: *(Aside)* I needed a name that was more melodic.

ART: The flowers I ordered didn't make it. But it's the thought that counts, and I've been thinking about this trip every minute of the week.

NORMA: Me too. *(Smiles)*

ART: Rough week at the bank?

NORMA: No.

ART: Your work is going...?

NORMA: Great. Fun. Great fun. *(Smiles)*

ART: Our car will be a couple minutes, so we'll have to wait here.

NORMA: Here?

ART: Is that a problem?

NORMA: No.

ART: You seem kind of uncomfortable being here.

NORMA: Oh no, I'm completely—

(JACKIE *enters,* NORMA *hides behind a painting.* JACKIE *grabs wax.*)

ART: *(To* JACKIE*)* Bravo.

(JACKIE *drops wax, hurries out.* NORMA *comes out of hiding.*)

NORMA: —comfortable. *(Smiles)*

ART: Sorry to make you meet me in such a depressing environment. I'm only here...cause we're bidding on a company that makes a hot new medication.

NORMA: Which one?

ART: Oh, it's called, uh—

NORMA: Not that I would know—

ART: *(Struggles to make up a name)* —flora—

NORMA: —anything about—

ART: —tri-ethyl—

NORMA: —anything involving—

ART: —bi-enzy—

NORMA: —whatever it is that—

ART: —pro-acta—

NORMA: —they take for those—

ART: —tetra-cycle-zeen.

NORMA: —whatever.

ART: Can you believe some people have to take medicine to feel happy?

NORMA: They can't just go outside and look at the sunshine? The birds? The worms? Being swallowed? Digested? Then excreted into the gaping wound of weeping, howling Earth?

ART: Huh?

(NORMA *smiles, giggles.*)

ART: That smile. It sets me free. I'm soaring.

(ART *grabs* NORMA *and starts dancing.*)

ART: I'm dancing without music. I've never done this before. I'm wild. I'm free. I'm embarrassing you.

NORMA: No.

ART: Then why are you looking around?

NORMA: I'm not looking around.

ART: I'm rushing things. I'm stupid. I'm awful.

NORMA: No. *(Looks around)*

ART: You looked around again.

NORMA: I didn't.

ART: You did.

NORMA: Did I? *(Looks around)*

ART: You're looking around right now.

NORMA: Oh that looking around...is just because...I don't want anyone to see me...doing this. *(Kisses his elbow)* And this. *(Kisses his elbow)* I'm kissing your elbow. Don't ask me why.

ART: We're wild. We're free.

NORMA: I'm kissing your elbow.

ART: I'm dancing without music.

NORMA: Now I'm chewing your shoulder.

ART: I'm dancing without—Ow.

NORMA: Back to kissing your elbow.

(JON *comes out of the supply closet with a large box.*)

JON: Norma?

ART: Norma?

NORMA: *(To* ART*)* They call me Melody, Mel, Melo, Norma...

ART: How do you know someone who works here?

NORMA: I'll tell you after you check if the car's ready.

(NORMA *hands* ART *her suitcase and hurries him away.*)

ART: I'll check if the car's ready. *(He goes.)*

NORMA: When he comes back, you've got to call me Melody.

JON: He can't come back.

NORMA: You don't like him, from one look?

JON: He looks like someone I hate: him.

NORMA: I finally met a guy who's decent and single....

JON: O for two.

NORMA: ...so if you could just—

JON: *(Flying into a rage)* I want him out out out out—

NORMA: Calm down or they'll chain you up.

JON: *(Contained rage)* I want him out out out out.

NORMA: We'll be gone in a minute if you'll help me think up an explanation for how I know you, a patient who—

JON: Not patient. Art therapist.

NORMA: Right right. So you're an art therapist. Who I know through your girlfriend, an actress named Madeline who went to drama school near my business school.

JON: Don't tell him actress Madeline my girlfriend. Madeline no girlfriend. Actress no Madeline.

(MADELINE *wakes, throws off the cover.*)

MAD: *(To* JON*)* This is how you watch over me? By standing there and mocking me, with her?

NORMA: *(To* MAD*)* I know you.

JON: *(To* MAD*)* She works here.

NORMA: *(To* MAD*)* I don't work here.

JON: *(To* MAD*)* Doesn't work here.

MAD: *(Clinging to* JON*)* I need you to stick to me like glue.

JON: I'm having trouble sticking to myself.

NORMA: *(To* JON*)* This is your actress?

JON: Not mine, not actress.

MAD: I'm not an actress?

JON: No. Yes.

MAD: *(Touching* NORMA*'s scarf)* She's taken my look.

NORMA: *(Touching* MAD*'s lips)* I know her face.

MAD: And now she's taken my friend. You like her.

JON: *(To* MAD*)* I don't like her. *(To* NORMA*)* I don't like *her.*

NORMA: *(To* MAD*)* I didn't come for Jon.

MAD: I think you're lying.

NORMA: I came for this guy I'm seeing. I'll introduce you.

JON: *(To* NORMA*)* Don't introduce. *(To* MAD*)* Don't see.

MAD & NORMA: Why?

JON: Because—

*(*ART *enters with* NORMA*'s suitcase, puts his arm around* NORMA*. * JON *drops the box over* MADELINE*.)*

NORMA: *(To* ART*)* I want you to meet Jon, who's an art therapist here, and this is—

*(*MADELINE *throws off the box.)*

ART: My wife.

MAD: My husband.

*(*MADELINE *charges* ART*.)*

*(*ART *drops* NORMA*'s bag and passes* NORMA *to* JON*.)*

NORMA: My life.

*(*JACKIE *enters, sees* NORMA *clinging to* JON*.)*

JACKIE: My Jonny.

JON: *(To* JACKIE*, re* NORMA*)* My scarf lady?

*(*JACKIE *pulls out her knife and tries to stab herself.)*

*(*THOMAS *enters with a crayon drawing of his princess—who looks exactly like Melody/the new* NORMA*, with blue scarf, etc.)*

THOMAS: *(Admiring the drawing)* My beautiful princess—

(JON *passes* NORMA *to* THOMAS, *grapples with* JACKIE.)

THOMAS: *(Seeing* NORMA*)*—has arrived!

(THOMAS *lifts up* NORMA *in his suddenly powerful arms.*)

(NORMA*'s bag falls open. White birds fly out. There's nothing else in there, except the image of a blue sky.*)

(NORMA *screams.*)

(*As* MADELINE *tugs the flesh on* ART*'s face,* ART*'s tape recorder starts playing, his phone starts ringing, and all six characters speak at once.*) ·

JACKIE: I saw yuh, Jonny. It's done now, Jonny.

JON: Get down. Get out. Don't look. Don't see.

ART: *(To* MAD*)* I'm all yours. *(To phone)* I'm all yours. *(To* MAD*)* I'm all yours. *(To phone)* I'm all yours.

MAD: You cut me open and I'm ugly falling out of all the particles that scattered from my face across the—

THOMAS: She's my beautiful princess and I'll be so happy forever and ever.

(NORMA *screams.*)

(*End of scene*)

Scene Two

(*Back in the common room*)

(ART*'s jacket hangs on the wall. Beside it, wrapped flowers with a note.*)

(JACKIE, JON, *and* ART *sit, bound in straight jackets.* MADELINE *sits, hands and feet loosely chained to the wall. In their various states of unconsciousness, these four characters mutter sporadic unintelligible phrases, and twitch.*)

(NORMA *sits on the floor in fetal position, rocking.*)

(*Suddenly,* NORMA *springs to her feet, starts to remove clothing as she charges out.*)

(*Though the other characters are still unconscious, their muttering becomes intelligible:*)

JON: Get down.

MAD: My...

JON: Don't look.

MAD:...face.

JACKIE: Stop.

(Silence)

ART: Sinking. Kicking.

(JACKIE *mumbles.)*

JON: Get get get get get get get get...

MAD: Particles.

ART: Kick in the—

JON & JACKIE:	MAD:
Don't.	*(Gasps)*

(They become quiet. THOMAS *enters.)*

THOMAS: Oh, Jon, my princess came, and now I just can't find her—

JON: *(Still unconscious)* Get down.

THOMAS: She was Norma, but she was all dressed in—

JON: Get out.

THOMAS: He's haloosirnating. *(To* MAD*)* My princess came, and she was—

(MADELINE *wails.)*

THOMAS: She's haloosirnating too. *(To* JACKIE*)* Oh, Jackie, my princess came, and you'll never guess who—

JACKIE: Stop.

THOMAS: — she—

JACKIE: I said.

THOMAS: —was.

JACKIE: Stop.

THOMAS: Cattertonic. Try try again. *(To* ART*)* Down from the sky, she was—

(ART *snores.)*

THOMAS: Fast asleep. This is like when I really wanted to tell my dad things but he was dead, but the priest said his body's right there so just tell him, so I did but it really didn't help because when I need to tell somebody things they just can't be haloosirnating or cattertonic or fast asleep or dead. I'm a perfectionist.

(THOMAS *waits near the door, looking out.* MADELINE *and* JACKIE *begin to awaken.)*

MAD: *(Half asleep)* He had someone else. Standing where I stand. He cut me out....

JACKIE: He did it.

MAD: *(Awake)* ...of my own life.

JACKIE: *(Awake)* He just. Did it.

MAD: We seem to have a lot in common.

(JACKIE *sobs, stops.*)

MAD: Did someone cut you out of your own life?

(JACKIE *nods vigorously.*)

MAD: With the swiftness of a—

(JACKIE *nods vigorously.*)

MAD: —and this after years of cramming his asinine dictates all over your—

JACKIE: Chair.

MAD: —to the point where every time you try to open up he's right there with his—

JACKIE: Chair.

MAD: —making it completely impossible for you to—

JACKIE: Magazines.

MAD: Exactly.

JACKIE: And so near my teeth.

MAD: So let's do something about it.

JACKIE: I got to strike myself, soon's I find my knife.

MAD: Don't you dare strike yourself. How can you swallow your true impulse like that? His shitty behavior was a request for information. So trust your impulse. Send a message. Strike him.

JACKIE: Huh.

MAD: Where's your knife?

(JACKIE *shakes her head.*)

MAD: Any other utensils?

JACKIE: *(Thinks)* Fork.

MAD: Excellent. Where?

(JACKIE *mumbles.*)

MAD: You're swallowing your impulse. And swallowing. And swallowing.

JACKIE: *(Calls to* THOMAS*)* Hey.

(THOMAS *turns to face them.*)

JACKIE: *(To* THOMAS*)* Under my bed, in my sculpture, there's a fork.

THOMAS: If I get it can I tell you about my princess?

JACKIE: No.

THOMAS: I'll get it anyway. *(He goes into* JACKIE's *room.)*

MAD: This is a big step for you.

*(*THOMAS *returns, puts a fork in* JACKIE's *mouth.)*

THOMAS: If anybody wants me...

*(*THOMAS *returns to the door, faces out.* MADELINE *takes the fork from* JACKIE's *mouth.)*

MAD: And now I strike my husband.

JACKIE: Him?

MAD: Why not.

JACKIE: Already...sick?

MAD: Very. What makes me sick is—

JACKIE: First strike the other one.

MAD: Him?

JACKIE: Why not?

MAD: Seems so...sweet.

JACKIE: He'd been showering her with gum.

MAD: If he hurt you, he should be stricken. But first I'll strike my husband, finally get through. Or not. It's your call.

JACKIE: *(Slipping into trance)* Got to hibernate.

MAD: Should we forget it?

JACKIE: If yuh don't, they'll just keep doing what they do.

MAD: You're right. It's time.

*(*JACKIE *slips into a trance.)*

*(*MADELINE *leans towards* ART *with the fork, reaching as far as the chains will allow her: inches from* ART's *face.)*

(She falls asleep with the fork clenched in her fist, right above ART's *face.)*

*(*ART *wakes, sees the fork at his face, screams.* MADELINE *sways towards* JON. JON *wakes, sees the fork at his face, screams.)*

ART: Why the hell didn't you tell me Maddy was in your art room?

JON: I was shocked. Shocked.

ART: How could you not know somebody was in that room?

JON: 'Cause she was hiding. Ashamed. Of her love, for art class. When you mentioned your girlfriend was coming, I begged her to run, to fly, to—

ART: Then you knew she was there.

JON: I did?

ART: You said you tried to get her to run.

JON: Right.

ART: If you knew she was there, why didn't you tell me?

JON: Because. Distracted. When I saw Norma.

ART: Melody.

JON: Melody. Right. Old friend. School friend. Met her through a girlfriend, actress named Madubuduhduhduh.

ART: However you did it, you really screwed up, so you've got to help me out with Maddy.

JON: Anything.

ART: Say Melody came to see you, because you and Melody have been going out.

JON: No problem. Yes problem. It would hurt Jackie, who's right there.

ART: The performance artist.

JON: We've been tasting each other's waters.

ART: So that's why she blew up when she saw you holding Melody.

JON: She blew up, right, because she counts on me. Devoted. Scrubs with every ounce, every muscle, every tissue, so I can walk on pure floor. She makes our floor a sky. Pure sky drips from her hands. But I filth it up. I filth it, just show up, and my actions, they take off and do stuff. I try to grab hold of my actions but even that becomes actions and before you know it I'm just a glop of jelly swarming with actions. She's grace. Pure sky but I'm tiny, a big wet tiny, a squid with nothing to clutch onto, my one rock is her but I blew it up and there's nothing I can say. I'm so disgusted with my actions I can hardly breathe. *(Panting)*

ART: In other words, you really like her.

(JON nods.)

ART: So if we can prove Melody's seeing some other guy, we'll save both our asses, right?

(JON nods.)

ART: But if we can't say it's you, and we can't say it's me, who can we get to go along with our story?

JON: *(Calls to* THOMAS*)* Hey.

*(*THOMAS *turns around.)*

ART: There's nobody else?

JON: We're working with a very small talent pool.

THOMAS: So can I tell you what happened?

JON: We need you to be in our play.

THOMAS: Oh goody goody.

JON: All you have to do is, make believe a woman came to see you this afternoon.

THOMAS: A woman did come to see me this afternoon.

JON: Perfect.

ART: Really she came to see me, but you have to keep saying—

THOMAS: Oh no, she came to see me.

ART: Right. And she works in a bank.

THOMAS: No she doesn't.

JON: Make believe, Thomas.

THOMAS: A bank. Make believe.

ART: She really goes for you, because you're....

JON: Why would a grinning banker go for a drooling idiot?

ART: Because...he has a quality that she....

THOMAS: I have no quality.

JON: She craves him because....

ART: Because...

THOMAS: Maybe she just doesn't know.

*(*MADELINE *stirs.)*

JON: Doesn't know.

ART: Feelings took her by surprise.

JON: Go with that.

THOMAS: But the really weird thing is, after she came all the way to see me, when I held her in my arms she only screamed and screamed.

ART: That they'll buy.

THOMAS: And then I couldn't find her.

ART: She came, they embraced, she ran screaming from the building.

JON: Bingo.

THOMAS: *(Leaving)* You think she's maybe running away?

ART: Where you going?

JON: It's show time.

(THOMAS tries to leave, ART and JON block his way.)

THOMAS: But my princess might be running away, and I've really really waited so long.

(THOMAS escapes. JON and ART fall on MADELINE and JACKIE, waking them.)

ART: Maddy.

JON: Jackie.

MAD: *(To ART)* Keep your words off my brain.

(JACKIE hisses at JON.)

ART: The woman you saw me with—

MAD: *(Screams to drown him out)* AAAAAAAAA.

JON: She didn't come to see me.

(JACKIE hisses.)

(All four, simultaneously:)

ART:	JON:
She came to see Thomas. The guy who was standing there. His name is Thomas. *(To JON)* What are you saying? *(To MAD)* She came to see Thomas—	She didn't come to see me, it was him, Norma came to see this guy *(Indicates ART)* him him him him—*(Responding to ART)* I mean Thomas Thomas Thomas Thomas—
MAD: *(Screams repeatedly)* AAAAA...	JACKIE *(Hisses repeatedly)*

(All four pause to catch their breathe. Then they resume, simultaneously:)

ART:	JON:
She really goes for Thomas, it isn't me it's the guy they call Thomas not me, really it's him—	Thomas Thomas Thomas that's the one not me not me not me not Thomas is the one she really—
MAD:JACKIE: *(Screams repeatedly)* AAAA...	*(Hisses)*

(Pause. They all just stand/sit/hang there.)

(ART *and* JON *open their mouths as though about to speak.*)

MAD: JACKIE:
(Short scream)   *(Short hiss)*

(ART *and* JON *give up, droop to the ground, exhausted. Pause*)

MAD: Thomas?

ART: That's right, it was him.

JON: She really did, she came for Thomas.

MAD: *(Moved)* Come here.

(ART *approaches* MADELINE *for a kiss.*)

ART: Maddy.

(MADELINE *wraps a chain around* ART's *neck,* JACKIE *snaps her jaws at* JON.)

MAD: Tell me the truth, or I'll read it on your cortex as it pops out your ear.

ART: She came for Thomas.

JON: Came for Thomas.

(THOMAS *enters carrying the clothes* NORMA *wore as Melody.*)

THOMAS: No, I think she really didn't come for me, because people don't really come for me, I just dream they do because look, she burst, just like a dream.

ART: What he means is...

JON: They embraced.

ART: She ran screaming.

JON: She ran miles from the building.

(NORMA *enters, dressed in hospital clothes again.*)

NORMA: No I didn't.

ART: Why are you here?

NORMA: I don't know. This afternoon I thought I was dropping by to escape. The path was clear. With Jon playing an artist, my lie was airtight. I was inches from freedom. Then I lost control, went plunging through someone else's dream, 'til I crashed into a new place where I was ripped open, pierced with feelings triggered not by my thoughts, but the thoughts of another. Thomas. What hurts you hurts me. What thrills you thrills me. It's glorious. It's creepy. I don't know what it is. I don't know anything. Why I plan. Why I gesture. Why the weight shifts around on my feet and moisture pops out on my shoulders. Why my lips shift into different shapes when my eyes notice certain hands and then words come. I don't know what the earth has to do with me or what my bones have to do with my thoughts. But I know what you have to do with me. I'm hooked. I'm here. I'm not alone.

(NORMA *frees* JACKIE, MADELINE, ART, *and* JON, *while humming a passionate Tchaikovsky melody and swirling around.*)

THOMAS: (*Pinching himself*) Pinchy pinchy. My cheeks aren't dreaming. Pinchy pinchy. My legs aren't dreaming. Oh, Jon. My princess really did come, and she turned right into Norma. And all because you set up a really fun office where magical things could happen.

NORMA: (*To* THOMAS) Time to wash up for bed.

THOMAS: Will you tell me a story?

NORMA: When your hair is all brushed, and your neck is all scrubbed, and your room is all tidied up, I will tell you a fairy tale.

(THOMAS *yelps for glee.*)

(THOMAS *and* NORMA *exit.*)

(JACKIE *crawls to her room.* JON *takes off his tie, sits at the table, and stares at a magazine, his energy level plunging.*)

MAD: So she's a hospital worker, who left. Then came back. To see Thomas.

ART: And the art teacher is a patient, who acted like an artist, to help the hospital worker. Somehow.

(MADELINE *kicks a chair.*)

ART: What.

MAD: If your excuse fell apart, I wouldn't have to keep seeing you and hearing you.

ART: Why don't you want to see and hear me?

MAD: Because I'm trying, with all my might, to figure out how to squirm back into my life. Your words mess up my concentration.

ART: If we don't talk, we get nowhere.

MAD: If we don't talk, we get nowhere; if we do talk, we get nowhere.

ART: Can I stay the night?

(MADELINE *shakes her head.*)

ART: (*To tape*) Cut out late calls. Cut down breakfast meetings. Make marriage work. (*Smashing the tape player*) Keep trying. (*Smashes*) Keep trying. (*Smashes. To* MAD) Now can I stay the night?

(*She shakes her head, gets his jacket from the door, notices the wrapped flowers.*)

ART: Oh Jeez. They delivered the flowers to the first floor at six instead of the sixth floor at one. I'm nailed. Don't read it, Maddy. I wasn't me. I was a child. Maybe I am a child. I'm a child, Maddy. But without you I don't have a face. Or legs. I have no face and no legs without you, Maddy.

MAD: *(Reads)* "Mad. For you. My melody." *(Moved)* I'm your melody? How did you learn to write poetry?

ART: It just came.

(MADELINE reaches her hand out to ART. ART takes her hand. Hands joined, MADELINE and ART exit.)

(JACKIE crawls out, scrubbing.)

JACKIE: It's a lie. Isn't it.

JON: What.

JACKIE: The whole day.

JON: Can't even remember.

JACKIE: Why do yuh lie to me, Jonny?

(JON shrugs.)

JACKIE: Yuh don't even know.

(JON shrugs.)

JACKIE: I lived on twigs. I lived on garbage. I lived on a soaked piece of cardboard. But I'd rather have nothing than you. Cause yuh don't know a single thing.

JON: I do.

JACKIE: What?

JON: It's something...I can't say.

JACKIE: How come?

(JON shrugs.)

JACKIE: Say it.

(JON's whole body shakes.)

JACKIE: What?

JON: This is it.

(JON puts his hand near JACKIE's shoulder. It shakes violently, and he pulls it away.)

(NORMA enters carrying a tray of pills, observes as:)

(JON stands before JACKIE and struggles to present a dance. Though it's jerky and awkward, it's the best he can do.)

JON: It's about you.

(JON *dances,* JACKIE *sways.*)

END OF PLAY

THE CHINESE ART OF PLACEMENT

Stanley Rutherford

ABOUT THE AUTHOR

Stanley Rutherford is the author of eleven plays, including A PENCIL FOR MISS SAPINGTON, TABLES AND CHAIRS, TEXAS FOX TROT, and BAD GUMS. His play BILLY NOBODY was produced by Woolly Mammoth Theater in 1992 and was nominated for a Helen Hayes Award for Outstanding New Play. He is a graduate of Stanford University and lives in Sonoma County, California.

ORIGINAL PRODUCTIONS

THE CHINESE ART OF PLACEMENT was originally presented at the
Phoenix Theater in San Francisco in February 1998, produced by Linda
Ayres-Frederick.

SPARKY LITMAN .... John Robb

Director .... Glynis Rigsby

THE CHINESE ART OF PLACEMENT had its East Coast premiere at
Woolly Mammoth on 7 June 1999.

SPARKY LITMAN .... Howard Shalwitz

Director .... Lee Mikeska Gardner
Set design .... Robin Stapley
Lighting design .... Jay Herzog
Sound design .... Hana Sellers
Stage manager .... Stephanie Nagle

THE CHINESE ART OF PLACEMENT *Show Sponsors*
Anonymous (2)
James and Marjorie Akins
Philip D Berlin
Tom Glass and Wendy Scoular
Gregg Hopkins and Murray Nimmo
James and Phyllis Kay
Roger and Eleanor Lewis
Beverly and Christopher With

CHARACTER & SETTING

SPARKY LITMAN
Setting: SPARKY LITMAN's *home*
Time: The present

(The stage is bare except for an old chair downstage right. At lights up, SPARKY LITMAN, a man in his late forties, stands studying the position of the chair. He crosses and moves the chair slightly upstage, stands back, studies its position, moves it slightly again, stands back and studies the whole space.)

SPARKY: I used to be a poet.

(He studies the placement of the chair again, then moves it slightly downstage, then walks away from it, turns back, and studies it for a moment.)

SPARKY: But the time came when I stopped being a poet, because I became normal, and after I became normal I didn't have anything to write poetry about anymore. And so now I have time to do other things.

(Beat, as he adjusts the position of the chair.)

SPARKY: And I for one am extremely relieved that I'm not writing poetry anymore, and there are a lot of other people who are extremely relieved that I'm not writing poetry anymore, because it was bitter poetry...angry, heart-wrenching poetry that caused a lot of people a lot of pain, and now that I'm not writing poetry anymore they don't have to suffer and neither do I.

(He crosses and moves the chair back to where it was at the start, stands back and studies it.)

SPARKY: It's important where you place the chair...and they don't tell ya' about that in school like a lot of other important things that they don't tell ya' about in school, and where you place the chair influences everything important like health, happiness, wealth and longevity, and I've been enjoying extremely good health, robust good health, and aside from the diet and the occasional exercise and the improved mental attitude now that I'm not writing poetry any more, I feel that a lot of it has to do with the fact that now I *know* that *where* you place the chair is important, and I've decided to place the chair in the position of the benefactors. And I've been spending a lot of time sitting here in the chair in the position of the benefactors, thinking about the benefactors, thinking about how if maybe they'd left me a little money, ya' know what I mean, everything'd be a whole lot different... .*(Beat)* I used to keep the chair up here *(He indicates.)* in the position of the children...which was stupid, and I'll admit that, because I don't have any children, and to place the chair in the position of the children when you don't have any children or want to have any children is like putting the chair on the north side of the tree when you want to be in the sun, O K. And if maybe you *wanted* to have children, and let me just say right now that I don't want to have children, I've never wanted to have children, and I've never understood people who *do* want to have children, and O K, you know what I mean, if you *wanted* to have children, then sure, O K, that's it, you *put* the chair in the position of the children and you sit there, and I'm not an expert in this stuff, let me just say that right now that I'm not an expert, but there's a system, there's a whole cosmological sort of system thing and it's an ancient Chinese cosmological system sort of thing and I read the book, O K...and they tell you on page twenty-seven, that a lot of what's goin' on here is intuitive...like you've got all these positions and rules about what goes where, and there's this thing called the *ch'i*, and it's a big deal thing and you want to place stuff so that the *ch'i* can move around the way it wants to move around, but ya' don't want it to move too fast either, and one thing influences another, and everything influences everything else, and, the bottom line here, and they're being very candid about this, is that you've got to rely on your own intuition. And lucky for me I'm an intuitive kind of guy kind of person, O K...and you sort of have to play around with the whole cosmological concept and find out what works for you, and not every day is going to be the same...things change... and that's what it's all about, things change, and maybe one day the chair's going to work for you better down over here and the next day it's going to work better for you up over there in the position of wealth, for example.

(He indicates upstage left, thinks for a moment, then moves the chair to a position upstage left in the position of wealth, then crosses away from it, turns back and studies it, then turns to the audience.)

SPARKY: I'd like to start with an understanding that this doesn't have anything to do with the sex thing or the gender thing....I mean I'm a guy kind of person and all that, but I'm not involved in any sort of relationship, sexual or otherwise with anyone male, female, or otherwise, and the main thing here is that I don't have any sex drive, and I'll just tell ya' that right now, O K...none. Absolutely none. And that didn't used to be the case when I was writing poetry...because when I was writing poetry I was controlled by relentless sexual urges, sexual images goin' through my head all the time, body-part kind of images, and since I've quit writing poetry, that's all gone. And it's a lot better now, really a whole lot better, and I figure that if you don't have any sex drive and aren't having any sexual relationships, then it means that the whole gender thing is irrelevant, and by saying that I'm not saying that I'm one of those cross-dressing kind of people, O K. I'm not saying that at all, and I just want to say right now that if the cross-dressing kind of lifestyle is something you're into then it's one-hundred-percent O K with me, because I think that everybody should be able to wear whatever they want to wear and be whatever kind of sex person they want to be, and whatever kind of racial-ethnic thing they want to be, Democrat, Republican, and if you want to make charitable contributions, O K...and if you don't want to...I mean, a whole lot of people are comin' on to ya' these days asking for charitable contributions, have you noticed this...and I'm one those kind of guys whose always willing to reach down into his pocket and pull out some change and give whatever I can to help another human being kind of person of whatever racial-ethnic-gender-socio-economic thing they're into...and I always give to organizations like Meals-on-Wheels...I *like* Meals-on-Wheels.... I think the whole Meals-on-Wheels concept is an A-number-one kind of multicultural humanitarian transgender concept... and I like knowin' that I'm helping some old lady, or whatever, and you just never know...*you just never know* whether one of these days you just might *need* Meals-on-Wheels, and I'd like to know that they're still going to be around when the time comes.

(Pause as he moves around the space for a moment, looking things over)

SPARKY: I've been thinking about creating an indoor garden...a lot of different plants, a grow light coming down from the ceiling, roses, lavender, foxglove, a whole English cottage garden sort of thing...and I've been thinking about putting it over here in the position of knowledge *(Indicating)* ...and then over here *(Indicating)* I'll have the books and the magazines, and up over here in the position of fame *(Indicating)* I'm going to keep the portfolio of high-quality blue-chip Fortune 500 stock certificates and high-yield bonds, and this is where I used to keep my poetry until I burned all of it last night, and over here in the position of marriage I'm going keep the cheese and crackers and tea bags and cocoa...the essential things...the alcohol...

(Beat, as he stops, looks around)

SPARKY: It's a funny thing being normal. All my life from babyhood on I was aware that I wasn't normal, and this can have a very disenfranchising effect on a person...you know you don't belong and you want to belong, at least you *think* you want to belong, because the adventure-and-romance video-and-film propaganda conglomerate is always tellin' ya' that you want to belong...and then there you are: *not* normal, *not* liked, *not* belonging, looking in through the window at the pretty party that's going on inside with all the pretty, nice, normal people to-ing-and-fro-ing and talking about their little normal things, and you're not one of them because you're not normal...and nobody wants to talk to you or look at you and you start to feel that you're invisible, which can give you a pretty bad attitude, O K...and your health suffers, and your nerves suffer, and your productivity suffers, and you think that if you could just write some really great poetry you wouldn't exactly be *normal*, but you'd be *special* and everyone would want to suck you off. And I went to college, O K, and I read Byron, and I read Keats and Shelley and Wordsworth and Coleridge and Whitman and Emily Dickinson and Anne Sexton and Allen Ginsberg and I even read some of those people who make absolutely no sense at all, O K...and they all thought that everyone was going to want to suck them off...and well, Ginsberg, O K,

Whitman, O K, maybe everybody *did* suck them off...but I don't think any of the rest of them got sucked off....Byron maybe, Anne Sexton maybe...but I know for a fact that Coleridge spent his whole life jacking off and I used to do that, and I want to say that right now, I admit it, I used to engage in that kind of hand job kind of behavior when I was writing poetry and, now, since last night, I don't. *(Long beat)* It's better. Really, the whole thing's a whole lot better now, and for the whole day since waking up I've had a good appetite, I've had a good attitude, and I've been quietly reviewing the political scene, the Dow Jones and the NASDAQ scene, and the whole diversified-investment kind of thing, and even though at this present moment I don't have any capital that's in a liquid sort of investment-ready condition, I've been making a lot of plans about when I *do* have some capital that's in a liquid sort of investment-ready condition...

(Suddenly stomping on an ant)

SPARKY: Fucking ants! Fucking goddamned ants. You know, I had the place sprayed...last week...the whole perimeter was sprayed with a really dangerous toxic pesticide that was absolutely guaranteed to kill fleas and ants and roaches and a whole lot of other things including small children, and I had to leave the premises, I'm serious about this...I had to vacate the premises for twelve hours and then ventilate the premises for an additional twelve hours, and it's not like I leave food lying, around because I take most of my meals out, O K, down at the Taco Bell... chicken burrito supreme, that sort of thing...and a certain number of my calories are from alcohol, I don't try to hide that fact...

(He picks up the phone.)

SPARKY: Hello...Gabriella...how you doin'? This is Sparky, listen, I wanted to invite you to a party, ya' know what I mean?... Really...my place...really, I'm serious...I'm going to be having a few friends over, and I thought if you wanted to come over and join in on all the fun we're going to be having...

(He hangs up the phone.)

SPARKY: And my whole social life has been on the upswing, because now that I'm normal I'm doing the things that nice normal people do when they're normal, like I'm going to have a party tomorrow night, a very nice party, and I'm inviting a number of old friends and some new friends, a nice mixture of nice, normal people, some of whom know each other, some of whom don't know each other, and it's going to be one of those stand-up affairs, with some nice wine and cheese-and-crackers and a casual but special kind of ambiance, a kind of a see-and-be-seen sort of thing...

(He picks up the phone.)

SPARKY: Randy, guy, how 'ya doin'...it's me, Sparky...*Sparky Litman*, remember me, from the bowling league, you remember the bowling league? ...Randy, listen, I'm going to be having a party over here at my place, one of those nice stand-up things with the wine and the cheese and the salted nuts, sort of a see-and-be-seen kind of meet-the-people kind of thing, completely nonthreatening...*(He listens for a moment.)* I don't know what kind of wine just yet, you know, some sort of selection of different kinds of interesting wines from around the world... *(He listens for a moment.)* Sure, you can taste them first if that's what you want, O K...it's going to be one of those nice wine-tasting, cheese-and-cracker-tasting sort of things, and you can bring your own, whatever, O K, no big deal.... Different people, Randy, just different people, O K, some of whom know each other, some of whom don't know each other, a nice selection of nice, normal people with the usual everyday selection of fears and neuroses....

(He hangs up the phone.)

SPARKY: And it makes me feel really good to be able to bring people together in a way that I didn't use to be able to do when I was a poet, because when you're a poet you have to spend all your time, every minute, sunup to sundown, being a poet, and it takes a whole lot of concentration to do that, because you've got to keep your mind wrapped around whatever painful, heart-rending kernel of truth you're trying to write a poem about, and you don't have any time to engage in a normal social life, and that's fine if you don't like people...but I like people, O K, all sorts of people, a lot of different, multicultural, transgender people...

(He picks up the phone.)

SPARKY: Jesse, this is Sparky...Sparky...Sparky Litman...Listen, Jesse, I'm having a party tomorrow night, because I'm not writing poetry anymore, and I'm inviting some people I know and some people I don't know to come on over and help me celebrate, and you're somebody I *don't* know, but you've come highly recommended, and I was wondering if you'd like to come on over, because it's going to be a very nice party, very nice, with a nice selection of wines from around the world...*(Beat)* Susan...Susan Milner... Susan Milner told me about you...she's a small woman, brown hair, says to say, "hi," she might be coming too...you don't think you know her...really... she said you were old friends...well, this could be a nice opportunity to meet her if you'd like, she's very nice, very small.... *(He puts down the phone.)* And you can't always predict what kind of reaction you're going to get, because some people are going to say "yes" and some people are going to say "no," and I try not to take it too personally, because I've always tended to be overly sensitive about everything, like rejection, for example, which is something I know a lot about, because it's been a major theme in my life, and I have to be careful...and so I'm only inviting people I know or people who have been recommended by people I *do* know, no open-door policy, because I did my time, O K...during the Vietnam business...and I served in a special capacity in the intelligence arena, in an underground bunker beneath the airport of a major metropolitan American city, the name of which *to this day* I'm not at liberty to divulge...and during my years as a super-secret intelligence operative I was exposed to extremely sensitive top-secret kind of information, and you've got to be careful about who you associate with and who you invite into your home, because there are people *to this day* who are going around out there trying to get their hands on this extremely sensitive top-secret kind of information, and these are not nice people...these are nefarious, evil, dangerous, not particularly good-looking people, and they could be walkin' down the street *at any time* pretending to be lookin' for a party to go to, trying to pass themselves off as regular party-goin' kind of people, and a guy in a position such as myself has to be on his guard...which is one of the reasons I've tried to create this sort of oasis here...a quiet space, a safe, protected space with a secure perimeter, but an interesting space, a stimulating space, a space where you can feel the pulse of life, the flow of the *ch'i*, and right here in the center is the *ba-gua*.

(He stands for a moment and studies the ba-gua.*)*

SPARKY: The *ba-gua* is the position of earth, the position of health, and it's the center and it's a special kind of sacred place, and every day I walk around the *ba-gua* twenty-seven times...clockwise twenty-seven times, because walking refreshes the *ch'i*, and helps to stimulate the flow of the *ch'i*, and I want my guests to experience the *ch'i* right when they come in the door, and they'll want to join in the flow of the *ch'i*, and I'm thinking about putting the food and drinks in the center, in the *ba-gua*, and the guests will move around the room in a clockwise direction and I'll be standing up here in the position of marriage *(Indicates)* ...a symbol of union between me and my guests...and at some point after most of the guests have arrived I'll start moving around too, mixing and mingling, chitting and chatting, and, of course, there are going to be people who will want to make a late entrance.

(He picks up the phone.)

SPARKY: I was wondering if I could speak with Miss Turner...Miss Tina Turner...I want to invite her to a party I'm having, and you can tell her that my name is Sparky Litman...S-P-A-R-K-Y L-I-T-M-A-N, and I'm one of her greatest fans, and I think that she's getting more beautiful and fabulous and sexy and wonderful every year, and I'm in love with her at a really deep level, that's sort of a cosmic kind of level, like a whole spiritual kind of love thing that's hard to define, because it's so deep and cosmic and spiritual that it's a religious kind of love, like some people have for the Virgin Mary.

(He puts down the phone.)

SPARKY: I think it would be nice to have music...and if you're going to have music you should have the best music, no imitations, and Tina's music comes straight from her gut and from her heart....

(He picks up the chair and moves it upstage center.)

SPARKY: Maybe Miss Turner would like to sit here in the position of fame....

(He sets the chair down, steps back and studies it.)

SPARKY: Maybe she would like to sit here when she's not singing and drink a little wine and eat some cheese-and-crackers and little wieners in sweet-and-sour sauce and talk to some of the nice, normal people who are going to be here and who will want to meet her and experience her life force...and some of them might want to tell her that they're wildly aroused by her and dream about her almost every night and are totally excited by the way she sings and moves around in that totally sexy, dirty-evil kind of way...and I've been under a lot of pressure lately, O K...a lotta stuff goin' on pertaining to my life-time goals and my precarious financial situation, and then last week I was walking along, and this was when I was still writing poetry and I was concentrating on my pain, trying to find the right words, the right images to describe the deep, deep hopelessness of my pain, and all of a sudden this woman walks over and starts givin' me the third degree about my dog taking a shit on her lawn...and I start tellin' her that I don't have a dog, and she starts yellin' at me, callin' me a spic, and it's, like, O K, I'm sayin' and I'm backin' away from her, and she's yellin' something about all you fuckin' spics comin' on up here lettin' your dogs shit on the nice, normal lawns, and the next thing I knew this neighbor guy comes out and *he* starts yellin' at me too, just because this woman's yellin' at me, and pretty soon they're chasing me down the street, yellin' at me about the dog I don't have, and this is in the same neighborhood that I've lived in my whole life...and O K...so maybe they've seen me goin' back and forth to the Taco Bell, ya' know what I mean...because I *do* go back and forth to the Taco Bell on a daily basis, two or three *times* on a daily basis, and the irony here is that just the other day this letter came in the mail from some genealogist kind of guy person who was trying to trace all the descendants of what turns out to be my grandfather's family tree...and the bottom line here, and I just want to be totally frank about this, is that my grandfather, my mother's father, the guy who was always referred to as "the Spaniard," ya' know what I mean... was really a Mexican Jew...and let me just say right now that I'm not circumcised, O K...we didn't know we were Jews, no one told us we were Jews, and nobody ever told us we were Mexican either, and the only thing grandpa ever knew was that he was born in L A...and so now I'm wanderin' around with this information that I don't exactly know what to do with, because, frankly, I'll tell ya', as far as I can figure I'm still the same mongrel-mix, chicken-burrito-eating American I always was...

(He picks up the phone.)

SPARKY: Hello, Gretchen...how ya' doin', Gretch, it's me, Sparky, long time no see, no talk...Sparky...*Sparky*...S-P-A-R-K-Y, listen, Gretch, you still single?... Look, Gretchen, I'm going to be having a little party over here at my place tomorrow night, and Miss Tina Turner's gonna be here, and I thought you bein' a real Tina Turner fan you'd want to be part of the crowd...Tina...Tina Turner...Tina Turner, Private Dancer, great legs, Ike and

Tina, T-I-N-A T-U-R-N-E-R...and she's going to be here and she's gonna
sing some of her favorite songs and talk to people, and it's going to be one
of those stand-up kind of things...stand-up...nice wine, different kinds of
imported and domestic cheeses and those nice little wieners in sweet-and-
sour sauce, everybody walkin' around with the flow of the *ch'i*, trying not
to spill anything...

(He puts down the phone.)

SPARKY: So I'm trying to be a little more open to people, a little more
accommodating, and I'm going to try to be a little more understanding
about them, because it's tough, ya' know what I mean...the whole life thing
is a real tough thing to put a person through, and I didn't use to have a
whole lot of sympathy for people when I was a poet, because you're not
supposed to have a whole lot of sympathy for people when you're a poet,
you're supposed to assault them, O K...you're supposed to brutalize them
and shock them and make them think about something or have a revelation
about something or at the very least *feel* something, preferably something
really painful...and last night I was walking around, and it was late, real
late, somewhere in the middle of the middle of a long, long, tortured,
dark-night-of-the-soul kind of night, and I hadn't written shit, O K...
not shit, not one crummy little stanza or verse or stinky little couplet
or anything, and for a while I had the chair up here—

(He indicates.)

SPARKY: —sort of halfway between the position of marriage and the position
of children, and you'd think that'd be a great place to sit, right? Creative,
right? Fecundity, union, offspring...and I kept moving the chair around and
I couldn't get comfortable, and I'm just new at this Chinese placement thing,
O K...it's a whole new thing for me, and it's not like you're expected to get
it all right off, because it's an art form itself, it's a spiritual sort of thing, and
ya' gotta keep trying, ya' gotta keep playin' around with it, and so I kept
moving the chair tryin' out different positions, and I couldn't find a single
word that was worth writing down, not one, and I tried all of 'em and I
moved 'em around and tried 'em in different combinations, old, tired,
stinking, worn-out, overused words that I'm sick of and everybody else
is sick of, and it started me thinking about when I used to spy on the
Hungarian Air Force...and I mean this is the sort of thing I'm not supposed
to talk about, because it's a secret kind of thing, and I guess they don't want
anybody to know that they wasted a whole lot of money spying on the
Hungarian Air Force...and I used to listen to these radio conversations
that these pilot guys were having when they were up there flying around,
and what these guys were doin' was talkin' in numbers, ya' know what
I mean...like seventeen...thirty-three...eighteen...code word...code word...
eighteen...thirty-two...forty-seven...code word... And I was supposed to
listen to this stuff, and it wasn't like it was all nice and crystal clear...this

was static, seriously un-Dolbyized static, and these Hungarian pilot guys were talkin' these numbers to each other in Hungarian, O K...Hungarian numbers, Hungarian code words, and I don't know any Hungarian, and they *knew* that we were listening to them, O K...they *knew* that, and so just to fuck with us they got in their airplanes, and they had about three of 'em, the whole lousy, stinking Hungarian air force had about three old World War II kinda planes, and they got up there on Monday, Wednesday, and Friday mornings, and sometimes on Saturday afternoons, but never on Tuesdays, Thursdays, or Sundays, and never when it rained, because they couldn't fly in the rain, and never at the end of the month, because they ran out of their gas allotment by the end of the month, and they were up there goin' code word, code word, number, number, and there were these people, O K...men and women kind of people, American kind of cross-cultural transgender kind of very *quiet* people who sat in the huge locked-up, super-secret, acoustical-tiled, no-window, concrete-walled room in the bunker underneath the major airport of the major American city...and these people spent the day poring over these printouts of number, number, codeword, codeword, looking for correspondences and configurations and repeated patterns, something that would make it appear that somehow somewhere something was making some sort of sense. And no one knew Hungarian, O K....*I* didn't know any Hungarian, the guy who intercepted the stuff didn't know any Hungarian, none of the people who sat in the huge, locked-up, super-secret, acoustical-tiled room knew any Hungarian, because all of this was such a big, special secret that the Central Intelligence people wouldn't let anybody who *knew* Hungarian listen to what the Hungarians were saying, because if they *knew* Hungarian, they probably *were* Hungarian, and if they *were* Hungarian then they were the enemy.

(Pause, as he picks up the chair and moves it down stage right and places it just so. He stands back and studies it.)

SPARKY: *(Very calmly)* Here is knowledge. *(Beat)* Here is the place where the wisdom of the ancient peoples comes together, a place where you can experience the deeper understandings that have been passed down from generation to generation, and you can sit here... quietly...consciously... intentionally...and you can feel the movement of the *ch'i*, the wind and the water, the life force...and you can breathe the air...

(He does so.)

SPARKY: ...slowly...quietly...consciously...intentionally...and contemplate the possibilities of where to place the chair, where to place the bed, where to place the bouquet of flowers and the light and the mirror to allow for the beneficial flow of the life-giving, beautiful *ch'i*....

(Suddenly stepping viciously on an ant)

SPARKY: Fucking ants! Fucking goddamn ants! And ya' know it pisses me off, because I spent one hundred thirty-seven dollars and eighty-three cents to have this outfit come out and spray the entire perimeter inside and out, the entire perimeter with this pesticide that has been banned, but this outfit is still using it...it's an underground kind of thing goin' on here, and you talk to somebody who talks to somebody else and then they drop ya' a note and make arrangements to come over for the "feasibility inspection" and ya' pay for this, ya' know, it's not cheap, one hundred thirty-seven dollars and eighty-three cents, and it's got a five-year guarantee, O K, that's what this guy said, five years, and he had these assistants, these guys all done up in these chemical warfare sort of suits, and they sprayed this totally toxic, cancer-producing pesticide all along the perimeter inside and out, and I've still got ants, whole platoons of 'em, battalions, and it's going on all over the neighborhood, that's the problem, the fucking neighborhood, and the filth that lives here, but it's all I've ever been able to afford as a poet, because you don't get to live in the real, hoity-toity, ant-free neighborhoods when you're a poet, you gotta live in the kind of neighborhoods where ya' got a lot of these people sittin' around in their homes at night, behind their barricaded doors, eatin' their Frito-Lays, watching the ants march across the room, and it's these same people who are watching all of those movies, you know what I mean, every night they're watching these romance-and-adventure propaganda movies, and now they don't just go *out* to watch 'em, they watch 'em *in* their homes, *in their homes*, night after night, munchin' away on their Frito-Lays, ants crawling around all over the place, and here I'm tryin' to have this party tomorrow night, tryin' to have a nice, tasteful, modest-but-not-too-modest kind of evening where people can meet and mingle and relate to one another on a one-to-one interactive kind of basis, and that can be kind of scary, O K...kind of scary for a lot of people, including myself, to try to relate to another person on a one-to-one interactive kind of basis, and that's what I'd like to be able to do without having to deal with a whole bunch of fuckin' stupid, goddamned fuckin' stupid ants!!

(He steps on another ant and then violently stomps all over a bunch of them. There's a pause, as he crosses, picks up the chair and moves downstage and sits on it, then pulls it closer to the audience to talk confidentially.)

SPARKY: Things were goin' pretty well for me until the whole puberty-adolescent episode, the seventh-grade hormone episode... And I was a pretty quiet kinda kid, because for the most part people made fun of me for one reason or another, and ya' just learn to keep quiet when people make fun of you, and this was during the period when everyone was getting their mannerisms down right, ya' know what I mean...like how you stood and how you walked and how you moved your arms and hands around and got the whole thing synchronized with what you're doing and saying...and I was having a pretty bad time gettin' the whole thing down right, O K...I was havin' a pretty bad time with the whole hand, eye, arm, leg, foot, mouth coordination thing, and, I'll tell ya' right now, I was spending most of my time lookin' at Mary Beth Latimore...three rows over, pink angora sweater, little blonde ponytail, Mary Beth Latimore, who spent most of her time looking at everyone else except me. And I'd smile at her, like I'd give her a real nice I-really-like-you kind of sincere-genuine kind of smile, and she'd look away real fast and pretend that she didn't see me, do you get this picture? And I was getting kind of desperate, O K...because the whole puberty-adolescent thing was goin' on and everybody was getting involved in boy-girl kind of relationships, going to parties, makin' out in the corner, stuff like that, and I was never invited to any of the parties and I never got to make out in the corner and develop a boy-girl kind of relationship, so I decided that the only thing to do in my situation was to ask Mary Beth Latimore out on a date...like a first-date sort of arrangement...and I thought that the Ringling Brothers Barnum and Bailey Circus would be a fun, wholesome, sophisticated sort of thing to do for a first-date kind of experience, and we could get there on the bus, and you had to think about that sort of thing in the seventh grade, the whole transportation issue, and we'd eat cotton candy and watch the aerialist people and the lion tamer people and maybe hold hands and she'd get to have the opportunity to realize what a really pretty decent kind of modest kind of guy I was. And I was saving my money, O K...the little bit I could scrape together from my crappy little nickel-and-dime allowance, and I was tryin' to get up my nerve to ask her, and it was scary, because I'd never really talked to her, and I knew I was never going to be able to talk to her, and so I decided to write her a note. And that was scary too because you gotta get the words just right, sort of easy-goin' but not too easy-goin', and after I'd written about thirty-seven drafts I finally had something I thought was really pretty nice, friendly yet respectful, not too formal, not too casual, and I put it in an envelope and carefully wrote her name and carried it around for a few days and took it out and looked at it a lot, because I didn't have the nerve to walk over and give it to her...and it got to be about two days before the circus, O K...and it was gettin' to the point where if I didn't give it to her it was going to be too late, and it was just before lunch, and the bell rang, and everyone was gettin' their stuff together and I held my breath and got up and tried to walk over to her real cool and casual and I was sweating, I admit that...I was sweating and my hands were kind of shaking, and I couldn't look at her, because I was too embarrassed, and so there I was all of a sudden standing right in front of Mary Beth Latimore staring down at the front of her pink angora sweater...and I handed her the note...and then I looked up and she was giving me one of these "why-are-you-bothering-me-you-repulsive-piece-of-shit" contemptuous kind of looks, d'you know this kind of look...and she took the note and opened it and read it and started laughing hysterically and ran over to Cynthia Petersberg and showed it to her, and they both started laughing hysterically, and then Cynthia Petersberg took it and showed it to every single other person in the entire class, and they all started laughing hysterically, and these are the same people who are running around today with big fat oversized 401K plans, O K...these are the same people who grew up all nice and normal with all the right mannerisms and the right voice and the whole social know-how thing at their disposal, and they all started putting handfuls of their discretionary income into big fat oversized 401K plans, and I never had any discretionary income, O K...I never had the opportunity to *be* in one of those employment situations where you could have discretionary income and put handfuls of cash into a big fat oversized 401K plan...

(He picks up the phone.)

SPARKY: Hello. This is Mr Sparky Litman. And I'm interested in getting one of those floral arrangement kind of things, maybe a couple of those floral arrangement kind of things...for a party, one of those nice stand-up affairs, hors d'oeuvres, wine, some nice flowers here and there, adding a little color and scent, creating an aura of exotic beauty and sensuous smells...

(He puts down the phone, then picks it up again.)

SPARKY: Hello. This is Mr Sparky Litman. And I'm interested in getting an assortment of canapés, some of those little cracker sort of things, little cheese spread, olives with the pimentos, that sort of thing...

(He puts down the phone.)

SPARKY: A little bit of preparation can prevent a lot of heartache. I want to say that again: A little bit of preparation can prevent a lot of heartache. And the thing is I didn't used to believe in preparation, O K...I believed in spontaneity...I thought that spontaneity was the morally and existentially superior way to go and that to plan for something merely reinforces the prevailing mythology that there is something to plan *for*...and, of course, I knew then and I know now that there isn't *really* anything to plan *for*... but what I didn't know then and what I do know now is that it's better to *prepare* for something even if you know it's never going to happen... because it gives you a feeling that something *is* going to happen, and if you just sit around all day being spontaneous nothing ever *does* happen, and then you're left sitting home alone with the ants, nursing a big dose of heartache.

(He picks up the phone.)

SPARKY: This is Mr Sparky Litman again...say, you don't have any of those puff pastry things that have those kind of nice, mystery fillings on the inside, those kind of things that you can't quite figure out what you're eating, but they're good anyway and they make nice little conversation-starters?

(He puts down the phone; there's a beat.)

SPARKY: I thought maybe I was going to die last week. I just had this queasy sort of gnawing-in-my gut kind of feeling that I was going to die, and I wasn't too sure whether it was going to be from natural causes or unnatural causes...but I felt like I was coming down with a really bad case of terminal mortality, and I'm ready, O K...Death is not a problem for me, I am not one of these people who has a problem with death and spends a whole lot of time all tied up in a knot about death, because *life* is the problem, O K...*death* is *not* the problem, *life* is the problem, and I've excavated an area down in the basement over here in the position of the children... *(He indicates.)* ...and it's where I'm going to be buried when the time comes, and it's all part of a very nice, very tasteful burial chamber that I've created down there for my family...each person's ashes at rest in a vessel that is appropriate for the personality and the occasion...all carried out in a nice Egyptian motif... *(He indicates.)*...and my grandmother the Norwegian is here *(He indicates.)* ...and my grandfather, the Mexican Jew from L A, is here *(He indicates.)* ...and over here are our neighbors, Doris and Sam Smedly, who, and I'll be brutally honest here, I never really liked...there wasn't much really to like about old Doris and Sam, but they used to hang out a lot with Mom and Dad, drinkin' and cussin', and gettin' into political sort of arguments with each other, and there was some kind of a sex thing goin' on between Doris and Mom, and Doris was always pawin' around at her, holding her hand, kissin' her and stuff, and you certainly couldn't blame old Doris, because Sam was one of those kind of guys who had a permanent really bad body odor kind of problem goin' on...and they'd watch T V and drink and argue and sooner or later Doris would fall asleep on the living room sofa, and at one point she moved some of her stuff into the spare room and started sleeping there, and not too long after that Sam moved some of his stuff in there too, and they never really left. *(Beat)* I never intended to be a hero, O K....I never had any fantasies about bein' a hero or had any plans to go out and do something that would make me a hero, I was just tryin' to do my best to be a regular kind of guy, writin' my poetry, sellin' Electrolux vacuum cleaners door to door, and I just want to say that this is a quality product...but then time and circumstance, and this is the thing, time and circumstance, it wasn't a planned sort of thing, O K...your country calls on you, and you do what you have to do, and they called on me, and we were at war against the so-called enemy in Vietnam, and I was called and I responded, and it didn't surprise me that they put me into the intelligence arena, O K...because I've got a first rate-kind of intelligence kind of brain, and the Army personnel people sensed that right off, and they pulled me aside and asked me very discreetly if I wanted to be involved in the intelligence arena, and I told them that if that's what my country wanted me to do...

(Beat)

SPARKY: So they sent me to spy school, and this is something I'm not supposed to talk about, that was somewhere in the middle of New Mexico, except I don't know exactly where, because they flew us to Albuquerque in the middle of the night and put us on these buses that had the windows painted over so we couldn't see where we were going, and it was me and a bunch of other guys, who ended up locked up together in these old World War II Army barracks that were surrounded by fourteen-foot-high electrified barbed-wire fences...and all day long, starting at five A M in the morning, they taught us the stuff that we needed to know about being a spy...like the secret hand signals, what to wear, who you could talk to, who you couldn't talk to, number, number, code word, code word, that kind of thing...and there was a lot of messin' around goin' on there, O K, a lot of queer stuff going on there, guys jackin' each other off and stuff, and at first, ya' know, I wasn't going to get involved in that sort of thing...but it was wartime...and there was a lot of stress and you never knew if you were going to get called to the front lines and have your head blown off, and you'd get back to the barracks after a long day of number, number, code word, code word, and there wasn't a whole hell of a lot ya' could do except smoke dope and drink a lot of tequila and get naked, and one thing led to another, and I'm only human, O K...and a lot of these guys were like that, kinda lonely, dealin' with the whole war thing, the whole life and death thing, just jackin' each other off, servin' their country... *(Beat)* And I've kept all of my medals, the special service, the duty above-and-beyond, and when you serve behind enemy lines they give you this very special medal that's got this fancy oak leaf cluster thing and a big, red ribbon, and they didn't tell me at first that they were going to send me behind enemy lines, they didn't mention that...and of course, they can't tell you a whole lot, because then it wouldn't be secret, and the idea behind the whole thing is secrecy, O K...and so one day they pulled me aside and started talkin' about how they needed a real special kind of guy, a dedicated, discreet, can-do kind of guy...somebody who could penetrate into the heart of the whole huge Red Commie Empire and figure out what, if anything, was goin' on.

(Beat)

SPARKY: Well, I wasn't so sure, I mean, you know...I wasn't exactly real crazy about the whole idea, and I told them quite frankly about Mom and Dad, and how I didn't think it would work out real well for me to be too far away from 'em, because they were gettin' along in years and needed someone to be there, and my parents, you know, god love 'em, didn't understand a goddamn thing, not a single goddamn thing...and you couldn't *tell* poor old Mom and Dad what was goin' on, god love 'em, and they were pretty dumb, I'll just have to say that, Mom and Dad were pretty dumb, and I don't mean that in a negative kind of way, just in a loving *objective* kind of way...and they tried, you know, and Mom was, well, you know, she had a mental condition and spent a lot of time hiding out under her bed...and it's not like I ever did real well in school, either, because I wasn't normal, and I knew I wasn't normal, and Mom and Dad knew I wasn't normal and they thought it was *their* fault, and frankly it *was* their fault, I'll just have to say that...because *they* weren't normal either, and neither were Doris and Sam Smedly or anybody else in the whole neighborhood for that matter, and the fact is that I didn't have one single, normal role model, not *one single, normal* role model, and so there I was with the Central Intelligence people tellin' me that I was exactly the right kind of special sort of anonymous, confused-looking kind of guy they'd been lookin' for. *(Beat)* You can appeal to my ego. I'll admit that. You say the right kinda stuff and I'll do just about anything, because I'm insecure, O K...and I've always been insecure, and I've always wanted to be liked by people and be special and you can really mess around with people like me...you can really screw people like me over, and the next thing I knew they were fixin' me up with this whole wardrobe of wash-and-wear polyester shirts and underpants and a pair of shoes that looked like a pair of shoes, except the right shoe was really a secret radio transmitter-receiver kind of thing...and then they gave me a one-way ticket on the Trans-Siberian Railroad, that I was supposed to take from this place called Nahodka to Moscow, eight days through the heart of the Red Commie Soviet Empire, and the whole thing was about trucks...because they thought that the trucks were being made someplace outside of Budapest, and they thought that they were being shipped by train through Poland and then traveled in caravans toward Minsk, but once the trucks left Minsk, no one could figure out what exactly was happening to them, except they thought maybe the Soviet Commies were shipping them to the Chinese Commies and the Chinese Commies were shipping 'em to the Commies in North Vietnam, big deal, O K, big international wartime political deal goin' on, and they wanted me to see what I could find out.

(Beat)

SPARKY: So the plan was that I was supposed to go ridin' along on the train, real cool, real noncommittal, pretending that I'm just one of those goin'-for-a-ride-on-the-Trans-Siberian-Railroad tourist kind of guys...lookin' out the window, chattin' it up with the other tourist kind of people, keepin' my eyes open to see if there were any trucks headin' to China or overhear any conversations about trucks heading to China, and in general keep an eye out for anything else that was suspicious, like any sort of unexplained counterintelligence espionage kind of activities, and I'm thinkin' ya' know that I don't speak any Russian, O K...and I'm not so sure if I'd recognize any sort of unexplained counterintelligence espionage kind of activity if I saw it, ya' know what I mean....I mean, does it look any different than what's going on all the rest of the time? So then they give me a ruble, ya' know, a Russian ruble, picture of Lenin, about the size of a quarter, and I'm thinkin' like maybe it's for makin' a phone call home...but then they tell me that they want me to give it to this guy named Boris, who's going to meet me in Moscow, and they show me that there's a secret little compartment sewn into my polyester underpants where I can keep the ruble and guard the ruble, and I wasn't supposed to show it to any body or tell anybody about it until I got to Moscow where this guy named Boris was going to meet me at the train station and whisper number, number, code word, code word, and then I was supposed to whisper code word, code word, number, number, and then he was supposed to say, "Welcome, comrade brother," and then I was supposed to give him the ruble. So I started to ask a few questions... and they told me I wasn't allowed to ask any questions, and I'm thinking like what if this ruble thing is some sort of explosive device, ya' know, like maybe they're really sending me off on some sort of suicide bombing mission or something, and I tried to explain that I had a certain right to know, and they said that I didn't have any right to know anything about anything and that the whole thing was super top-secret and I was just supposed to shut up and do what I was told. *(Beat)* I mean, it's O K, ya' know...you can only assume that somebody somewhere knows what in the hell they're doin', and I was fully aware that I was just a pawn in the military-industrial-espionage complex, and it's then that I started having the serious acid-reflux indigestion that I'd never had before that point in time, and it's not like I had a choice about any of this, O K...I mean, these were orders, this was the army, this was wartime, this was the enemy, this was the objective, and I was Communications Specialist First Class Sparky Litman, and I was the man who they called on to get the job done.

(Long beat, as he moves the chair closer to the audience and leans in to talk very confidentially.)

SPARKY: It was winter, O K...and they bundled me up in this Eskimo kind of jacket and gave me some luggage and a camera and a passport that had my picture in it but with a different name that was hard to pronounce... and then they put me on a plane for Tokyo where I stayed for two days and then got on a Japanese ship that took me to this place called Nahodka that's north of Vladivostok where you catch the train...and it was cold, O K...real cold, like forty-seven degrees below zero cold, and it was snowin', and I was scared, and I'll just say that right now, because I was pretty sure that at any moment some sort of ugly-lookin' K G B kind of operative person was goin' to come along and hold a gun to my head and take me off to some sort of Siberian torture chamber...and so I'm goin' along tryin' to act like a simple-minded tourist kind of guy takin' a nice trip in minus forty-seven-degree weather...and they show me to this train compartment, and it's like one of those European trains with four people in a compartment and there were these two big Russian soldier guys and an old, old, old Russian crone kind of lady, and I sat down, and everybody started noddin' and smilin' and I started noddin' and smilin', and they all started talking in Russian, and this one soldier guy offers me a drink from his bottle of vodka and I'm thinkin' that ya' know it's a friendly kind of gesture and so I take a little drink and thank him and he urges me to take some more and I do and then the soldier guy passes the bottle to the old lady and she drinks a little and

they keep passin' this bottle around, and then another bottle, and this is
pretty much what went on for the next eight days, O K...and this was a Red
Commie Soviet Empire train...I mean, it wasn't exactly one of these scenic-
cruiser-dome-car-nice-linen-napkins-with-a-bar-car-in-the-rear sort of
trains...it was one of those kind of trains that barely had any heat, for
example, and there was about eighty feet of snow outside and ice on
the windows, and you'd sit there rockin' back and forth drinkin' vodka,
noddin' and smilin', tryin' to keep warm, and three times a day you'd have
the pleasure of going down to the so-called dining car where the only thing
they served was tongue. Beets and tongue. Potatoes and tongue. Pimentos
and tongue. Green-yellow weedy mystery vegetables and tongue...and after
a while you'd sort of start to wonder: What in the hell are they doin' with
the *rest* of the animal, huh? Who's gettin' to eat that, huh? And it's not that
you could even *tell* what *kind* of animal it was...it was just tongue, O K,
fat, ugly, pink, pulled-out-by-the-roots tongue, and at one point it sort of
occurred to me that maybe it wasn't even *animal* tongue...maybe it was
dead human capitalist pig *spy* tongue, ya' know what I mean? And I wasn't
sleepin' very well to begin with, because every night at exactly 0130 A M
in the morning I had to get up and go down to what they called the toilet,
which was one of those holes-in-the-floor sort of deals that ya' gotta squat
over when the time comes...and I stood there and took off my shoe that was
really a transmitter-receiver and radioed back to the underground bunker
that I hadn't seen any trucks, because most of the time you couldn't see
out the windows because of the ice and snow, and I hadn't heard anyone
talking about any trucks either, because, let's face it, I don't speak any
Russian, O K...I don't speak any Russian or Hungarian or Polish or
Czechoslovakian or Serbo-Croatian, and there was this woman in dark
glasses who started followin' me around, and she was a knockout drop-
dead fasten-your-seat-belts kind of woman, nice legs, nice thighs, nice
calves, nice ankles, real red lipstick, real thick and wet. And she started to
make it a point to sit across from me in the dining car, and I'm just a modest
kind of guy, O K, and I'm not used to women payin' a whole lot of attention
to me, because they never *have* paid a whole lot of attention to me, and this
woman was makin' me real nervous because I'm a spy, O K, and I'm on
a top-secret intelligence mission, and this woman was pretending to read
this book, and it was one of those big thick Russian novel sort of books
with Cyrillic kind of letters all over the front cover, but the point is that
she wasn't actually *reading* the book...she was just *pretending* to read the
book while the whole time she was peekin' around at me, checkin' me out,
watchin' me real closely as I was starin' out the window lookin' for trucks...
and they warned me about this kind of person, O K...they showed me actual
pictures of this kind of person, and told me about how this kind of person
operated, and how this kind of person would lead you on with alcohol and
drugs and red lipstick...and so I'd try to make sure that I sat in a different
place at every meal...kind of moved around a bit, tryin' to keep her guessin',

but she was smooth, O K...smooth, slick, professional, cold-blooded, and dangerous, and every time she'd find a place somewhere within eyeshot of where I was sittin', *every time*...and if she was sittin' at a table at one end of the car and I came in and sat down at a table at the other end of the car, she'd get up and move over by me, and then one night I look up and find her sittin' right next to me, and she looks at me and licks her lips and gives me one of those I-know-what-you-want kind of smiles, and I'm scared, O K...I just want to say that right now that I was scared and even under normal conditions I'd have been scared, and I'm thinkin' ya' know that this woman is working for the other side...I mean, let's face it right now, this woman is some sort of Russian secret service counterintelligence espionage kind of agent sort of woman and she knows who I am, she knows that I'm Communications Specialist Sparky Litman First Class, and she knows that I'm here on some sort of super-secret special sort of assignment, and she knows that she's got ways of making me talk.

(Beat)

SPARKY: So, she pulls out a pack of those ugly little black Sobrane cigarettes and asks me if I'd like a smoke...in English, she says this in English, kind of heavily accented English, but not exactly Russian-accented English, but more sort of Eastern European sort of accented English, and she's lickin' her lips and smilin' and then she sort of crosses her legs, you know how women do that, cross their legs real sort of slow and dirty...and then she moves closer to me and tells me that her name is Eva and that I shouldn't be afraid.

(Suddenly stamps viciously on a bunch of ants)

SPARKY: Fucking ants! Fucking goddamn ants! You can't win. There's no fuckin' hope. Fuckin' everywhere, and it doesn't make any difference what ya' try to do... *(He stomps around some more, then stops and picks up the phone, very irritated.)* Hello, this is Mr Sparky Litman, and I want to express my extreme dissatisfaction with your services. One hundred thirty-seven dollars and eighty-three cents! *One hundred thirty-seven dollars and eighty-three cents!* That's what I paid, *one hundred thirty-seven dollars and eighty-three cents!* And I *still* have ants, millions of ants, and I am having a party tomorrow night, and a number of very nice, very attractive, very clean people are going to be here, including Miss Tina Turner, who will be providing entertainment in her own unique, inimitable style, and I want you to come over here right now, this minute, this absolute minute, and bring your men and your equipment, and I want you to spray every square inch, and I want you to spray until *every single, solitary, wretched, filthy, disgusting, little ant is dead! Dead! Dead!*

(He slams down the phone, walks back to the chair, picks it up, moves it, stands there and takes a deep breath or two, slowly calms down, and then sits and then pulls the chair up closer to the audience.)

SPARKY: So, this Eva woman offers me a Sobrane, O K...and I say, sure, and I take it, and then she pulls out one of those fancy Dunhill lighters and lights mine and lights hers, and I take a drag and start coughin' real bad 'cause I don't smoke, but I wanted to play like I was real cool...and she starts laughin' and all of sudden I realize she's got her hand on my thigh...and I'm just a guy, O K...I'm just a human being kind of guy person, and I never had what you'd call a real sex life, a normal kind of boy-girl kind of sex life even though I had all of the usual sort of urges and some pretty unusual sort of urges, and she starts kind of feelin' me up, ya' know what I mean...and I'm gettin' aroused, O K...it's a natural kind of response, and she's gettin' her hand up there somehow or another, and she's kind of rubbin' it around, and I was tryin' to be cool, because there's this conductor kind of guy, who's a pretty scary-lookin' kind of guy, who comes along every hour or so checkin' the passports, and you could see him comin' on down the aisle, and this Eva woman's got her hand in my lap, and I've got a serious erection, O K...a *real, real* serious erection and she's rubbin' it and lickin' her lips and crossin' her legs and tellin' me how big it is, which it's not, and I'll just say that right now...I mean it's not exactly little or anything, it's a pretty regular-size kind of penis thing, and this scary-lookin' conductor guy's comin' down the aisle, and this Eva woman is rubbin' it harder and harder and faster and faster... and this is one of the reasons I started to write poetry...because of the frustration...because I've never been successful with women, and I'd never, up until that time in my life, had regular normal boy-girl kind of sexual relations with a woman...and so there was this woman comin' on to me in a serious sort of way, and we're sitting there on the Trans-Siberian Railroad and the conductor was comin' down the aisle, and this woman *knew* I was a spy, and *I* knew that *she* was a spy, and she knew what *I* was doin', and I knew what *she* was doin', and I knew that she wasn't really interested in me, O K, I knew that she wasn't really turned on to me, she just wanted my secrets, that was the only thing she was interested in, and I wanted her, and I'd just like to say that right now, because I was seriously excited by this woman, seriously aroused by this woman, because she was a beautiful-angelic-earth-goddess-Marlene-Dietrich kind of woman and I was falling in love...at that moment, it was love, true love, and my heart was pounding, and she was rubbing my thing, which was getting bigger and bigger and harder and harder than it had ever been in my entire life up to that time, and I'm not one of those kind of guys who just thinks about sex, O K...I think about love...I think about love and the whole beautiful heart-body-and-soul package, and I'm like reaching over there getting my hand up under her skirt, sort of a reciprocal kind of thing going on here, ya' know what I mean...and I'm startin' to get a real good feel up there, and I figure out pretty quickly that she's not wearin' any underpants, and she's like all wet and frothy and breathin' hard and smilin' and laughin' and things are gettin' real serious now, and I'm gettin' real worked up, and she's getting real worked up, and both of us have completely forgotten about the scary-lookin' conductor kind of guy who all of a sudden is standin' there, and he's watchin' us, and we just keep on goin' for it, and this Eva woman is starting to moan and sigh, and some of the other passengers have started to look and a few of 'em have stood up and come on over to stand around and catch the action, and I've got most of my hand up inside her now, and she's unzipped my pants and pulled out my big, huge, enormous, throbbing penis thing, and she's pumpin' it and pumpin' it and she's going "yes, yes, yes, yes, yes..." and I'm feelin' like I can't hold it a second longer and just as I feel her insides start heavin' and quakin' like they're about to explode, I blow my wad all over the fucking train.

(Long pause as he moves the chair, pauses, sits on it, then pauses.)

SPARKY: I wasn't really planning on having a career in the military. I mean I knew I wouldn't be any good at that kind of thing, and *they* should have known that I wouldn't be any good at that kind of thing, and so there I was in the middle of Siberia with my dick hanging out and this scary-lookin' conductor guy is smilin' and laughing and breakin' out the vodka and this Eva woman has disappeared down the aisle, and I'm sort of tryin' to put myself back together when I realize that the ruble is gone, just gone. And I start searchin' around, thinkin' it might have fallen on the floor or somethin', and it only takes me a couple a seconds to realize that this Eva woman, the enemy counterintelligence agent, has taken it, and that's what this whole thing was all about, to distract me so she could get her hands on the ruble, and now it's in the hands of the enemy and I don't have anything to hand over to the guy in Moscow when he says number, number, code word, code word, and this is trouble, O K...this is big, huge, major, bad trouble, and I'm going to end up in front of a firing squad or something worse, and I panicked...and I just want to say that right now that I did not handle this in a cool, calm, professional, James Bond kind of manner, I started screaming, *(And he does)* "Where's the fucking ruble! Where's the fucking ruble!" And I started trying to run down the aisle to find this Eva woman, and these other people are all blocking my path, O K, like they're not gonna let me through, and they're all drinkin' and laughin' and it's like they're in on the whole thing, like everybody on the train is in on this whole thing, everybody in the whole Soviet Commie empire is in on this thing, and this Eva woman has disappeared. Gone. Lost. Nowhere. Never to be seen again.

(Long beat)

SPARKY: You can begin to get the picture. I can tell, ya' know, that you're beginning' to really get the idea here of what it's been like for me, and I'm not complaining, I want to make that real clear right up front, that I'm not complaining, O K...ya' just start learnin' when you're real young that you're a dupe. I mean, that's what I was learnin', and that's what life was teachin' me, that I was one of those people who was born to be a dupe, somebody you could really take for a ride, because I never learned how to play the game, O K. I wasn't playin' the game, I didn't even know that there *was* a game...I was just innocent and stupid and terrified, the kind of guy who doesn't realize that everyone else is into something that requires some sort of *strategy*, ya' know what I mean? I didn't have a strategy. I didn't have a plan. I didn't know I needed one. And it turns out that there weren't any trucks, O K...it turns out that the Commies barely had any trucks, because they spent all their money on missiles and tanks, and the Central Intelligence people knew this, they knew this all along, but they wanted me to *think* that this whole thing was all about trucks, because it turns out they *wanted* the Commies to get the ruble, O K...they actually *admitted* this to me that they *wanted* the Commies to get the ruble, because there were secret *plans* of something big and important and classified top-secret top-secret microscopically engraved around the picture of Lenin...which was information that the Central Intelligence people just *happened* to *plant* in the *ear* of one of their operatives who they also knew was a *double agent* who would tell the Commies anything that he found out about, which included the fact that I was carrying this ruble with the secret plans in my underpants... But the plans were a fraud, O K...the plans were a red herring, O K...and they put me on the train knowing that the Commies knew who I was and what I was doing and that they'd drug me or something or kill me or something, and they'd get the ruble and think that they'd really gotten something big and important, and all along it was all part of big fat United States of America trap...And *they* were a dupe, and *I* was a dupe, and ultimately *everybody* in the whole entire world was a dupe. *(Beat)* So then they gave me a medal...for "valor and courage behind enemy lines"...and Mom and Dad were real proud, because it was the first time in my whole life that I'd ever done something that they could be proud of, and it's not like I could really *tell* anybody about what I actually *did* to get the medal for valor and courage behind enemy lines...And it was then that I started staying awake at night, because I was afraid to go to sleep, because whenever I closed my eyes angry little voices started talking to me in my head, little voices speaking in little rhymed couplets all night long, and my appetite started going, and I'll tell you right now that there are a whole lot people who I really admire who killed themselves in one way or another... like Jackson Pollock...Jackson Pollock drank himself into a stupor and drove into a tree, and Mark Rothko drank himself into a stupor and slashed his wrists and bled to death, and the thing is I drink, O K...but I don't drink myself into a stupor...I just drink until the voices inside my head either take over completely or disappear completely...

(Suddenly, furiously starts stepping on ants, shouting)

SPARKY: Fucking ants! Fucking goddamned fucking fucking goddamned ants!

(In a frenzy, he picks up the chair and starts smashing the ants with it, pounding it against the floor over and over until it breaks apart. Long beat as he regains his composure and moves downstage.)

SPARKY: I went down into the basement last night. *(Beat)* And I was lookin' things over and thinkin' about Mom and Dad and Grandma and Grandpa and the whole mortality situation, the whole life-and-death sort of thing... and I was thinking about the fact that everybody in the extended family unit is dead except me...I'm the last one...and I'm the only person who really knew them, because they didn't exactly have a lot of friends, in fact they didn't have *any* friends, and I didn't exactly know them real well either, O K...I mean, at one point or another we all lived in the same house and ate at the same table, and there was the whole sort of genetic thing going on, the whole D N A sort of thing, but you kinda got the feeling that nobody really *wanted* to get to know anybody real well, because they spent a lot of time yellin' at each other, and Mom couldn't think very well, couldn't figure stuff out real well, but she always tried to see to it that I got a good little breakfast and had a little peanut butter sandwich and an orange in a little bag to take to school for lunch... *(He gets teary-eyed, almost starts crying, and then holds back.)* And Dad was always wantin' to play catch with me...but I didn't want to play catch with him, because I couldn't catch...and he'd say that I'd never be *able* to catch unless I *tried* to catch, and I didn't care whether I could catch or not, and he'd get pissed, and then he'd start yellin' at me, and then Mom would start yellin' at him, and then he'd start yellin' at her, and then I'd go hide in my room, and they'd go on yellin' at each other, and how are ya' supposed to get to know anybody in that sort of environment, you know what I mean? I mean, *I did not know these people.* They were my parents, fine...they were Doris and Sam the neighbors who I didn't like very much, fine...they were my grandfather the Mexican Jew from L A and my grandmother the Norwegian, and *I did not know these people! Who were these people?!* And everybody's goin' on these days about *their* heritage, and *their* culture, and *their* traditions and history and people, and how special their people are, and my people weren't special, they weren't special at all, they were just unhappy, scared, terrified, lost, little people...and every night after Mom and Dad and Doris and Sam and Grandpa the Mexican Jew had pretty much passed out, Granny the Norwegian and I would sit up and watch wrestling matches on T V... which I pretty much hated, but Granny wanted to watch 'em, and I was the kind of kid who wanted to make his poor old confused granny happy, and so we'd watch wrestling, and she'd sit there rocking back and forth saying,

(Mimicking, distressed Norwegian)

SPARKY: "Vhy, vhy, vhy d'ese men kill each other...vhy, vhy, vhy?" And then she'd go on watching while these guys kept pounding away at each other, and she'd be shaking her head and beating her breast, saying, "Vhy, Vhy, Vhy d'ese men kill each other...vhy, vhy, vhy?" And I'd tell her, ya' know, like Granny, O K, like maybe we could change the channel, ya' know what I mean, like there's a whole lot of other, better stuff goin' on, and so I'd try to change the channel, but she wouldn't let me, and then she'd stare at the screen some more going, "Vhy, Vhy, Vhy d'ese men kill each other... vhy, vhy, vhy?" *(Beat)* So I was thinkin' that maybe tomorrow night, like when the people come to the party that maybe at some point they might like to come on downstairs and pay their respects to the dearly departed...and this could be sort of an optional kind of thing, O K...like maybe at some point after Miss Tina Turner has sung a few songs, and there's a little break for more conversation, another glass of wine, I could sort of casually mention to a few people that I'd like to introduce them to my extended family unit...and I'd invite them downstairs and show them around, and the whole place is lookin' real nice down there, O K...candles and incense, and everybody's urn is set out real nicely right here in the *ba-gua (Indicating center stage)* ...the center, the earth, the position of health...*(Then indicating specifically and reverently)* ...Mom and Dad...Grandma and Grandpa...Doris and Sam Smedly...*(Beat)* And I thought I could introduce my friends to them and tell people their names, sex, date of birth, date of death, country of origin, some brief biographical information...because the thing is, I never used to bring any of the kids from school home, O K...I never used to do that, because I didn't want them to meet my parents...and I didn't want them to meet my Grandpa and Grandma or Doris and Sam, because I was ashamed of them, and I just want to admit that...I was ashamed of my Mom and Dad and Grandpa and Grandma and poor old dumb Doris and Sam, and I never brought anybody home to meet them and I tried to pretend that I didn't even know them...in fact I *didn't* know them, I didn't know them at all, but you don't *realize* that while they're still alive, you don't *think* about that kind of stuff while they're still alive, and now that they're dead ya' realize that *you do not know these people*! And there they are down in your basement and you don't know who in the hell they are, and when they were alive you were ashamed of them, and it was a pretty crappy thing to do now, wasn't it? A pretty fucking crappy thing to do, and I was that kind of guy, O K...I was that kind of crappy, selfish, ashamed-of-my-people kind of guy, and it's sad, pretty fuckin' pathetically fuckin' sad...and I'm thinking now that it'd be pretty damned nice of me to introduce Mom and Dad and the whole extended family unit to these people who are comin' to this party sort of thing tomorrow night...sort of a pay-our-respects kind of thing, a moment of silence kind of thing, a little way for me to ask Mom and Dad to forgive me, and Grandma and Grandpa and poor old dumb Doris and Sam...

(Getting teary-eyed)

SPARKY: And you gotta kinda hand it to 'em, ya' know what I mean...they kept on doin' it, O K...they kept on gettin' up in the morning, doin' their sad little bullshit lives, and I'm the only one who's left who knows their sad little stories...and after I'm gone their sad little stories will be gone...and I thought it would be nice to share some of their sad little tragic everyday little heartbreaking stories with the people who are coming tomorrow night, because, I'll tell ya', these people have stories too...these people who are coming tomorrow night all have sad little tragic everyday little heartbreaking stories and they're suffering...these people are suffering, and this is from personal observation: The average guy on the street kind of person is suffering, and the average woman on the street kind of person is suffering, and there's an isolation there, O K...there's a fear there...and they'll be coming out of their little houses tomorrow night all scared and apprehensive, reaching out, hoping to connect with other sad, apprehensive, isolated, wounded, suffering people...so they can tell each other their sad little tragic everyday little heartbreaking stories...and I want them to know that they're not alone.... I want them to know that it's O K to be scared and isolated, it's *normal* to be scared and isolated, because I'll tell ya', night after night these people are locked up in their little homes tuning in for another episode of fear and chaos and random acts of violence, and they get all worked up about it and pissed off about it and terrified about it, and then they try to go to sleep and forget about it, and all they can hear are the voices screaming inside their head and the *pound, pound, pound, pound, pound of their angry...hungry... lonely...heart.*

(*Long beat as he crosses, picks up the pieces of the chair and carries them downstage center and dumps them over the front of the stage. There's a beat.*)

SPARKY: I'm feeling a lot better now. Everything's been goin' a whole lot better lately, and the thing that turned the whole thing around was figuring out that my bed was supposed to be placed so that it was *facing* the door, but not *directly* facing the door, but sort of *kitty-corner* to the door, because there's a whole system, O K...a whole ancient Chinese system and they have the whole thing figured out, and the position of the children is over here (*Indicating*), and the position of knowledge is down here (*Indicating*), and the position of health is here in the center (*Indicating*), and it's a reassuring kind of thing in an unreassuring kind of world...and it gives the whole thing a sort of a meaning, and I'd been looking for meaning for a long time, and that's what a lot of my poetry was all about, and I couldn't find meaning and so I suffered and then I learned that if ya' get everything in the right place, facing the right way, in the right segment of the room, then the *ch'i* moves around the way it's supposed to move around, then everything else takes care of itself.

(*He picks up the phone.*)

SPARKY: Hello...Is this Mary Beth? Mary Beth Latimore?...I bet you'll never guess who this is....I bet you'll never guess who this is, because you never knew that I even existed, O K...but I was in love with you...totally completely forevermore in love with you, and I used to cry myself to sleep at night, because I wanted to take you to the Ringling Brothers Barnum and

Bailey Circus and you just laughed at me and broke my little heart. Do you know what that means? Do you know what it means to have your little heart broken and lose all hope, and because of you I became a poet... *(Beat)* Sparky Litman...*Sparky Litman*, S-P-A-R...listen, Mary Beth, I was just thinkin', ya' know, that maybe you might like to come on over tomorrow night and join me and some nice, normal, isolated, wounded, suffering friends of mine and the fabulous Miss Tina Turner for a little party sort of thing...just a nice easy-going wine and cheese kind of stand-up thing, because I'm trying to create some nice memories, O K. I never had any nice memories, and there are a lot of other people who've never had any nice memories, and I'm inviting a few of these people over and I thought maybe you'd like to come over too...

(He hangs up the phone.)

SPARKY: I always like to give people a second chance. I want to say that again: I always like to give people a second chance...because you never know what could have happened, maybe it was a misunderstanding... maybe it was a miscommunication, and she was just as scared as I was and as overwhelmed as I was, and she knew I was looking at her and she wanted to look back, but that whole puberty-adolescence-hormone thing was going on and it was embarrassing, ya' know what I mean...and I didn't used to feel that way about giving people a second chance when I was writing poetry...because when you're writing poetry you're only thinking about revenge, O K...and it's all payback time, every line, every stanza, every word is like a perfectly poisoned arrow aimed at somebody's rotten little unforgiving heart, and I was writing some really vicious, hateful, not-at-all-uplifting kind of poetry that had a lot of dirty words, body-part kind of words, and I was sending it to people, signed and inscribed... And then last night all of a sudden I couldn't do it any more. Something snapped. It just snapped. And I was sitting there writing this really poisonous, foul, nasty, take-no-prisoners kind of verbal swill, and I just stopped. Just stopped. And there weren't any more words, O K, no more words, not a single word, not a single thought, no hate, no anger, no remorse, no nothin'...and I put down my pencil and realized that I'd never write another word again. Not a word. Again. Ever. *(Beat)* And for the first time in my life...I felt like I was free. *(He looks down, sees an ant, and quietly steps on it.)*

(Blackout)

END OF PLAY

THE GENE POOL

Christi Stewart-Brown

THE GENE POOL
©1999 by Christi Stewart-Brown

For all rights please contact Ron Gwiazda, Rosenstone/Wender, 3 E 48th St,
NY NY 10017, 212 832-8330, fax 212 759-4524.

ABOUT THE AUTHOR

Christi Stewart-Brown is a critically acclaimed playwright who has had over thirty-five productions of her plays across the U S, in Canada, and at the Edinburgh Fringe Festival in Scotland. Stewart-Brown is a three-time Helen Hayes Award nominee and is the former Artistic Director of Consenting Adults Theatre Company in Washington, DC.

Her plays include: MORTICIANS IN LOVE, which ran Off-Broadway in 1995 at the Perry Street Theatre, THREE MORE SISTERS, SWEET LAND OF LIBERTY, FULL OF GRACE, STEAK! (co-author), a country-western musical about cattle-rustling vegetarians, and DO NOT USE IF SEAL IS BROKEN, which was made into a film entitled *Loungers*. *Loungers* was featured at the 1996 Slamdance Film Festival in Park City, Utah, where it won the Audience Award and placed second for the Jury Award. MORTICIANS IN LOVE has been optioned for a movie and THE GENE POOL will also be made into a feature film.

Stewart-Brown holds an M A in Theater from the University of Colorado in Boulder and has taught Playwriting for Johns Hopkins University, Woolly Mammoth Theatre Company, and the Theatre Lab.

ORIGINAL PRODUCTION

THE GENE POOL premiered at Woolly Mammoth on 12 January 1998. The cast and creative contributors were:

CLAIRE . . . . Kimberly Schraf
MIRA . . . . Jennifer Mendenhall
PETER . . . . Jeff Lofton
PAIGE . . . . Tina Frantz
HAROLD . . . . Michael Russotto

Director . . . . Lee Mikeska Gardner
Set design . . . . Robin Stapley
Costume design . . . . Lynn Steinmetz
Lighting design . . . . .Marianne Meadows
Sound design . . . . Hana Sellers
Stage manager . . . . John "Scooter" Krattenmaker

THE GENE POOL *Show Sponsors*
Susan and Dixon Butler
Wade Carey and Ted Coltman
Andy and Nancy Colb
David Marshall and Alan Wiesenthal
Gilbert and Jaylee Mead
Herbert and Nancy Milstein

THE GENE POOL has also been produced at Mixed Blood Theater Company in Minneapolis, Borderlands Theater in Tucson, The Kitchen Theater in Ithaca, Phoenix Theater in Indianapolis, and the Waterfront Playhouse in Key West.

.

CHARACTERS & SETTING

CLAIRE GRAY
MIRA GRAY
PETER GRAY
PAIGE
HAROLD CARTER

Setting: The living room of the GRAY's *house*

Time: The present

ACT ONE

Scene One

(At rise: Lights come up on an empty living room, perhaps even while the audience is still settling in. The opening bars of Doris Day's "Everybody Loves a Lover" blast. MIRA dances across the stage in ratty work clothes, carrying a varnish-covered paint brush. She exits.)

(She comes back on, half dressed, struggling into a nice shirt. She sings and bops her way back across the stage, picking up things, straightening the room, etc. She finds a lipstick and smears some on. She dances off.)

(She returns with a large cooking spoon and an oven mitt shaped like some sort of animal. She dims the lights, straightens more things, looks around to make sure everything is perfect, fluffs her hair. When the part of song plays in which Doris sings a round with herself, MIRA sings one part and puppets the oven mitt to "sing" the other. "They" share the spoon as a microphone. After the round is over, perhaps the oven mitt sings backup vocals as they head off. MIRA has exited by the time the final "Call me a Pollyanna..." is sung.)

(Sound of a door slamming, cutting the chorus off after the final "Pollyanna." Silence)

(CLAIRE enters with a briefcase, blinks at the dimness, and turns the lights up brighter.)

CLAIRE: Honey, I'm home!

MIRA: *(Off stage)* Be right out!

(CLAIRE sits at the table and takes some bills out of her briefcase. MIRA enters and dims the lights again. She tip-toes up behind CLAIRE and nuzzles her neck.)

CLAIRE: Hi, sweetie.

MIRA: Hi there. How was your day?

CLAIRE: Oh, the usual. What'd you do today?

MIRA: Oh, this and that.

(CLAIRE continues to do paperwork. MIRA continues to nuzzle, then starts massaging CLAIRE's back, then works her way down to her breast.)

CLAIRE: Mira, what are you doing?

MIRA: Rubbing your breast.

CLAIRE: Why?

MIRA: Because it's nice.

CLAIRE: I'm trying to do bills.

MIRA: Can't you do them later?

CLAIRE: I'd like to do them now.

MIRA: You know what I'd like to do now?

CLAIRE: Mira...

(MIRA *sighs, releases* CLAIRE's *breast, and tries another tack.*)

MIRA: I got your bookshelves finished.

CLAIRE: That was quick. Thanks, sweetie.

MIRA: The varnish isn't dry, so don't put anything on 'em yet.

CLAIRE: O K.

MIRA: Oh, I just picked the last of the zucchini—I hope. Could you please take some into work with you? Give some to Sally or Blake or one of your patients' owners or something?

CLAIRE: Sweetie, nobody wants zucchini. Everybody plants it and it goes crazy and then they try to give it away. It's like some big fall ritual. Nobody actually eats that stuff.

MIRA: We eat it.

CLAIRE: No. You cook it, then Peter and I push it around our plates.

MIRA: You do?

CLAIRE: Yep.

MIRA: You just push it around?

CLAIRE: Mira... Could you just let me finish these—

MIRA: Yet the two of you encourage me to slave over a garden every spring...

CLAIRE: You like to garden.

MIRA: I like fresh vegetables. Do you two even like fresh vegetables?

CLAIRE: I like the broccoli, I like the carrots, the occasional beet. All I'm saying is that you can stop with the zucchini.

MIRA: O K.

(*The phone rings.* MIRA *picks it up.*)

MIRA: Hello?...Hello?...*Helllll-ooooh? (She hangs up.)*

MIRA: I hate that.

(CLAIRE *focuses more intently on her bills.* MIRA *puts on some soft music and dims the lights again.* CLAIRE *can't see what she's writing and puts down her pen, exasperated. She massages her neck with both hands. While she is doing this,* MIRA *sneaks up behind her and snaps a pair of pink furry handcuffs onto* CLAIRE's *wrists.)*

CLAIRE: What the hell—?

MIRA: Now I've got you!

CLAIRE: What are you doing?

MIRA: *(Straddling* CLAIRE's *lap)* How about a quick game of Master and Servant before Peter gets home?

CLAIRE: What?! Take these off me right now!

MIRA: Oh, c'mon Claire, I'm just trying to spice up your life.

CLAIRE: With handcuffs?

MIRA: Would you prefer silk ropes? They have some at the—

CLAIRE: No, I would not prefer ropes! What in the world have you been reading now?

MIRA: Nothing.

CLAIRE: Yes you have. Tell me.

MIRA: Nothing.

CLAIRE: Mira...

MIRA: Just a book.

CLAIRE: A book about...

MIRA: Just a book.

CLAIRE: Mira, take these off and tell me what the book is about.

MIRA: *(Mumbling quietly, unlocking the cuffs)* Bed Death.

CLAIRE: Oh, God! You have got to stop reading those books!

MIRA: But we never make love anymore...

CLAIRE: We do too.

MIRA: When?

CLAIRE: You want an exact date?

MIRA: Yes.

CLAIRE: I can't give you an exact date.

MIRA: I can't either.

CLAIRE: I've been busy.

MIRA: We have Bed Death.

CLAIRE: We do not.

MIRA: They list the symptoms in my book.

CLAIRE: Work has been crazy, that's all.

MIRA: We have all the symptoms.

(PETER *enters unnoticed. He's carrying a book bag.*)

CLAIRE: I am not going to listen to this right now.

PETER: Hi, Moms.

CLAIRE: Oh, hello, dear.

PETER: What are you fighting about?

CLAIRE: We're not fighting, we're arguing. How was school?

PETER: Boring. What are you arguing about?

MIRA: Bed Death.

PETER: God, Mom! You can't talk about that stuff in front of your kid! Fuckin-A... *(He exits in disgust.)*

MIRA: Well, he's certainly in a bad mood.

CLAIRE: He's been in a bad mood since he was thirteen.

MIRA: *(Whispering)* I think it's because of his...you know....

CLAIRE: His what?

MIRA: *(Pointing to her crotch)* You know...his...

CLAIRE: Oh...do you think?

MIRA: He can't leave it alone.

CLAIRE: What do you mean?

MIRA: He masturbates *all the time!*

CLAIRE: I don't wanna hear this, Mira...

MIRA: *All the time.*

CLAIRE: How do you know?

MIRA: I wash the sheets around here.

(CLAIRE *makes a face of disgust.* PETER *returns, eating a snack, carrying a piece of paper, and scratching and rearranging his genitalia.* MIRA *and* CLAIRE *watch, fascinated.)*

PETER: What's for dinner, Mom?

MIRA: Um...Coquille Saint Jacques.

PETER: Yuck. Why are you guys staring at me?

CLAIRE: Um...you're getting so tall.

PETER: Duh, Mom. Mom?

MIRA: Hm?

PETER: *(Handing her the paper)* I don't get this question I missed on my calculus quiz.

(MIRA studies the paper for a moment.)

MIRA: This isn't a *nonlinear* differential equation, it's linear.

PETER: But this function is raised to a power, that makes it nonlinear.

MIRA: But it's raised to the power of *one*. It has to be raised to a power other than one to make it nonlinear. That's the oldest trick question in the book.

PETER: That is so totally rude, to trick people like that.

MIRA: It's how teachers get their kicks.

PETER: I guess. Mom?

CLAIRE: Yes, dear?

PETER: There's a guy at school who's selling his motorcycle really cheap—

CLAIRE: No.

PETER: Aw, c'mon, Mom! I can pay for most of it, and you can pay for the rest for my birthday.

CLAIRE: I am not buying you a death machine for your birthday, there's no logic to that.

PETER: It's not a death machine. *(He looks to MIRA for help.)*

MIRA: My brother had a motorcycle, and he never got hurt.

CLAIRE: I don't want Peter riding one of those things. Buy yourself a car.

PETER: I don't want a car. I want a motorcycle.

CLAIRE: What's wrong with a car?

PETER: I don't want a car.

CLAIRE: Why not?

PETER: Cuz.

CLAIRE: I see.

PETER: I'm gonna be eighteen, you know. I don't even need your permission.

CLAIRE: But you do need a place to live. And you will not live here if you buy a motorcycle.

PETER: Maaaaaaa!

CLAIRE: You are not getting a motorcycle. End of discussion.

PETER: Fuckin'-A!

(PETER *stomps off.* CLAIRE *returns to her bills.*)

MIRA: Honey, he'd be careful.

(CLAIRE *stops writing and sighs.*)

CLAIRE: I had to put Molly to sleep today.

MIRA: Molly Malone?

CLAIRE: Mm-hm.

MIRA: Oh, Pookie, I'm so sorry. Why didn't you say so?

CLAIRE: You didn't ask.

MIRA: Sh, sh. Poor darling.

CLAIRE: *(Scribbling out a bill)* Y'know, the worst part about this profession is charging people for putting their pets to sleep. Billing for killing. It's so absurd.

MIRA: I know, sweetie. How's Mrs Dalton?

CLAIRE: How do you think she is? She's upset!

MIRA: Sh, sh. Poor pumpkin.

(PETER *enters eating something different.*)

PETER: What's the matter?

MIRA: Your mother had to put Molly Malone to sleep today.

PETER: Who's Molly Malone?

MIRA: Old Mrs Dalton's cat.

PETER: Bummer. Moms?

MIRA & CLAIRE: Yes, dear?

PETER: Can Paige come over tomorrow?

CLAIRE: Who's Paige?

PETER: My girlfriend.

MIRA: You have a girlfriend?

PETER: Yeah.

CLAIRE: You've never mentioned her.

PETER: She's new at school.... We just sorta...you know...I mean she wasn't really my girlfriend until today.

CLAIRE: Why? What happened today?

PETER: I asked her to be my girlfriend.

CLAIRE: Oh.

PETER: She wants to meet you guys. Can she come over?

MIRA: She *may*. For dinner?

PETER: Yeah, I guess so.

MIRA: How exciting! I'll cook something extraspecial.

PETER: Can't you just make something normal, like hamburgers, or macaroni and cheese?

MIRA: No.

PETER: Can you make something I can pronounce?

MIRA: Roasted chicken?

PETER: No zucchini.

MIRA: No zucchini.

CLAIRE: So tell us about Paige, dear.

PETER: *(He shrugs.)* She's just a girl.

MIRA: Well, she must be a special girl, if our Peter likes her.

PETER: *(He shrugs.)* Yeah. She's pretty cool. When's dinner?

MIRA: In about half an hour.

PETER: I'm gonna have a snack, then.

MIRA: Just a little one.

PETER: O K.

*(*PETER *exits.* MIRA *runs to* CLAIRE *and hugs her from behind.)*

MIRA: This is so exciting! Peter has a girlfriend.

CLAIRE: *(Disentangling herself)* Uh-huh.

MIRA: You don't love me anymore.

CLAIRE: What? Look, I just killed Molly Malone, I don't love anyone right now, O K?

MIRA: O K.

CLAIRE: I had a bad day.

MIRA: Well, I'm trying to cheer you up.

CLAIRE: Sweetie, furry handcuffs do not cheer me up. They're probably made out of somebody's cat I killed.

MIRA: I don't think so, honey—it's fake fur.

CLAIRE: I just...it seems like all I ever do anymore is put animals to sleep. I like the giving-birth part of my job. I delivered a beautiful, healthy foal at the Robbins place this morning, then I euthanized three cats and one dog this afternoon.

MIRA: Poor dear.

CLAIRE: And do you know why I got into this profession?

MIRA: The money?

CLAIRE: Because I love animals. And look around! Do you see a single pet? We don't have a single pet!

MIRA: Peter's allergic.

CLAIRE: You'd think we'd have a million pets. Strays. Cripples. Orphans. Sometimes I just want to come home to my own animals, not these...*transients* I deal with every day—

MIRA: But Peter's allergic. Anyway, pets shed so much.... And they smell.

CLAIRE: Not all of them.

MIRA: They drool. They whine. They meow. They eat the furniture. They want things, but they don't speak English. They poop...

CLAIRE: So do babies.

MIRA: I guess I've never really understood their purpose. I mean—"pets." What an odd name. "Pet." Some creature sits around waiting to be "pet." I'm going to pet my pet—

CLAIRE: This is what I'm saying!

MIRA: What?

CLAIRE: My career revolves around animals! You don't like them, and Peter's allergic to them! What have I been doing for twenty years?!

MIRA: You're having a crisis, aren't you?

CLAIRE: I built this practice thinking my child would take it over! James Herriot's son took over *his* practice....

MIRA: But Peter's allergic.

CLAIRE: I know he's allergic—

MIRA: You think I'm saggy—

CLAIRE: So what am I supposed to do?—

MIRA: I do my Jane Fonda tape everyday—

CLAIRE: My son is allergic to my entire career!

MIRA: —but I'm still saggy—

CLAIRE: I'll never be able to retire—

MIRA: Sometimes I have to rewind the tape—

CLAIRE: I'll have to go on killing cats until I'm ninety!

MIRA: —because I'm getting slower...and saggier—

CLAIRE: I want my son to kill cats for me!—

MIRA: He can't do that. He's allergic—

CLAIRE: You are not saggy! And I know Peter is allergic to animals, O K?! I'm just trying to communicate that I'm a little bit depressed that our only offspring is not going to follow in my footsteps and that you have no connection whatsoever to my life's calling!

MIRA: I have a connection. I do.

CLAIRE: Phht! Every time I suggest going riding, you find some excuse.

MIRA: Horses are so sweaty...

CLAIRE: So are you when you walk around in the hot sun for a couple hours!

MIRA: I don't know what to say.

CLAIRE: I don't want you to say anything, I'm just venting! You always say you want me to talk more. WELL, I AM TALKING AND YOU ARE NOT LISTENING!

MIRA: If Peter wore a gas mask, he might be able to kill cats...

CLAIRE: There's a little more to it than that! I do not just go to my office and KILL CATS!

(PETER *enters eating something.*)

PETER: Something's burning.

MIRA: Oh, no! *(She runs off.)*

CLAIRE: Peter?

PETER: Mom?

CLAIRE: Do you want to be a vet?

PETER: I don't wanna kill cats...

CLAIRE: Because we can get you allergy shots...

PETER: Fuckin'-A, Mom. I don't wanna kill cats. I like cats.

CLAIRE: I also help give birth to animals, I make sick animals well. I encourage life, I don't just put an end to it.

PETER: Yeah, but...I'm allergic...

CLAIRE: There are shots...

PETER: I'm afraid of needles...

CLAIRE: O K, fine. What *do* you want to be, Peter? You're going to college next year...somewhere. What do you want to study?

PETER: I dunno. That's so far away.

CLAIRE: It's not far away. It's next year.

PETER: I can't think that far ahead.

CLAIRE: What *do* you think about, Peter?

PETER: Sex.

CLAIRE: Is that all?

PETER: Pretty much.

CLAIRE: Have you...um...ever...*had*...sex?

PETER: No. I'm a virgin. Can you believe that? I'm almost eighteen!

CLAIRE: Uh-huh. Speaking of which, what do you want to do on your birthday? Shall we go out to dinner?

PETER: Nah. I'm gonna hang with Paige.

CLAIRE: Oh.

PETER: I wanna lose my virginity on my birthday, and Paige said she'd help me.

CLAIRE: Help you?

PETER: You know what I mean.

CLAIRE: Uh-huh. And is Paige the right girl?

PETER: Right girl? She's a girl. I like her a lot. She likes me a lot. We want to have sex.

CLAIRE: Well, there you go.

(MIRA *enters carrying a pot holder.*)

MIRA: It was just the rice. I had to start a new batch, so it'll take another half hour. You'd better have a snack, Peter.

PETER: O K. (*He starts to exit.*)

CLAIRE: Wait a second, Peter. Tell your mother what you want to do for your birthday.

MIRA: Dinner at Hamburger Heaven? Friday the Thirteenth, Part 47?

PETER: I wanna lose my virginity.

MIRA: With Paige?

PETER: Yeah.

MIRA: Wow.

PETER: Is that O K?

MIRA: Shoot yeah. Can't think of anything I would've rather done when I was eighteen. Except I was sixteen. Eighteen is a little late for a guy, isn't it?

PETER: That is so sexist, Mom! Eighteen is late for everyone these days!

MIRA: Yeah, I guess so.

PETER: *(Starts to exit, then stops)* Oh, yeah. Can one of you guys buy me some condoms?

CLAIRE: Why can't you buy your own?

PETER: Fuckin'-A, Mom. That would be so embarrassing!

CLAIRE: Well, if you're old enough to have sex—

MIRA: Oh, I'll get some at the Safeway.

CLAIRE: Mira...

MIRA: He's embarrassed. But if he's gonna ride, he has to wear a helmet.

PETER: Maaaaa! *(He exits.)*

CLAIRE: So when he's away at college, you'll Fed-ex him condoms?

MIRA: Sure.

CLAIRE: You can't be responsible for your son's sex life, Mira.

MIRA: Maybe I'm just glad someone's getting it around here.

CLAIRE: Jesus, Mira. Look, sweetie, I've just been busy and distracted and neglectful and I'm sorry. How about we go dancing Friday? We'll go to the country-western place and you can twirl me 'round the dance floor.

MIRA: Really?

CLAIRE: Really. Dinner and dancing.

MIRA: You're on! Give us a kiss, and I'll go back to my kitchen.

(CLAIRE gives MIRA a kiss. MIRA jumps up, energized. She charges off to the kitchen, clutching her pot holder.)

(Blackout)

Scene Two

(The next evening)

(Music plays: Doris Day's "Que Sera, Sera". The stage is lit primarily by candles. CLAIRE enters, carrying a briefcase. Her right hand is bandaged. She is bewildered by the darkness and bumps into things, groping for the light switch.)

CLAIRE: Honey, I'm home! Why are the lights off? Hello?

(She finds the switch and turns on the lights. The phone rings. CLAIRE picks it up. Throughout the conversation, she continually glances around, trying to figure out where MIRA is.)

CLAIRE: Hello? *(Her voice drops to a whisper.)* You have to stop calling me... No...just call Blake if one of the horses is sick... No... Look, I'm sorry.... Because I just can't anymore, we've gone through this.... Well, I'm sorry, but there's nothing I can do.... I have to go.... No, absolutely not...don't cry... I'm hanging up, now, O K?... I'm sorry... *(She hangs up the phone. She is shaky and upset.)* Mira?

(She heads for the table to put her briefcase down. The lights go off. She goes to the switch and turns them on and heads back toward the table...they go off again. MIRA enters in the candlelight. She creeps up behind CLAIRE and hugs her. CLAIRE screams. MIRA screams.)

CLAIRE: Good God!

(CLAIRE turns the lights on. MIRA is wearing Saran Wrap. Underneath the Saran Wrap, she is wearing a bra and panties. She strikes a "sexy" pose when the lights come on.)

MIRA: Hi, honey.

CLAIRE: Hi. Where were you—? My God, what are you wearing?

MIRA: Saran Wrap.

CLAIRE: Have you been reading *The Total Woman* or something?

MIRA: Maybe.

CLAIRE: That book is hopelessly out of date, Mira.

MIRA: I thought she had some very good ideas....

CLAIRE: You're not supposed to wear anything underneath.

MIRA: What?

CLAIRE: You're wearing underwear.

MIRA: They're sexy underwear.

CLAIRE: I think the idea is to...never mind.

MIRA: Does it turn you on?

CLAIRE: No, Mira, it does not "turn me on." You've got to stop reading those books.

MIRA: *(Slinking up and putting her arms around* CLAIRE.*)* If I took off the underwear would it turn you on?

CLAIRE: No.

MIRA: Well, can you give me some idea of what would?

CLAIRE: I said I'd take you dancing.

MIRA: Fine. But I also want some spontaneity. You can't just take me out dancing when you feel guilty about neglecting me.

CLAIRE: You're right. Mira, I need to talk to you.... I don't know how to say this—

*(*PETER *enters. He stares at* MIRA.*)*

PETER: Holy shit, Mom! Have you been reading *The Total Woman* or something?

CLAIRE: How do you know about that?

PETER: I had to read it in my Women's Studies class. Fuckin-A, Mom! That book is so out of date.

MIRA: Well, I liked it.

PETER: Mom, tell her to change. Paige is coming over. She can't dress like that in front of Paige!

CLAIRE: Mira...

MIRA: I'm going. I'm changing. *(She exits in a huff.)*

PETER: *(Yelling off toward* MIRA*)* And you're not supposed to wear underwear! *(To himself)* I'm hungry.

*(*PETER *exits to get a snack.* CLAIRE *sighs and sits at the table with her briefcase. She begins taking papers out. She rubs her injured hand and checks the bandage. The doorbell rings.* CLAIRE *waits for* PETER *to get it. The doorbell rings again.)*

PETER: *(Offstage)* Mom! Someone's at the door!

CLAIRE: She's your girlfriend, Peter. Let her in and introduce her to us properly.

PETER: *(Offstage)* Fuckin'-A.

(After a moment, PETER *enters, followed by* PAIGE. PAIGE *carries a motorcycle helmet.* CLAIRE *stands and smiles.)*

PETER: Hey, dude.

PAIGE: Hey.

PETER: Mom, this is Paige.

PAIGE: Hi.

CLAIRE: Nice to meet you, Paige.

(CLAIRE *starts to shake hands, then remembers the injury and just sort of waves at her.*)

PETER: What happened to your hand, Mom?

CLAIRE: Dog bite.

PAIGE: Oooo, bummer. You're a vet, right?

CLAIRE: That's right.

PAIGE: I'm thinking about becoming a vet.

CLAIRE: Really?

PETER: Why do you wanna do that? Dogs'll bite you.

(MIRA *enters, dressed normally. Stuck to the bottom of her shoe is a long piece of Saran Wrap, which* CLAIRE *will spend the better part of the scene trying to surreptitiously remove.*)

MIRA: Hello, hello! You must be Paige.

PETER: Mom, this is Paige.

MIRA: How lovely to meet you.

PAIGE: Hi.

MIRA: Shall we sit? Have you offered Paige something to drink, dear?

PETER: You want something to drink?

PAIGE: Coke?

PETER: O K. Be right back. Uh...anyone else?

MIRA: I'm fine, thanks.

CLAIRE: No, thanks.

(PETER *exits.*)

MIRA: What happened to your hand, Claire?

CLAIRE: Dog bite.

MIRA: Pets! (*To* PAIGE) Sit, sit, sit! Make yourself at home.

PAIGE: Thanks.

MIRA: So...you're Peter's girlfriend.

PAIGE: Yes, ma'am.

MIRA: She's so polite! I love that.

(PAIGE *looks around, unsure where to put her helmet.*)

PAIGE: Mrs Gray...I mean...I'm sorry...I never asked Peter what your last names were.

MIRA: You were right. Gray. We're all Gray here!

PAIGE: That's a coincidence.

CLAIRE: Well, we weren't born with the name Gray.

MIRA: No, no. Ironically, my maiden name is *Black* and hers is *White*, isn't that funny? So when we got together, we met in the middle.

PAIGE: Cool.

MIRA: Get it? Black and White together make—

CLAIRE: She gets it, dear.

PAIGE: Yes, ma'am.

CLAIRE: I notice you have a motorcycle helmet there.

PAIGE: I was gonna ask where to put it...

CLAIRE: Anywhere's fine.

(PAIGE *places it on the coffee table,* MIRA *picks it up and puts it on the floor under the coffee table.*)

PAIGE: Sorry.

MIRA: No, no. That's a nice helmet.

CLAIRE: So...you ride a motorcycle...

PAIGE: Yes, ma'am.

MIRA: How do your parents feel about you riding a motorcycle?

PAIGE: Well, my mom rides a Harley...

MIRA: Wow. Where're you from?

PAIGE: South Dakota. Near Rapid City.

MIRA: Great place to ride. The Black Hills...we were there years ago.

PAIGE: Yeah, that's a great ride through there.

(PETER *enters with two Cokes. They watch him sit. Silence.*)

MIRA: So...tell us what you like about our Peter.

PETER: Fuckin'-A, Mom...

PAIGE: Umm...he's cute.

CLAIRE: Is he?

MIRA: Claire! He's gorgeous!

PETER: I am not "cute."

MIRA: Of course you are.

PETER: Mom...

(Pause. Nobody knows what to talk about. PAIGE gropes for a topic.)

PAIGE: So...um...which one of you is Peter's real mother?

(Total, utter, complete, dead silence. MIRA fidgets with the helmet with her feet. PETER sticks a finger in his Coke and stirs the ice. CLAIRE stares at PAIGE.)

PAIGE: Oh, God. Sorry. Wrong question.

CLAIRE: We are *both* Peter's mothers.

PAIGE: I'm sorry.

CLAIRE: It's O K.

PAIGE: No, I...um...

(More silence. MIRA tries to help.)

MIRA: Say, Peter, did we ever tell you the story of how you got your name?

PETER: Grandpa's name is Peter.

MIRA: Oh, my God, you're right! But that's not how you got your name.

CLAIRE: Mira...

PETER: It isn't?

MIRA: This is a cute story, Paige. You'll like it.

CLAIRE: Oh, Mira...

MIRA: When we were pregnant, we naturally thought we'd have a girl. I mean...you know... *(Gesturing as if to say that two females would naturally have another)* Anyway, we had all these girls names picked out...and then in the delivery room the doctor says, "It's a boy!" and we just stared at him. We couldn't believe it was a boy. And I said to Claire "It's got a peter!" And so—

PETER: That is not true!

MIRA: It is.

PETER: Fuckin-A, Mom! You named me after my...my—?

MIRA: Well...in a way...no, not really...

PETER: I don't believe this! Nice embarrassment job in front of Paige, guys. Let's go. We're going to my room to listen to music. Call when dinner's ready.

MIRA: O K.

(PETER *and* PAIGE *start to exit.*)

CLAIRE: Sweetheart?

PETER: Yeah?

CLAIRE: It's a beautiful name. It's a saint's name.

PETER: Whatever.

(PETER *and* PAIGE *exit.*)

CLAIRE: You shouldn't have told that story. And you have Saran Wrap stuck to your shoe.

MIRA: I shouldn't? I do? (*She pulls the Saran Wrap off of her shoe and plays with it.*)

CLAIRE: You embarrassed him.

MIRA: I didn't mean to.

CLAIRE: People take their names seriously.

MIRA: I suppose...

CLAIRE: We named him after his penis—and while it is a lovely name— I don't think he appreciates that.

MIRA: I'll apologize.

CLAIRE: After Paige leaves...

MIRA: After Paige leaves.

(PETER *enters the living room. His clothes and hair are a bit disheveled.*)

PETER: Mom? Did you get the...the "you knows"?

MIRA: The condoms?

PETER: Yeah.

MIRA: They're for your birthday.

PETER: Yeah, but...

MIRA: Dinner's almost ready. You don't have time, and this is something I really want to stress: You *have to take the time.* When you masturbate, it may take you five minutes—

PETER: Fuckin'-A, Mom!

MIRA: But when you're with a girl, you need to make sure she's satisfied. And that takes more than five minutes.

PETER: O K.

MIRA: Are you listening?

PETER: Yeah.

MIRA: I mean are you really listening?

PETER: Yes!

MIRA: You don't want to be a bad lover, do you?

PETER: Mom!

MIRA: You get the condoms on your birthday.

PETER: O K! Can we go for a ride on Paige's bike then?

MIRA: Dinner'll be ready soon.

PETER: Just a quick ride. I just gotta do *something*—know what I mean?

MIRA: Uh-huh. O K, a quick ride.

CLAIRE: Does she have an extra helmet?

PETER: Yes, Mother. *(He grabs the helmet from under the coffee table and exits.)*

MIRA: Should I have given them to him?

CLAIRE: They're a birthday present.

MIRA: Right.

CLAIRE: Right.

MIRA: Come help me get dinner on.

CLAIRE: I need a drink.

MIRA: *(Flicking the Saran Wrap at her playfully as they exit)* Would it loosen you up?

CLAIRE: Mira, please...

MIRA: It was just a joke, Claire. Lighten up.

(They exit.)

(Lights up on the motorcycle. PETER and PAIGE are standing by the bike. PAIGE unlocks a second helmet and hands it to PETER.)

PAIGE: I'm sorry I fucked up in there? I shouldn't have asked that.

PETER: No biggie.

PAIGE: But I'm totally curious. I mean, like, which one is your mother?

PETER: They both are.

PAIGE: Yeah, yeah. But which one gave *birth* to you?

PETER: Both.

PAIGE: That's not possible.

PETER: It's complicated.

PAIGE: *(Getting on the bike)* I'm sorry. There I go again. Total diarrhea of the mouth.

PETER: It's O K.

PAIGE: Who's your father?

PETER: I don't have a father.

PAIGE: Dude...*that* is not possible.

PETER: Well, I don't know who it is.

PAIGE: Aren't you curious?

PETER: No.

(PAIGE cranks the engine and revs it. They have to yell over the noise. PETER climbs on behind PAIGE and wraps his arms around her waist. PAIGE takes off, and they both jolt slightly backward. Throughout this next they lean around curves in unison, etc.)

PAIGE: What about your medical history? You should have your medical history.

PETER: I'm not sick.

PAIGE: For the future. It's always good to know that sort of stuff just in case.

PETER: Never thought about it.

PAIGE: God, I'd be obsessed.

(PETER shrugs.)

PAIGE: What if you look like him? You don't really look like your moms.

PETER: I look like me.

PAIGE: Was it a guy they knew?

PETER: I don't think so. It was all artificial insemination and stuff like that. I was conceived in a lab.

PAIGE: Just an anonymous sperm donor?

PETER: I guess so.

PAIGE: What if your dad is a Nobel Prize winner or something?

PETER: That'd be cool. But what if he's a serial killer or something?

PAIGE: Don't even joke about that shit. God, this is driving me crazy. It's like a big mystery!

PETER: Are we still gonna have sex on my birthday?

PAIGE: Sure. Are you gonna get the...?

PETER: My mom has 'em.

PAIGE: You told your mom?

PETER: Sure.

PAIGE: Which one?

PETER: Both.

PAIGE: God, I'm so embarrassed.

PETER: They're cool.

PAIGE: I can't eat dinner with them. I'm mortified.

PETER: Don't be.

PAIGE: I feel like such a slut.

PETER: That is so—

PAIGE: Sexist, I know. O K. O K, if you don't feel like a slut, I don't. I'm fine. Really.

PETER: O K.

PAIGE: O K.

(PAIGE *stops at a stop sign. They jolt a bit forward, put their legs down on the ground to balance the bike, look both ways, etc.*)

PETER: How long does it take?

PAIGE: What?   ·

PETER: Sex. How long does it take for girls?

PAIGE: What do you mean?

PETER: My mom said it takes longer for girls...

PAIGE: O K, now I'm mortified.

(PAIGE *peels out.* PETER *is thrown backwards and almost loses his seat. He grabs onto* PAIGE *and holds her tighter.*)

(*Blackout*)

Scene Three

(*Evening. The living room is dark.* CLAIRE *enters with her briefcase.*)

CLAIRE: Honey, I'm? (*She sees the darkness again. She sighs. She stands, not even attempting to turn the lights on.*) Mira, don't do this to me. I had a terrible day. There was an accident. One of those double-decker-horse-carrying-truck-things overturned on the highway.

There were horses everywhere. Horses missing legs...heads...tails. I had to euthanize fifteen of them. Four died on their own. One horse lived. One damn horse out of twenty. And the asshole driving the truck was mad because his truck was totaled! Mira?

Are you listening to me? I mean, there's death and destruction everywhere, and he's upset about his goddamned truck! Those poor horses are dead, and they didn't understand what was happening to them. They don't understand traffic. They just...they just got on the truck because some other asshole told them to. Mira?

(She stumbles to the couch, sits, puts her head in her bandaged hand, and sobs. After a moment, PETER enters carrying a motorcycle helmet. He turns on the lights. CLAIRE jumps.)

PETER: Hey, Mom.

CLAIRE: Oh, hello, dear.

PETER: Why're you sitting in the dark?

CLAIRE: I thought...well, I thought your mom had them off on purpose to be romantic and—

PETER: I don't wanna hear that stuff—

CLAIRE: No, I mean...Mira!? Maybe she's not even home.

(PETER picks up a note from the table and reads.)

PETER: "Be back soon, pardner. Went to rustle up some new duds." She's not here, Mom.

CLAIRE: Guess not. *(Noticing the helmet)* What's that?

PETER: A helmet.

CLAIRE: A motorcycle helmet.

PETER: Paige didn't feel like driving me home, so she gave me the bike.

CLAIRE: I thought you were having dinner with Paige and her family.

PETER: I did. They eat, like, right when you walk through the door. No conversation, no "How was your day, honey?" It's, like, dinner is *there*. Eat it now or *starve*. So I ate it. And then there was nothing to do. I'm not allowed to go to her room, and I didn't wanna watch T V with her family, so I came home.

CLAIRE: Why can't you go to her room?

PETER: I dunno. Guess they figure something might happen, which it might.

CLAIRE: So you took the motorcycle...

PETER: It's such a rush, Mom! Have you ever been on one?

CLAIRE: No.

PETER: God, it's like the wind is right there in your face, and you totally notice what color the leaves are, and how buildings are built, and drops of water on the pavement, and everything around you—

CLAIRE: And the other people in traffic?

PETER: Don't be such a drag! Of course I notice the traffic.

CLAIRE: Good.

PETER: Man, you look like you killed a hundred cats today.

CLAIRE: Something like that.

PETER: You need a ride.

CLAIRE: A ride where?

PETER: On the bike. C'mon, I'm gonna take you for a ride!

(PETER *hands the helmet to* CLAIRE. *She fidgets with it.*)

PETER: C'mon, Mom! You'll love it. You'll forget all about the cats.

CLAIRE: Horses.

PETER: Whatever. Put it on.

(CLAIRE *hesitates, then puts the helmet on.*)

PETER: How's it feel?

CLAIRE: Scary.

PETER: C'mon, let's go.

CLAIRE: What about your head?

PETER: There's an extra helmet on the bike.

CLAIRE: I don't know...

PETER: *(Heading out)* Come on, Maaaa!

(CLAIRE *follows* PETER *off. They reappear by the motorcycle, and* PETER *unlocks the second helmet.*)

CLAIRE: No, wait. What if we crash and there's arms and legs and tails everywhere?

PETER: God, Mom. You ride horses all the time. You could get thrown from a horse and break your neck!

CLAIRE: But horses just seem so much more reasonable than motorcycles. You can talk to them and pet them and all that.

PETER: They still do whatever they want. You can control a bike easier than a horse.

CLAIRE: But I can relate to horses. I can't relate to machines. I can't even work the microwave unless you help me.

PETER: Maaa!

CLAIRE: I'm not a modern woman, Peter.

PETER: *Carpe diem*, dude. That's Latin for—

CLAIRE: I know.

PETER: C'mon, Ma. I'll go slow. I promise.

CLAIRE: Very slow.

(PETER *cranks the bike up and revs the engine.*)

PETER: Get on.

(CLAIRE *climbs on behind* PETER. *She holds onto him very tightly.* PETER *gasps for air.*)

PETER: I can't breathe, Ma!

CLAIRE: Sorry.

PETER: O K, here we go!

(CLAIRE *lets out a shriek as they pull out. She buries her head in* PETER's *shoulder and won't look at the road. They lean around a few curves, and* CLAIRE *gradually looks around her. She breathes deeply and smiles.* PETER *turns around and smiles at her, she immediately points for him to look at the road, not her. She sits up straighter and loosens her grip on* PETER. *Suddenly, she lets go of* PETER *and puts her hands straight up in the air and yells, "Wheeee." She loses her nerve and grabs* PETER *again. They both laugh.*)

(*Lights fade on the motorcycle and come up in the living room.* MIRA *enters, wearing a country-western outfit and carrying a shopping bag. She pulls a cowboy hat out of the bag and plunks it on her head.*)

MIRA: Claire? Sorry I'm late! Let's go show them cowpokes how to dance! Claire?

(MIRA *wanders offstage, then back on, calling for* CLAIRE. *She finds her own note, then looks around for a reciprocal one. She goes to the telephone and dials.*)

MIRA: Sally? Hey, it's Mira. Sorry to call you at home. I'm just wondering if Claire had an emergency or something. We were supposed to—oh, dear. How awful. So they're still there. Oh. What time did she head home, then? I see. Well, maybe she went for a beer with Blake after all that. I sure would. Thanks anyway, Sally. Say hey to Tim for me...O K. Bye.

(MIRA *hangs up the phone, then picks it up and dials another number.*)

MIRA: Oh, hi, Blake...you're home...It's Mira. Sally told me about the accident, so I thought maybe you went out for beer—Oh. O K. Say hey to Max for me...O K. Bye.

(MIRA *hangs up the phone, then picks it up and dials another number.*)

MIRA: Hey, it's me.... No, nothing's wrong.... No, Peter's fine. I'm just calling to say hey. Nothing's wrong, Mom.... Yeah... A little... Uh-huh... She's a lot like Daddy.... Yeah, I tried that.... No, nothing... Really? *(She laughs.)* Daddy? I can't imagine.... O K... Well, I'd better go. We're supposed to go dancing tonight. Say hey to Daddy for me... I know, Mother. I meant next time you visit his grave.... O K, I will.... Love you, too.

(MIRA *hangs up and wanders around aimlessly for a bit. She goes to the stereo and puts on some country-western music. She sings along with the music and dances around a bit by herself. Suddenly, she sits down and starts crying.*)

(Lights come up behind her on the motorcycle. CLAIRE *is driving. She applies the brakes, and the bike wobbles a little bit.)*

CLAIRE: Whoa, girl.

(PETER *puts his feet down to steady the bike, then reaches around and switches off the engine.* CLAIRE *pats the bike like it's a horse, then pulls her helmet off, grinning.*)

CLAIRE: I did it!

PETER: You were awesome, Mom.

CLAIRE: It did what I told it to!

(PETER *laughs. They head inside, chattering.* MIRA *hears them coming and wipes her nose on her sleeve.*)

CLAIRE: *(Offstage)* That was really amazing! What a rush! Is that what it's called?

(They enter the living room.)

PETER: See? I told you— *(He spots* MIRA.*)* Hi, Mom!

CLAIRE: Mira, guess what? I rode on Paige's motorcycle, and then Peter taught me how to drive it, and I went around the block all by myself and—

MIRA: Peter, I'd like you to go to your room.

PETER: Is Mom in trouble?

MIRA: She is.

CLAIRE: *(Looking at her watch, suddenly remembering their date)* Oh, God, I'm so sorry, I—

PETER: Well, it's probably my fault, whatever it is, 'cause I—

MIRA: GO!

PETER: I'm totally gone. *(He hustles off.)*

CLAIRE: Oh, sweetie, I'm so sorry. It's not that late, let's go now.

MIRA: Forget it. That's not the point.

CLAIRE: I'm sorry, I just had a bad day, and Peter—

MIRA: You always have a bad day!

CLAIRE: No, I mean a *really* bad day. There was this big accident with a horse trailer—

MIRA: I don't care if every horse in the county keeled over dead today!

CLAIRE: Don't say that.

MIRA: *(Hurling her cowboy hat at CLAIRE.)* WE HAD A DATE!

CLAIRE: I said I'm sorry!! Look, I came home, I felt lousy, and I went for a ride with Peter. You weren't even home!

MIRA: I left you a goddamned note! You could've at least done me the same courtesy! But no! You're as thoughtless as your son! Both of you just go off and leave me whenever you feel like it!

CLAIRE: What's Peter got to do with this?

MIRA: I spend all day at home, trying to make it a nice place for you two ingrates. I clean, I cook, I empty the trash, I mow the lawn, I plant the garden, and you both take it for granted that I'll just be here to listen to your problems when you get home.

CLAIRE: I think you're having a midlife crisis, Mira—

MIRA: But nobody wants to listen to my problems! No one asks if *I've* had a bad day and need some help feeling better!

CLAIRE: Or pre–empty-nest syndrome or something—

MIRA: I'm your doormat! Your faithful dog, who gets a pat on the head now and then by its two thoughtless owners!

CLAIRE: Well, if it's so terrible for you, Mira, why don't you get out of the house more? Join a club! Take a class! Have an affair! Get a job! Get a *life*, for Christ's sake!

(MIRA is stunned.)

MIRA: How *dare* you! YOU are my life! Peter is my life!

CLAIRE: I'm sorry—

MIRA: And you're both wandering away from me. God! I'm gonna be totally alone!

CLAIRE: I'm sorry, sweetie, I shouldn't have—

MIRA: Wait a second. Did you just tell me to have an affair?

CLAIRE: Well, I didn't mean—

MIRA: Why did you say that?

CLAIRE: It's just something you say...like, I didn't really mean "get a life"... I was just saying....

MIRA: What an odd thing to say to me. I would never think of saying something like that.

CLAIRE: It was just a—

MIRA: And I would never think of...

(MIRA *narrows her eyes and stares at* CLAIRE *for a long time. This makes* CLAIRE *very uncomfortable.* MIRA *looks a little dizzy. She sits.*)

MIRA: When?

CLAIRE: It's over, Mira.

MIRA: When, goddammit?!

CLAIRE: It didn't mean anything...

MIRA: Tell me *when!!!*

CLAIRE: It was stupid, it was just—

MIRA: Are we talking recent here?!

CLAIRE: Mira...

MIRA: It's over since *when*?!

CLAIRE: Last week.

MIRA: Last week? Last *week*?!!!

CLAIRE: It didn't mean anything.

MIRA: Were you planning to tell me about this?

CLAIRE: Yes. I was going to...I tried...

MIRA: Who was she?

CLAIRE: I can't tell you that.

MIRA: Oh. Yes, of course. By all means, protect *her*. It's O K if I go to the grocery store or the video store or the hardware store and run into her and smile like a fool. That's O K. Just make sure to protect *her*.

CLAIRE: You don't know her.

MIRA: Oh, good. Now I feel better. A complete stranger has made a fool of me. God, you probably gave her some of my zucchini! Did you give her some of my zucchini?

CLAIRE: Of course not.

MIRA: Wow. You actually...? *(She sits silently for a moment.)* With someone else...? You actually...I can't even say it. This is really beyond my comprehension. I don't know what to say. I don't even know where to begin....

CLAIRE: It didn't mean anything.

MIRA: Stop saying that! It devalues whoever it was. And you. I don't think I really want to know you're that shallow.

CLAIRE: I think I just felt like I needed—

MIRA: You needed something, and it couldn't come from me.

CLAIRE: No.

MIRA: Yes.

CLAIRE: Maybe. I don't know. I can explain—

MIRA: You can?! You mean there's actually a valid explanation for this behavior?

CLAIRE: I just meant—

MIRA: Well, as long as you have a good explanation, Claire, I'm sure everything'll be just fine and dandy!

CLAIRE: I'm only trying to—

MIRA: Shut up, Claire! Right now I'm just trying to grasp this. How about if I just ask you for details when I'm ready to hear them?

CLAIRE: O K.

MIRA: I need to think.

CLAIRE: O K.

(MIRA stands. She's a bit wobbly.)

MIRA: In the meantime, I think you're probably right. I should go out and get myself a life.

CLAIRE: Mira, I didn't mean that—

MIRA: Maybe I need more than just the two of you. Obviously, you need more than just the two of us...

CLAIRE: I'm so sorry.

MIRA: Me too, Claire. Maybe I'll get a job.

CLAIRE: I don't want you to get a job.

MIRA: You just told me to get a job, among other things...

CLAIRE: I was angry. I didn't mean it.

MIRA: I think it's a good idea.

CLAIRE: Well, I don't.

MIRA: *(Glaring at her)* Well, too bad.

(MIRA goes to the table and picks up the newspaper. She rifles through it until she finds the classified section.)

CLAIRE: Mira, don't do this just because you're mad at me.

MIRA: I'm not. I've been thinking about it anyway. I need to have something to do when Peter leaves home. I don't think either of you realize how hard that's going to be for me. Typical of you both. I bet she was young. Was she young?

CLAIRE: *(Ignoring the question)* What kind of job are you going to get? What can you do?

MIRA: I'm a math whiz.

CLAIRE: I know, but you can't just look in the want-ads under "Math Whiz". You haven't been in the job market for...? Have you ever been in the job market?

MIRA: Nope. Daddy supported me in college, then you supported me. But I *want* a job. I hear that people who are unemployed don't really *want* jobs. I *want* a job, therefore, I will get one. The power of positive thinking. Was she a blonde? At least tell me she wasn't a blonde.

CLAIRE: She wasn't a blonde.

(MIRA abruptly tucks the newspaper and starts to exit.)

MIRA: Good. I'm gonna go read these in bed. You'll be sleeping out here, of course.

CLAIRE: No, wait, Mira. Stay and talk to me. Don't go to bed angry.

MIRA: Don't go to bed angry?! You know what, Claire? If I wait until I'm not angry about this to go to bed, I won't get any sleep for months! Did she have one of those Rubenesque figures?

CLAIRE: Oh, for God's sake. If you want to talk, let's talk. Don't just keep throwing out these—

MIRA: Or maybe she one of those "horsey women" who go everywhere dressed like they're fox hunting.

(CLAIRE looks away. MIRA notices and drops into a chair.)

MIRA: Oh, my God. I'm right, aren't I?

(CLAIRE nods.)

MIRA: I thought you hated those clothes.

CLAIRE: It wasn't about clothes—

MIRA: Of course not. She probably wasn't even wearing clothes most of time. It was about horses.

CLAIRE: Not just horses. Animals in general. I was attracted to her love of animals. We just had so much in common...

(MIRA *clamps her hands over her ears and closes her eyes.*)

MIRA: No more.

CLAIRE: And I felt like I could talk to her about things I can't talk to you about.

MIRA: *That's enough!*

CLAIRE: I need to talk to you about this.

MIRA: I don't care what you need! You should have told me about your needs before you went off and found someone else to take care of them! This is about *my* needs now. And right now I need to get away from you!

(MIRA *stomps off, clutching her newspaper. After a moment,* PETER *enters.*)

PETER: Hi, Mom. Where's Mom?

CLAIRE: She's reading want ads, looking for a job.

PETER: Do we need money?

CLAIRE: She just wants a job.

PETER: Is she having a midlife crisis?

CLAIRE: I think she just wants to get out more.

PETER: Oh.

(*The phone rings.* PETER *picks it up.*)

PETER: Hello?... HELLO?... Get a life! (*He slams the phone down.*)

CLAIRE: No one there?

PETER: I hate that. What's for dinner?

CLAIRE: You already had dinner at Paige's.

PETER: I'm hungry again, so I'll have some of whatever you guys are having.

CLAIRE: Your Mom didn't cook anything.

PETER: What are you gonna eat?

CLAIRE: I'm not hungry.

PETER: Fuckin-A... What am I supposed to eat?

CLAIRE: Look, sweetie, I'm sorry there's no extra dinner for you. I'd make you something, but I don't know how to cook. I'm a terrible mom, I know—

PETER: It's not your job, it's Mom's job.

CLAIRE: Well, that may have to change. Put something in the microwave, O K?

PETER: I guess.

(MIRA *enters, dumps a pillow and blanket on the floor, then exits.*)

PETER: You sleeping out here tonight?

CLAIRE: Yeah.

PETER: Just 'cause you rode a motorcycle?

CLAIRE: It's complicated. Don't worry about it.

PETER: O K. Mom?

CLAIRE: Yes, dear?

PETER: Who's my father?

CLAIRE: Oh, God. Can we talk about this later?

PETER: Yeah, sure.

CLAIRE: It's a long story. Your Mom should be here for it, but now is not the time. O K?

PETER: O K.

CLAIRE: O K. I'm gonna turn in now. It's been a hard day.

PETER: *(Looking for reassurance)* The horses, huh?

CLAIRE: Yeah. It was pretty yucky. 'Night, sweetie. Love you.

PETER: Love you back.

(PETER *scratches and adjusts his genitalia. He is only vaguely satisfied by* CLAIRE'S *answer.*)

PETER: *(To himself)* Fuckin-A.

(PETER *shuffles off.* CLAIRE *tips over and curls up on the couch.*)

(Blackout)

END OF ACT ONE

ACT TWO

Scene One

(At rise: the next evening. CLAIRE *sits doing paperwork at the table.* PETER *watches her as he eats a snack. The house already looks messier.)*

PETER: How much do you charge to kill a cat?

CLAIRE: Twenty-five dollars.

PETER: Fuckin-A. You could tie a rock around its neck and throw it in the river for free!

CLAIRE: Don't talk like that.

PETER: How much do you charge to kill a dog?

CLAIRE: Same.

PETER: A horse?

CLAIRE: Fifty dollars.

PETER: That seems reasonable. Do you shoot 'em or stick 'em?

CLAIRE: Stick 'em...unless it's an emergency. I had to shoot a horse at the accident the other day.

PETER: Mom with a gun! Way cool! Um...how much do you charge to help give birth to a baby horse?

CLAIRE: A *foal*. Are you bored?

PETER: I'm hungry. Fuckin-A. For eighteen years there's always been food waiting for me, or at least in the oven cooking for me. Suddenly, there's no food. What's for dinner?

CLAIRE: Maybe we can order out.

PETER: I want a burger.

CLAIRE: Nobody delivers burgers, sweetie. Why don't you have a snack?

*(*PETER *sighs and exits.* MIRA *enters. She is quite chuffed with herself.)*

MIRA: Hello!

CLAIRE: Hi.

MIRA: Oh. Hi. Where's Peter?

CLAIRE: Getting a snack. How'd it go today?

MIRA: Fine. PETER*!!!*

(PETER *enters, eating a snack.*)

PETER: Hey, Mom.

MIRA: I have an announcement.

CLAIRE: You got a job.

MIRA: Of course I got a job. I start day after tomorrow, and let this be a lesson to you, Peter. Your mother got a job because she *wanted* one.

PETER: O K.

CLAIRE: What kind of job is it?

MIRA: I'm working down at Tom's Tow Lot.

PETER: What's that?

MIRA: That's where they take cars that have been towed. When people come to get their cars, they have to ask me for their cars, and they have to give me money to get their cars back. I have this adorable little Airstream trailer all to myself, and I'll be meeting people from all walks of life—I mean anyone can get their car towed, it crosses all socioeconomic boundaries.

CLAIRE: I thought you wanted to use your math, sweetie.

MIRA: Well, that's the great part. I do get to use my math. Tom and I talked for a while about how mad people get at him when all he's doing is towing cars that the police tell him to tow. So I came up with this really neat sliding scale system for the customers, and Tom agreed to try it out, but to use it you have to be able add in your head really fast, and I can do that because I'm a math whiz, so I got the job!

PETER: Cool. What kinda system?

MIRA: Well, if people get mad about being towed there are certain rules. Like if they use the S-word, I tell them there's an extra twenty-dollar charge for towing during rush hour. And if they use the F-word, I tell them there's an extra fifty-dollar charge for having to break into their car to put it into neutral. And if they *physically* threaten me, I just push this secret button under my desk and, before Tom brings the car up from the lot, he puts a dent in it with a baseball bat. Isn't that clever? And there are all sorts of other extra charges that depend on other types of behavior. It's like combining psychology and math! I evaluate their mental condition, then charge 'em for it! Isn't that a great system?

CLAIRE: Very clever, sweetie.

PETER: Yeah. That's cool, Mom. What's for dinner?

MIRA: I thought we'd go out to dinner. To celebrate.

PETER: Cool. I want a burger.

MIRA: Hamburger Heaven! Let's go!

PETER: Oh, wait. I gotta ask you guys an important question before we go. Maybe I should get a snack.

MIRA: O K.

(PETER *exits to get another snack.*)

CLAIRE: I'm so proud of you, sweetie.

(CLAIRE *tries to hug* MIRA. MIRA *pushes her away.*)

MIRA: Look. I'm being civil to you for Peter's sake. Don't touch me. And will you please stop calling me "sweetie"?

CLAIRE: No, I won't. We need to deal with this!

MIRA: Tell me she didn't have washboard abs and perky breasts.

CLAIRE: Look, just talk this out with me, or—

MIRA: Or what, Claire? You'll start cruising chicks at the Humane Society?

CLAIRE: Stop it, Mira.

MIRA: Or you'll start hanging out at a petting zoo, looking for a new housewife?

CLAIRE: Stop it, goddammit!

(PETER *enters, eating something.*)

PETER: Are you fighting again?

CLAIRE: No.

MIRA: Yes.

PETER: Do you want me to leave?

MIRA: No, honey. You have an important question.

PETER: Yeah. O K. So...who's my father?

MIRA: You don't have one.

PETER: Dude, that is totally impossible.

CLAIRE: Peter, you don't have a father, you have a *sperm donor*.

PETER: O K, I'll buy that. Who's my sperm donor?

CLAIRE: We don't know. Donors are anonymous.

PETER: Can I find out who he was?

MIRA: No.

CLAIRE: Yes.

MIRA: Yes?

CLAIRE: Yes. We have what's called a "yes" donor. Someone who will allow his records to be unsealed at the time of his child's eighteenth birthday.

MIRA: We do?

CLAIRE: Didn't you read the contract?

MIRA: No. That was your job.

CLAIRE: Well, anyway—

PETER: Whoa. So, like, in a few days I can ask for the records?

CLAIRE: Yes.

MIRA: No!

CLAIRE: Yes.

MIRA: Boy, Claire, I'd say you're battin' a thousand around here.

CLAIRE: *(Ignoring her)* I'll give you the number of the clinic.

MIRA: I don't believe this. Why do you want to know?

PETER: Just curious. I need my medical history. Paige was saying that, like, what if my father—

CLAIRE: Sperm donor.

PETER: What if my sperm donor had a history of some weird illness...

MIRA: Then they wouldn't let him donate sperm...

CLAIRE: They're pretty careful about that stuff, Peter. They only allow men with very healthy backgrounds to donate.

PETER: Yeah, but what if in the meantime *his* father died of some rare blood disease or some weird cancer or something? Medical histories can change, you know.

CLAIRE: Do you want to meet this man, or just get his medical history?

PETER: Well, I wouldn't mind meeting him, I guess. Maybe I look like him. I don't really look like you guys.

MIRA: You look like you.

PETER: Fuckin-A, Mom. Wouldn't you be curious?

MIRA: No.

PETER: I'm not gonna run away and live with him. I just want to meet him.

MIRA: So Paige put you up to this?

PETER: No.

MIRA: You've never asked before.

PETER: Never thought much about it before.

MIRA: But Paige thought about it, didn't she?

CLAIRE: Mira, it's O K....

MIRA: Hussy!

PETER: Fuckin-A, Mom. That's pretty harsh.

CLAIRE: Let's just go to dinner, shall we?

MIRA: Shall we invite *Paige*? Maybe she has more things for us all to worry about. I find these sorts of discussions are particularly helpful for the digestion.

PETER: God, Mom! What's the big deal?

MIRA: What's wrong, Peter? Aren't we good enough for you now that youre becoming a man? You need someone around with a penis, is that it?

PETER: Whoa, Mom. You are way outta line.

MIRA: No, *you're* out of line! I am your mother!

CLAIRE: Mira—

MIRA: Stay out of this! How do you think it makes me feel with you running around looking for another parent?

PETER: Well, how do you think it makes me feel to know I *have* another parent out there that I've never met?!

MIRA: He is not a goddamned parent! You call sperm a parent? Is that what a parent is to you, Peter? Sperm?!

PETER: I'm just talking about the biology, Mother!

CLAIRE: Mira, I don't see why—

MIRA: Shut up!

CLAIRE: Don't tell me to shut up—

MIRA: *(Ignoring* CLAIRE*)* A parent is someone who changes your diapers and bandages your scrapes and wipes your tears and your nose and feeds you and puts up with you when you're being a jerk!! Do you think that's how Sperm-Man feels? Do you?

PETER: Don't call him that.

MIRA: I'll call him whatever I want to!

PETER: Fuck you.

(MIRA *slaps* PETER's *face.* PETER *just stares at her. His lip quivers, he's about to start crying.*)

CLAIRE: Jesus, Mira...

MIRA: Don't you *ever* speak to me like that! *(Heading out)* I'm going out. *(She stomps off.)*

(PETER *sniffles and* CLAIRE *goes to him.*)

CLAIRE: Oh, sweetie, I'm so sorry. She didn't mean to hit you.

PETER: *(Rubbing his cheek)* Sure feels like she meant to.

CLAIRE: She's just upset lately.... She's mad at me about something, and she's taking it out on you....

PETER: Yeah, well you must've done something pretty bad, 'cause she's never hit me before.

CLAIRE: I'm sorry....

PETER: What'd you do?

CLAIRE: You don't wanna know that stuff. Remember?

PETER: Whatever. Just don't do it again, or I'll end up with a black eye.

CLAIRE: I won't. You want to go get some dinner?

PETER: I'm not hungry. I'm gonna go take a walk. Maybe I'll go over to Paige's.

CLAIRE: O K.

PETER: 'Night.

CLAIRE: Love you. I'm sorry about....

PETER: *(Shrugging)* Whatever.

(PETER *exits.* CLAIRE *sits on the sofa and stares into space. The phone rings.* CLAIRE *glances toward it, but doesn't move to answer it. It rings and rings and rings....)*

(Blackout)

Scene Two

(Evening. PETER's *birthday.* PETER *is on the phone. He looks upset.)*

PETER: But, I— ... But—... Uh-huh...O K. Bye.

(PETER *hangs up.* MIRA *enters unnoticed. She is carrying a birthday cake in a box.)*

PETER: Fuckin-A. Happy Birthday to me.

MIRA: Hey there.

(PETER jumps.)

PETER: Hey, Mom.

MIRA: You O K, sweetie?

PETER: Yeah, I'm fine.... You scared me.

MIRA: Sorry. What's up?

PETER: Nothing.

MIRA: Yes there is.

PETER: No there's not.

MIRA: Yes there is. I can tell. I can always tell.

PETER: *(Impatiently)* I'm fine!

(MIRA eyes him suspiciously.)

MIRA: *(Touching his cheek)* Peter, we used to talk.... I don't understand what's happening to you lately.

PETER: Me? What's happening to *you*? It's like you're mad all the time. You're mad at me about the sperm donor thing, and you're mad at Mom about that and something else.

MIRA: I have a pretty good reason.

PETER: Fine. Don't listen to me, I'm just a stupid kid! Just walk around here mad and make everyone miserable and hit people! Whatever.

MIRA: I'm so sorry about that, Peter.

PETER: Whatever. It's like walking in a minefield around here. So whatever it is, just get over it, Mom.

MIRA: Is that what you do, Peter? Whenever you have a problem, you just "get over it?"

PETER: No, Mom. I *talk* about it, because you *make* me talk about it. So *talk* to Mom!

MIRA: It's not quite that simple!

(The phone rings. MIRA answers it.)

MIRA: Hello?...Hello?....Look, I don't know who you are, but... Oh, God, wait! I *do* know who you are! You listen here, you little... Hello? *(She hangs up the phone. She is shaking.)*

PETER: What was that about?

MIRA: *That* is why I'm mad at your mother.

PETER: Because some psycho keeps calling us?

MIRA: Your mother had an affair.

PETER: What?

MIRA: I said—

PETER: *(Furious)* I heard what you said! Why the hell did you tell me that?!! Oh, God!!! I can't believe you just told me that!! I don't wanna know that stuff!!! Fuckin-A, Mom!

(MIRA starts to cry. PETER is hopping around, grabbing his hair, trying to erase this information from his brain.)

PETER: Shit! God! Aw, Mom. Don't cry. God!

(PETER pats her on the shoulder awkwardly.)

PETER: It's O K, Mom. don't cry. Please? Shit! God!

MIRA: I'm sorry.

PETER: It's O K.

MIRA: I shouldn't have told you that—

PETER: It's O K.

MIRA: You're right. I should talk to her and—

PETER: Can we please stop talking about this?!

MIRA: Sorry. Umm... What time is Paige coming over?

PETER: In about an hour.

MIRA: We'll have your cake when she gets here, then get out of the way.

PETER: O K. So...um...where are the...uh...?

MIRA: What?—oh. You'll get them when you open the rest of your presents.

PETER: Can't I just look at them? I've never really seen one up close.

MIRA: Do you know how to put one on?

PETER: Won't it be obvious?

MIRA: I don't know. You should read the instructions.

PETER: I don't wanna sit and read the instructions in front of Paige.

MIRA: I guess you should have them now.

PETER: Yeah, then I could get used to them. This is making me nervous....

(MIRA retrieves a small gift-wrapped box and hands it to PETER.)

PETER: You didn't need to wrap 'em, Mom....

MIRA: It's your birthday.

(PETER *tears off the wrapping and studies his brand-new box of condoms.*)

MIRA: I hope they're the right kind. There were some that were extra large. You're not extra large, are you?

PETER: *(Opening the box and pulling out the instructions)* I don't think so.

MIRA: Do you like them?

PETER: Totally. Thanks a lot, Mom.

(MIRA *runs off briefly, then runs back on carrying a large zucchini, which she hands to* PETER.)

MIRA: Here. Practice with this. Then you won't get nervous later.

PETER: O K.

(PETER *wanders off, holding the zucchini and reading the instructions.* CLAIRE *enters with a large box.*)

CLAIRE: Where's Peter?

MIRA: He's practicing his condoms.

CLAIRE: Oh. Have you been crying?

MIRA: We can talk about it later.

CLAIRE: O K.

MIRA: Did you get it?

CLAIRE: Well...no...I got him something different.

MIRA: Without asking me?

CLAIRE: Don't get mad. It was a spur-of-the-moment sort of thing.

MIRA: Lemme see.

(CLAIRE *takes the lid off the box and* MIRA *looks inside.*)

MIRA: Wow.

CLAIRE: Is it O K?

MIRA: He'll love it. Are you sure about this?

CLAIRE: Yeah, I'm sure. Is it O K with you?

MIRA: It's the perfect present. Let's give it to him.

CLAIRE: O K.

MIRA: Peter!

PETER: *(Offstage)* Just a sec!

MIRA: How'd you get it home?

CLAIRE: Paige brought it. She's out there now. I called her and she came and helped me pick it out.

MIRA: Oh, did she now? How sweet.

CLAIRE: She's really a very nice girl, Mira.

MIRA: She's a troublemaker.

CLAIRE: Well, Peter likes her, and we owe it to him to like her too.

MIRA: Hmph.

(PETER *enters, holding a condom-encased zucchini. He behaves coolly toward* CLAIRE *throughout the following.*)

PETER: *(Waving the zucchini)* Think I got it. Oh, hi, Mom.

CLAIRE: *(Holding out the box)* Happy Birthday!

PETER: Thanks. Can I open it now?

MIRA: You *may.*

(PETER *takes the lid off the box and looks into it. His eyes get very big.*)

PETER: Holy shit! Are you serious?

MIRA: Yes.

PETER: Where is it?!

CLAIRE: In the driveway.

PETER: Whoa. *(He pulls a motorcycle helmet out of the box. He's completely spastic and tears offstage.)*

PETER: Thanks, Moms!

(PETER *finds* PAIGE *wheeling out his new bike. Throughout the following,* PETER *checks out the bike, etc.*)

(Pause. MIRA *looks at* CLAIRE *expectantly.)*

CLAIRE: What now?

MIRA: Well?

CLAIRE: Well, what?

MIRA: Aren't you even going to ask me? See? That is so typical of you. Do you see what I'm talking about?

CLAIRE: What've I done now?—Oh my God! Your first day at work! How was it?

MIRA: It was really fun!

CLAIRE: Yeah?

MIRA: It was great! There are a lot of angry people out there, let me tell you.... I was racking up charges right and left. Tom was thrilled. He said I'd made more money on my first day than the last woman did in a week!

CLAIRE: That's great.

MIRA: And on my lunch hour I picked up the cutest curtains at K-Mart for the trailer. It makes all the difference. Tom liked them a lot.

CLAIRE: That's great, honey.

MIRA: How was your day?

CLAIRE: Quiet. A couple of neuterings, a teeth cleaning, and a Husky who swallowed a pair of socks.

MIRA: This is kinda fun. Talking about our jobs. It's so grown-up.

CLAIRE: Yeah...it is...it's kinda...sexy.

MIRA: Don't use that word around me.

CLAIRE: She weighed seven hundred pounds and had long, greasy, black hair.

MIRA: You think that's funny?

CLAIRE: No, I just... No...nothing's funny. I don't know what to say.... I love you, Mira.

MIRA: Duh, Claire.

(CLAIRE *can't help but laugh. She puts a hand on* MIRA'*s knee.* MIRA *shies away, and* CLAIRE *takes her hand away.*)

MIRA: I don't trust you anymore.

CLAIRE: Can you trust me enough to take you to dinner?

MIRA: I suppose.

(*They rise and head out.*)

CLAIRE: Oh, wait, we have to have Peter's cake first.

MIRA: Oh, Claire, Claire, Claire. Peter's got a motorcycle, a girl, and a brand-new box of condoms...the cake can wait.

CLAIRE: Yeah, I guess you're right.

(*They exit and reappear by the bike. They go to* PETER, *who is sitting on his new bike.*)

CLAIRE: What do you think? Pretty spiffy, huh?

PETER: (*Shrugs*) Yeah.

MIRA: Peter, don't be rude...

PETER: *(Forced smile toward* CLAIRE*)* Thanks, Mom.

CLAIRE: *(Completely confused)* You're welcome.

(MIRA *pulls* CLAIRE *off.)*

CLAIRE: What was that about?

PAIGE: *(Waving to them)* 'Night.

(CLAIRE *and* MIRA *are gone.* PETER *and* PAIGE *head back inside.)*

PAIGE: So anyway, the sperm dude...

PETER: I only talked to him for a little bit....

PAIGE: And?

(PETER *shrugs. He starts to cry.* PAIGE *holds him.)*

PAIGE: What's the matter?

PETER: He said he doesn't want to meet me. He said he'd send me his medical history, but he thinks it's best if we don't meet. And he said his wife doesn't want him to meet me and he had to honor her wishes and shit like that.

PAIGE: Phht! What a dickhead. Dude, I'm so sorry.

PETER: It's O K. Doesn't matter.

PAIGE: Fuckin-A.

PETER: It's O K. I mean, it's not like I'm his son or anything. I was just curious to see what he looks like. I never thought about it before, and now I think about it all the time.

PAIGE: That's my fault. I shouldn't have bugged you about it.

PETER: Nah, I would've thought about it on my own sooner or later. *(He disentangles himself and wipes his nose on his sleeve.)*

PAIGE: I can't believe him. What a dickhead. Fuckin-A. I mean, why is he a "yes" donor if he's just gonna say "no"?

PETER: He said, "Things change." But he also said that he thinks I should have my medical history, and that's mostly why he became a "yes" donor in the first place. He's gonna mail it to me.

PAIGE: Well, isn't that swell of him.

PETER: Well, at least I have that. I could've had a total "no" donor.

PAIGE: What a dickhead. Fuckin-A.

PETER: Isn't it weird that guys can have kids they've never seen? Girls can't do that.

PAIGE: Yeah.

PETER: I mean, I can make life just by...by...you know...but you can only make life by carrying it all around for nine months. It's like you're making soup and I would just be one of the ingredients, but you would be the soup pot. That's weird as shit! Fuckin'-A...

PAIGE: It's totally not fair.

PETER: Not at all. But, you know it's also totally cool that you can do that. I wouldn't mind being able to do that...

(PAIGE *lunges at* PETER *and kisses him.*)

PETER: Whoa.

PAIGE: You are so cute.

PETER: Naw...

PAIGE: Yeah... Um, I really want to....

PETER: Me too...

PAIGE: When are your moms coming back?

PETER: Not 'til late.

PAIGE: Do you have the...?

PETER: Yeah, Mom bought me like a whole case of 'em.

(*They embrace and kiss passionately.*)

(*Blackout*)

Scene Three

(*Late, that night. The stage is lit only dimly.* PETER *sits alone in the living room. He has a nearly empty cakeplate on his lap and is finishing it up with a fork. He looks depressed.* MIRA *and* CLAIRE *enter, stumbling over things. They fumble for the lights and do not see* PETER.)

CLAIRE: Sh, sh! They might still be—

PETER: We're not.

(CLAIRE *and* MIRA *scream.*)

CLAIRE: Oh my God! I didn't see you!

PETER: You didn't wait for cake.

CLAIRE: What—? You were busy with Paige and the new bike and we figured we could eat it later.

PETER: I already ate it.

MIRA: Well, let's have some more.

PETER: I ate all of it.

MIRA: You ate the whole cake?

PETER: I didn't know when you were coming home, if ever. Are you still fighting?

MIRA: Not at the moment.

CLAIRE: *(Turning the lights up a little brighter)* Peter, what's the matter?

MIRA: Did you have a good time? Was it...fun?... Was it what you thought it would be?

PETER: I'm still a virgin.

MIRA: What? Why? Did Paige change her mind, that—

PETER: I couldn't get it up.

MIRA: Oh.

CLAIRE: That happens sometimes, sweetie, it's nothing to worry about...

(CLAIRE isn't actually sure if that happens, she shrugs and looks to MIRA for help. MIRA nods.)

PETER: But I've had at least five erections a day since I was thirteen!

MIRA: I'm sure it was just nerves. Don't take it so hard.

PETER: Maybe I'm gay.

CLAIRE: Do you think you are?

PETER: I don't know. I must be.

CLAIRE: Are you attracted to other boys? Men?

PETER: No.

CLAIRE: But you're attracted to girls?

PETER: I thought I was....

CLAIRE: Peter, you mustn't make such a big deal out of this.

(PETER shrugs.)

MIRA: Paige was O K with it, wasn't she?

PETER: I guess. I don't know. I started crying and I think it wigged her out, and she left.

MIRA: She just left without saying anything? That—

PETER: She said I was making a big deal out of it.

MIRA: Oh. Well, she's right. I remember I had this boyfriend in high school who—

PETER: God, Mom! How many times do I have to tell you? I don't wanna know that stuff!

MIRA: Sorry.

PETER: *(Rising)* I'm going to bed. Thanks for the bike. It's totally awesome.

CLAIRE: Good night, dear.

(PETER exits.)

MIRA: Poor guy. Peter's peter petered out and performed poorly.

(MIRA and CLAIRE collapse on the couch, laughing.)

(Blackout)

Scene Four

(The next day. An empty living room. PETER's motorcycle helmet sits on the coffee table. CLAIRE enters with a large box.)

CLAIRE: Hello?! Anybody here?

(CLAIRE hides the box behind the couch as PETER enters, wearing an apron and an oven mitt.)

PETER: Hi, Mom. How was work?

CLAIRE: Great. I saved a horse's life today!

PETER: Cool. What's in the box?

CLAIRE: A present for your mom.

PETER: 'Cause she's so pissed about the affair?

(CLAIRE is quite taken aback.)

CLAIRE: What did you say?

PETER: You heard me.

CLAIRE: I'm sorry your mother told you that.

PETER: Me too. But that was way uncool of you.

CLAIRE: It was. But how about we talk about this when you're forty?

PETER: Phht!

CLAIRE: I'm sorry. Do you want to talk about it now?

(The phone rings. They both look at the phone, but do not move to get it. They look at one another.)

PETER: Don't you want to get that?

CLAIRE: No.

PETER: *(Moving toward the phone)* I bet.

CLAIRE: Peter—

(PETER *picks up the receiver and immediately drops it back into the cradle without putting it to his ear. He watches* CLAIRE *the whole time.)*

CLAIRE: I'm sorry.

PETER: You messed everything up around here. First, you were hardly ever around all summer, because you were "working" so much—yeah, right —and now Mom went and got a job because she's mad at you, so *no one's* ever around!

CLAIRE: Look, Peter, I don't I want you to worry about this. We'll get through it, and we'll always be here for you. Together.

PETER: Promise?

CLAIRE: Give it some time, sweetie. *(Smiling, trying to jolly him up)* Just promise me you won't run away and live with your sperm donor or something—

(PETER'*s eyes well up and he looks like he's about to cry.)*

CLAIRE: It was just a joke.

PETER: I talked to him.

CLAIRE: You did? I didn't know you even had his number. What's his name?

PETER: Harold Carter. Is Harold, like, the stupidest name there is or what?

CLAIRE: Well, what did he say?

PETER: He won't meet me.

CLAIRE: He won't? Why not?

PETER: What do you care?

CLAIRE: I care a lot. I think you should meet him.

PETER: Yeah, right.

CLAIRE: Who signed the contract, Peter? *(No response)* Who?

PETER: *(Quietly)* You.

CLAIRE: That's right. *(She gives him a hug)* Why are you wearing an apron?

PETER: I'm making dinner.

CLAIRE: Oh. Why?

PETER: Because no one else was.

CLAIRE: Ah. How lovely. Thank you, Peter.

PETER: You're welcome.

CLAIRE: How are you doing that?

PETER: What?

CLAIRE: Making dinner.

PETER: Duh, Mom. I'm following a cookbook. I'm eighteen. I can read now.

MIRA: *(From offstage)* Hello?

PETER: Can we tell Mom about the Harold thing later? She'd probably be all happy that he won't meet me, and I can't deal with that right now.

CLAIRE: O K.

(PETER exits. MIRA enters.)

MIRA: Hi.

CLAIRE: Why did you tell him?

MIRA: What? Oh.

CLAIRE: That was out of bounds.

MIRA: I'm sorry...it just slipped out. I was upset.

CLAIRE: This has nothing to do with Peter.

MIRA: I know. You're right. I'm sorry. I'm so sorry.

(PETER enters, looking for his oven mitt.)

PETER: Hi, Mom. How was work?

MIRA: I got fired.

PETER: Bummer.

CLAIRE: Fired?! Why? Tom loves you!

MIRA: I fed the dogs.

CLAIRE: You what?

MIRA: Tom has these two Dobermans. I thought they seemed awfully testy, and so I figured they might just be hungry. They looked a little skinny to me...so, anyway, the other day I picked up a bag of dog food on my way to work, and you should have seen them go at it! So for the past couple days I've been feeding them, and let me tell you they've been a lot more pleasant to be around! They've been hanging out with me in my trailer...you know, just snoozing, I mean, that's what dogs do, don't they?... And then today Tom walks in and sees Slasher and Basher asleep by my desk and he goes ballistic!

CLAIRE: Mira, I think the idea is that—

MIRA: You know why he has those dogs?

CLAIRE: To guard the lot.

MIRA: To guard the lot! And he tells me they won't guard the lot if they're all fat and happy and he can't believe I'm *feeding* them. And he said that last night four cars were taken out of the lot and now he knows why! Like it's my fault! I mean, we're a pretty high-tech country.... Hungry dogs is kind of a primitive security system, don't you think?

PETER: It's pretty common practice...

MIRA: To starve dogs?

PETER: So they'll be meaner.

MIRA: That's disgusting.

CLAIRE: Yes, it is.

PETER: What happened to them?

MIRA: I called the Humane Society after Tom fired me.

PETER: Go, Mom.

CLAIRE: Good for you.

(MIRA *looks at* PETER.)

MIRA: Why are you wearing an apron?

CLAIRE: He's making dinner.

MIRA: Really? Why?

PETER: No one else was. Oh yeah, and Paige is coming over.

CLAIRE: Great.

MIRA: Uh-huh. What are you making?

PETER: Pot roast.

MIRA: Yum! You found my Fannie Farmer Cookbook, didn't you?

PETER: Yeah. It seemed like the easiest one.

MIRA: It is. A well-written cookbook, that one. Good choice.

PETER: Thanks. I gotta go check on it. (*He exits.*)

CLAIRE: I'm sorry about your job, sweetie.

MIRA: I'm sorry I told Peter about your...the...you know...

CLAIRE: I'm sorry about the...you know...

MIRA: We're a pretty sorry pair, aren't we? Come talk to me while I get out of these clothes.

(They exit. After a moment, the doorbell rings.)

PETER: *(Offstage)* I'll get it!

(PETER enters with PAIGE, who carries her helmet.)

PAIGE: Nice apron, dude.

PETER: I'm making dinner.

PAIGE: Cool.

(They sit on the couch. Awkward pause)

PETER: Thanks for ditching school with me today. I had a nice time.

PAIGE: Don't be so weird, it was fuckin' amazing!

PETER: Yeah, I guess it was.

PAIGE: My friend Carla-May was saying that the first time for girls wasn't so great, but I totally had a great time.

PETER: Totally.

(They kiss. MIRA enters, straightening out her clothing.)

MIRA: Oops! Sorry, kids.

(PETER breaks away from PAIGE.)

PETER: No prob.

(Something occurs to MIRA as she looks from PETER to PAIGE and back. While she is scrutinizing them, CLAIRE enters.)

MIRA: *(To CLAIRE)* Look at them!

CLAIRE: What?

PETER: Mom...

PAIGE: What?

MIRA: Am I right?

PETER: Yeah, yeah. Old news.

CLAIRE: What are you talking about?

PETER: Nothing.

MIRA: Can't you see?! Peter's lost his virginity!

PETER: Fuckin-A...

CLAIRE: Ohhhh! Yes, now I see it. Well, congratulations, dear.

PETER: Maaaaaaaa!

PAIGE: I am totally mortified.

MIRA: Was it fun?

PETER: Maaaaaaaa!

PAIGE: I can't even make eye contact, I am so mortified.

CLAIRE: Don't be silly, Paige. Look at me....c'mon...look at me... Paaaaaige...talk to me Paige.

PAIGE: Hey, Dr Gray, Mrs Gray.

MIRA: Hey.

CLAIRE: That's better. How are you, dear?

PAIGE: Fine. I'm great. I'm fine.

PETER: Fuckin-A, I gotta check the roast. *(He exits.)*

CLAIRE: Have a seat, Paige.

(The women all sit.)

PAIGE: So, whaddaya think about this dickhead?—sorry—*guy*.

MIRA: What guy?

PAIGE: Peter's sperm donor.

CLAIRE: Mrs Gray just got home, she hasn't heard the news.

PAIGE: Oh, sorry.

MIRA: What news?

CLAIRE: Peter's sperm donor refuses to meet him.

MIRA: Why?

PAIGE: "Things change."

MIRA: Is Peter upset?

PAIGE & CLAIRE: Yes.

CLAIRE: He cried.

MIRA: He cried?

PAIGE & CLAIRE: Yes.

MIRA: Why didn't he tell me?

CLAIRE: You just got home—

MIRA: Why didn't *you* tell me?

CLAIRE: Mira, you weren't exactly thrilled about the whole thing....

MIRA: What?... But that doesn't mean... I mean...I want what Peter wants... he's my son—I can't believe he won't meet Peter! What a jerk...what a...

PAIGE: Dickhead.

MIRA: Right. Peter is a wonderful kid! Why the hell won't he meet him?

CLAIRE: I don't know...he just won't.

PAIGE: Part of it's 'cause of his wife.

MIRA: Phht! What a...

PAIGE: Dickhead.

MIRA: Right. The nerve of this guy! What? He just wants to ejaculate into a Dixie Cup and not deal with the results? What is that all about? What a...

PAIGE: Dickhead.

MIRA: Right.

CLAIRE: Mira, you didn't even want them to meet!

MIRA: But what right does this guy have to make my son cry? What right does he have to just refuse to meet such a beautiful boy? He signed a "yes" contract!

PAIGE: Yeah, and then he says "no." What a—

MIRA: Dickhead!

PAIGE: Right. Peter's totally upset.

MIRA: Well, we'll just have to do something about that.... *(She gets a perfectly diabolical gleam in her eye.)*

CLAIRE: You have a plan, don't you?

MIRA: I think so. I'd need your help.

CLAIRE: O K.

MIRA: You too, Paige.

PAIGE: O K.

(PETER enters in his apron. The three women turn toward him and smile hugely.)

PETER: It's almost ready. What? What are you staring at?

(Blackout)

Scene Five

(The living room is empty. MIRA tiptoes in. She looks around. Listens. She hears nothing.)

MIRA: *(Whispering loudly)* Coast clear! Come on!

CLAIRE: *(Offstage)* You have to help me!

MIRA: Right.

(MIRA runs back off. MIRA and CLAIRE enter shortly thereafter, carrying the inert body of HAROLD. He's wearing the fur-covered handcuffs from Act One. HAROLD looks more like PETER than either of the women do.)

CLAIRE: Where should we put him?

MIRA: I don't know. How long 'til he wakes up?

CLAIRE: I'm not sure.

MIRA: You're not sure? You're a doctor, you're supposed to know these things!

CLAIRE: I'm a *vet*! I gave him the dosage for a Great Dane. I didn't think he'd stay under even this long.

MIRA: You didn't kill him, did you?

CLAIRE: Can we just put him down?

MIRA: On the couch.

(They trundle him over to the couch and dump him onto it.)

CLAIRE: Do you think he'll be mad when he wakes up?

MIRA: *If* he wakes up...

CLAIRE: He was pretty mad when I gave him the shot...

MIRA: He was just surprised. He's drooling on the cushions.

CLAIRE: Drool is a good sign. Means his body is functioning normally again.

(They hear the sound of PETER's motorcycle pulling up and toss HAROLD over the back of the couch to hide him.)

PETER: *(Offstage)* Hello?!

(PETER and PAIGE enter the living room, carrying their respective motorcycle helmets.)

PETER: Hi, Moms.

MIRA: Hello, dear.

PETER: Paige is here.

MIRA: I see that.

PAIGE: Hi.

MIRA: Hi.

PETER: Can she stay for dinner?

MIRA: She *may*.

PETER: What's for dinner?

MIRA: Whatever you want. Pizza?

PETER: Cool. Why are you acting so weird?

MIRA: *(Signalling to* PAIGE *to get* PETER *out of the room)* I'm not.

PAIGE: C'mon, dude. Let's go to your room.

PETER: O K.

(HAROLD *starts to stir behind the couch. The women resettle themselves on the couch and make noises [coughing, etc] in an attempt to mask* HAROLD's *movements.)*

CLAIRE: Don't...um...don't start anything...

PETER: Fuckin-A, Mom...

CLAIRE: We have a suprise for you and it'll be ready soon, so I'm just saying...

PETER: You're acting totally weird. C'mon, Paige.

(PETER *and* PAIGE *exit.* HAROLD *lets out a loud groan. They drag him from behind the couch.)*

MIRA: It's alive.

CLAIRE: Thank heavens.

MIRA: Harold? Harold, can you hear me?

HAROLD: *(Groggily)* Fuckin-A! Where am I?

CLAIRE: You're here, Harold. With Claire and Mira Gray.

HAROLD: Who're they?

CLAIRE: They're us, Harold.

HAROLD: Don't call me Harold.

CLAIRE: Mr Carter, we—

HAROLD: Hal.

CLAIRE: Hal, we're not going to hurt you—

HAROLD: *(Noticing the handcuffs and starting to panic)* What the—? Who the fuck are you?

CLAIRE: We're Peter's parents.

HAROLD: Peter? Oh, shit...the kid who called me.

CLAIRE: Correct. The result of your sperm donation, for which we are eternally grateful, but now we just have one more favor to ask...

HAROLD: Where is he?

MIRA: In his room.

HAROLD: Did he see me like this?

MIRA: No.

(HAROLD *is a little more focused now. He struggles against the handcuffs and tries to rise. They push him back down.*)

HAROLD: You kidnapped me! That's a federal offense!

MIRA: Yes, Hal, it is. But try to see things from our point of view—

HAROLD: And you drugged me! That's assault and battery!

MIRA: Not necessarily. She's a doctor.

HAROLD: Oh.

CLAIRE: I'm a vet.

MIRA: Claire...

HAROLD: A vet?!! Fuckin-A! A *vet*?!!!

CLAIRE: It's harder to get into vet school than med school, you know.

MIRA: Claire...

HAROLD: I want you take off these handcuffs right this second!

MIRA: I'll take them off if you'll agree to meet Peter.

HAROLD: I don't wanna meet Peter.

MIRA: Then why were you donating sperm?

HAROLD: I needed money. I was in college.

MIRA: So why did you sign on as a "yes" donor?

HAROLD: Because...I don't know...things were difficult back then...I let my emotions decide for me...I thought...I thought that kids should know who their parents are...I...but...*things change*...and I still want him to know his medical history, but not *me*.

MIRA: I'm not following.

HAROLD: I'm an orphan.

MIRA: What?

HAROLD: That's why I signed the "yes" contract. At the time, I figured if I had kids somewhere they would feel like orphans if they didn't know who I was, and I didn't want them to feel like that because I always felt like that because I *was* an orphan. But *things change.*

CLAIRE: I wouldn't think they'd let orphans donate. You don't have the medical history....

HAROLD: I lied.

CLAIRE: You lied.

HAROLD: Well, I didn't actually lie, I just didn't tell them. They didn't ask outright. Well, sort of...but not really...Mostly they were just interested in my sperm count and my I Q. I have a high I Q. Anyway, I'm healthy.

MIRA: But how do we know you'll stay that way?

HAROLD: How do we know *you* will?

MIRA: It's not fair to Peter.

HAROLD: Water under the bridge. What do you want, a refund? I've survived with less knowledge than Peter will have. Would you please remove these handcuffs? I'm allergic to fur. *(He sniffles to prove his point.)*

MIRA: It's not real fur.

HAROLD: Oh.

CLAIRE: You're allergic to animals?

HAROLD: Yes.

CLAIRE: Figures.

HAROLD: Could I at least call my wife? I'm usually home by now. She'll probably be calling the police soon, and then you'll be in big trouble—hey, how am I gonna get out of here anyway?

MIRA: I drove your car here. We took your keys after you passed out.

HAROLD: Oh.

CLAIRE: Promise to meet Peter and you can call your wife.

HAROLD: I don't wanna meet him.

CLAIRE: I think you do.

HAROLD: Of course I do! But I promised my wife...

CLAIRE: Your wife isn't here.

HAROLD: A promise is a promise.

CLAIRE: Does she have a promise in writing...like Peter does?

(HAROLD sighs, defeated.)

HAROLD: Fine. I'll meet him. Briefly.

CLAIRE: O K.

HAROLD: *Briefly.*

CLAIRE: Fine.

MIRA: *(Handing him the phone)* No funny stuff. Any funny stuff and she shoots you up again. Got it?

HAROLD: Got it. *(He dials, with some difficulty.)* Hi, Cookie.

MIRA: Cookie?

HAROLD: I'm gonna be a little late. I'm, uh...over at some friends' house.... No, you don't know them...I met them at the office today...well, I sort of met them in the parking lot.... Yes, it is a strange place to meet people, an entirely new experience for me, but maybe I could explain it later? Hm? Uh, Claire and...and...

MIRA: *(Whispering)* Mira.

HAROLD: Claire and Mira. Hm? Yes....uh-huh... I'll be home in about....

(He looks to CLAIRE *and* MIRA *for help,* MIRA *holds up one finger.)*

HAROLD: ...in about an hour...Uh-huh. Good...What's for dinner?...God, you know I hate brussels sprouts. O K. Sorry. No. Right. Uh-huh. No. Yeah... Well, I'll tell you whole fascinating story when I get home, O K? Bye-bye, Boo-Boo. See you soon. *(He hangs up.)*

MIRA: Peter hates brussels sprouts too.

HAROLD: Who doesn't?

MIRA: Why doesn't your wife want you to meet Peter?

HAROLD: It's an uncomfortable situation for her.

MIRA: Do you and your wife have children?

HAROLD: She can't have children.

MIRA: Oh, God, I'm so sorry—

MIRA: God, that must be terrible for your wife, knowing that you've got a—

HAROLD: Look, I said I'd meet Peter. Let me meet him and go home.

*(*MIRA *takes a key from her pocket and starts to uncuff* HAROLD.*)*

MIRA: He's a great kid, I think you'll really like him.

HAROLD: Uh-huh. *(He stretches out his freed wrists.)* Thank you.

MIRA: I'll call Peter. Oh, this is so exciting. PETER!!!!

PETER: *(Offstage)* What?

MIRA: Your surprise is ready!!!!

PETER: *(Offstage)* Be out in a minute!

MIRA: No. *Now!!!*

PETER: *(Offstage)* Fuckin'-A, Mom!!!

MIRA: NOW!!!

(PETER *and* PAIGE *enter, looking rumpled.* PETER *notices* HAROLD. HAROLD *stands. He looks miserable.)*

PETER: Whoa.

MIRA: Peter, this is—

PETER: Harold.

HAROLD: Hal.

PETER: Hal.

MIRA: How'd you know?

PETER: He looks like me. Or moves like me. Or something...

HAROLD: *(Holding out his hand, which* PETER *shakes.)* It's nice to meet you, Peter.

PETER: You too...um...this is my girlfriend, Paige.

HAROLD: Hi.

PAIGE: Wow. Hi. This is so totally cool of you to do.

PETER: Yeah, thanks. I know you didn't want to.

HAROLD: Well, your...uh...*they* talked me into it.

PETER: Yeah?

CLAIRE: It was your Mom's idea.

PETER: Really?

MIRA: Really.

PETER: Wow. Well, hey, sit down. Are you staying for dinner?

HAROLD: No. My wife doesn't know I'm here, and—

PETER: Oh, well, that's O K...

HAROLD: It's a little weird for her.

PETER: Yeah, I bet. I mean isn't it totally weird that guys can have kids they've never seen? Women can't do that.

HAROLD: Exactly. *(Suddenly standing)* Well, it was nice meeting you all.

MIRA: Oh, have a seat, Hal. Stay awhile longer. *(Hissing)* Sit!

(HAROLD *sits.)*

MIRA: So...Hal was just telling us his wife can't have children.

HAROLD: Jesus—

PETER: Oh, man, I'm really sorry, I mean, this must be really—

HAROLD: Could we talk about something else?

MIRA: Sure. Talk to Peter. You two need to...catch up.

HAROLD: Yeah...so, um...are you happy, Peter?

PETER: About what?

HAROLD: I don't know...with your life, I guess.

PETER: Oh. Well, sure...I guess...I mean, I'm not one of those suicidal teenagers or anything....

HAROLD: Good, good.

PAIGE: What do you do for a living?

HAROLD: Oh, nothing exciting. I'm an engineer. I was always good at math, so...

PETER: I'm good at math too.

MIRA: I'm a math whiz.

HAROLD: Great, great. So you must be about to go to college.

PETER: Next year.

HAROLD: What do you want to study?

PETER: I dunno. Whatever.

HAROLD: Well, I'm sure you'll figure it out eventually. Don't rush it.

PETER: O K.

CLAIRE: What sort of things do you like to do? When you're not engineering something...

HAROLD: Oh, this and that. I like to listen to music. Go to concerts.

PETER: Me too!

PAIGE: What's your all-time favorite album?

HAROLD: Um..let's see...probably Meatloaf's "Bat Out of Hell."

PETER: No way! That's mine!

HAROLD: No way!!

PETER: Way! It's an amazing album.

HAROLD: Truly amazing.

PETER: During "Paradise by the Dashboard Lights," when he does that baseball thing—

HAROLD: Oh, that's just so—

PETER: Sometimes I listen to it over and over—

HAROLD: Oh, me too. It's great.

PETER: Totally.

HAROLD: Yeah.

(They smile and nod. Awkward pause)

HAROLD: *(Starting to rise)* Well, I should—

MIRA: Don't you have something to tell Peter? Hal has something to tell you, Peter.

PETER: O K.

HAROLD: I do?

MIRA: Your parents...

HAROLD: Oh, yeah. Um...I'm an orphan, Peter.

PETER: An orphan?

HAROLD: Well, you know...I was adopted and everything...

PAIGE: Whoa.

HAROLD: But I have no idea who my biological parents are, or *were*.

PAIGE: Whoa.

PETER: Whoa.

HAROLD: Sorry, but your history sort of starts and ends here as far as your paternal line goes.

PETER: O K. That's cool. I can deal with that.

CLAIRE: But he's very healthy, Peter.

PETER: Yeah, that's cool. I don't even think about that medical stuff really, I was just wondering about...I dunno...I was just...*wondering*, I guess.

HAROLD: Yeah, tell me about it. I wonder all the time. It can drive you crazy.

PETER: Yeah.

HAROLD: Look, can I ask a question?

MIRA: You *may*.

HAROLD: I'm curious how this was done...

MIRA: Meaning "How was Peter done?"

HAROLD: Yeah, did you just walk into some fertility clinic and end up with my sperm?...or...I dunno...I don't know how it works...

CLAIRE: A friend of ours, Bill—

HAROLD: Doctor Bill! I remember Doctor Bill!

CLAIRE: Right. I went to school with him. We branched off, obviously. I inseminate horses, he inseminates women. Anyway, he was working on a new procedure.... Peter, do you want Paige to hear this?

PAIGE: What? I wanna hear it. Can I hear it?

PETER: Yeah, it's O K.

CLAIRE: O K. So we really wanted a child, and, to make a long story short, Mira gave physical birth to Peter, but we don't know whose biological child Peter is, because Doctor Bill inseminated Mira, but he also inseminated my eggs in his lab and implanted them in Mira at the same time.

HAROLD: Whoa.

PAIGE: Whoa.

CLAIRE: We have no idea which conception happened, and we've never had a D N A test or anything to find out. Once we saw Peter, it didn't really matter. He was ours.

HAROLD: Whoa.

CLAIRE: I know that procedure happens more these days, but it was new back then.

HAROLD: That is so intense! I mean, you can just give someone your sperm, and they can do all sorts of weird shit with it. Fuckin'-A! What a trip!

PETER: A long trip.

MIRA: Isn't he the cutest?

HAROLD: He is. He really is.

PAIGE: Totally. And he looks like...

HAROLD: Like me. Yeah, he does, a little.

PETER: *God, you guys....*

HAROLD: I feel like crying. (*He puts his head in his hand and sniffles.*)

PETER: Moms! Check it out.

CLAIRE: We're checking.

HAROLD: What?

PETER: I cry sooooo easily.

PAIGE: Totally.

HAROLD: *(Wiping his eyes and lurching to his feet)* I have to go.

PETER: No.

HAROLD: I have to. Look, Peter, I have another life....

PETER: I know. But maybe we could get together sometime?

HAROLD: No.

PETER: No?

HAROLD: I don't think so.

PETER: You mean like *never*?

HAROLD: Right.

PETER: Fuckin-A. But I'm your...

HAROLD: You're not my son, Peter. Biologically you are, but realistically you're not.

PETER: But—

HAROLD: Look, I'm glad I got to meet you, but I didn't raise you and I can't start playing Dad with an eighteen-year-old. That's not fair to you, to me, to my wife, or to your...uh...moms. I just donated sperm. I needed money and I donated sperm.

PETER: Children! Sperm becomes children, dude! That is just so random to just give your children away.

HAROLD: Well, you wouldn't exactly be here if I hadn't!

PETER: I just think it's pretty irresponsible....

HAROLD: Are you listening to me? You wouldn't be here! And maybe some other couple wouldn't have a kid if I hadn't donated!

CLAIRE: He's right, Peter. You wouldn't be here if he hadn't donated sperm.

PETER: WELL, MAYBE I DON'T CARE IF I WOULDN'T BE HERE!

(MIRA, CLAIRE, and PAIGE took at him with expressions of utter horror. PETER realizes what he has said and starts to cry. HAROLD reaches for him, then checks himself. MIRA, CLAIRE, and PAIGE do the same.

HAROLD: This is very hard for me, Peter. Part of me wants to give you a big hug and sit and talk to you for hours. God, it's fascinating for me just to look at you! But you're not my son, and I have to go on with my life, and you have to go on with yours.

PAIGE: What about if you just got together once in a while and...played football or something—

CLAIRE: *We* play football with him....

HAROLD: No.

PETER: It's O K, guys. He doesn't wanna see me.

HAROLD: I *do* want to see you....

MIRA: So how can you just—?

PETER: It's O K! He's right. He's not my father. I don't even know what I was expecting. I don't even need a father...it's just so weird.

HAROLD: I'm sorry it's so weird.

PETER: It's O K. Look, could you do me a favor? Could you maybe send me a picture every year? Like maybe on my birthday. I just wanna see what I'm gonna look like when I get old.

HAROLD: When's your birthday?

PETER: Last week. The fourteenth.

HAROLD: Oh. Happy Birthday. Yeah, I can do that.

PETER: Thanks.

HAROLD: Well, I should...uh... *(Looking pointedly at* MIRA*)* Hm. I don't seem to remember where I put my *car keys.*

MIRA: I'll get em. *(She runs offstage.)*

HAROLD: Thanks. And how do I get back out of here?....I can't remember....

CLAIRE: Right at the stop sign. Left at the light. You'll see the signs for the highway.

HAROLD: Oh, that's right.

*(*MIRA *runs back on, carrying* HAROLD*'s keys and a small white garment. She hands both to* HAROLD*.)*

HAROLD: What's this?

MIRA: It's Peter's christening dress. I thought you might want it.

HAROLD: No...I can't....

MIRA: Sure you can.

HAROLD: Please don't do this to me.

MIRA: I want you to have it. It'll be good luck.

*(*HAROLD*'s eyes start to water. He holds the dress to his face and smells it.)*

HAROLD: I...I have to go.

*(*PETER *holds out his hand for* HAROLD *to shake.* HAROLD *starts to hug him instead but changes his mind and shakes* PETER*'s hand.* HAROLD *exits.* PETER *starts to cry. The women all rush toward him.)*

PETER: Don't. I'm O K.

(They all move away. No one knows what to do.)

CLAIRE: He's a nice fellow.

MIRA: He really is.

PETER: Yeah.

PAIGE: Sorry I called him a dickhead.

PETER: 'S O K.

(PETER takes a deep breath and looks at the women, who are staring at him intently...he wants them to stop.)

PETER: Thanks, Moms.

CLAIRE: Oh, sure.

MIRA: No problem.

PETER: I know it was hard for you.

MIRA: It wasn't so bad.

PETER: He's a pretty good-looking guy. At least I know I'll look halfway decent when I'm old.

CLAIRE: He's younger than we are.

PETER: *(Smiling)* Like I said... I need to get outta here. I wanna go for a ride or something.

CLAIRE: A ride! I almost forgot!

MIRA: What?

CLAIRE: Wait!

(CLAIRE retrieves the present that MIRA never opened and hands it to her.)

MIRA: What's this?

(MIRA opens the box and takes out two motorcycle helmets.)

MIRA: You bought me a motorcycle?

CLAIRE: I bought one bike for the both of us.

PETER: Go, Mom!

PAIGE: Way cool.

CLAIRE: I want you to ride around the countryside with me. I want us to experience it together. It's really amazing.

(MIRA strokes a helmet and starts to cry. PETER signals to CLAIRE that they'll wait outside and leads PAIGE out.)

MIRA: That's the sweetest thing you've said or done in ten years.

CLAIRE: Is it? I didn't mean to wait so long.

(MIRA cries harder. CLAIRE goes to her and holds her.)

CLAIRE: I love you so damn much, Mira.

(The phone rings. MIRA and CLAIRE look at one another. MIRA answers it.)

MIRA: Hello?...This is she...Oh, hi!...Uh-huh...Yes, I'm still interested. Definitely...Great!...How's nine o'clock?...O K...Great!...Thank you so much. Bye-bye. *(She hangs up the phone, beaming.)*

CLAIRE: Who was that?

MIRA: The Humane Society. I told them if no one adopted Slasher and Basher, that we would.

CLAIRE: You did?

MIRA: No one will take them, so I'm going to pick them up tomorrow morning.

CLAIRE: Really?! But Peter's allergic.

MIRA: Well, he'll just have to get shots. He's eighteen now, and it's time for him to get over his silly fear of needles.

CLAIRE: You mean we're really gonna adopt two dogs?

MIRA: Yep! What do you think?

CLAIRE: I think you're beautiful.

MIRA: Oh, stop it.

CLAIRE: I'm gonna ravage you any second now.

MIRA: You are not.

CLAIRE: *(Lunging for her)* I am.

(CLAIRE grabs the furry handcuffs and goes after MIRA. MIRA shrieks with delight and runs. CLAIRE catches up with MIRA, throws her onto the couch and pounces on top of her. CLAIRE snaps one cuff onto MIRA's wrist and the other onto her own, then kisses MIRA. They begin making out heavily. They roll around on the couch, they roll off of the couch, they roll across the floor....)

MIRA: I think you're having a midlife crisis, Claire.

CLAIRE: No, you are.

(They continue making out while saying, "No, you are," back and forth.)

(PETER has gotten impatient and heads back inside to see what's keeping his moms. He enters unnoticed and sees what's keeping them. He smiles, then closes the door quietly and returns to PAIGE.)

PAIGE: Are they coming?

PETER: Um... They'll catch up. Let's go.

(Music starts: The Shangri-Las (or Bette Midler) singing "Leader of the Pack." PETER *and* PAIGE *put on their helmets while* CLAIRE *and* MIRA *continue to wrestle around on the floor, trying to pull clothes off over the handcuffs, etc.* PETER *cranks up the bike.* PAIGE *climbs on, and they take off as the lights dim and the music blares....)*

(Blackout)

END OF PLAY

THE LAST ORBIT OF BILLY MARS

Robert Alexander

ABOUT THE AUTHOR

Robert Alexander is the author of twenty-one plays, including SERVANT
OF THE PEOPLE (a play about the rise and fall of Huey Newton and
the Black Panther Party) and the widely seen I AIN'T YO' UNCLE;
THE NEW JACK REVISIONIST UNCLE TOM'S CABIN and SECRETS IN
THE SANDS, the latter two originally written for the San Francisco Mime
Troupe. He is also the author of the very popular and much-produced THE
HOURGLASS. As the playwright-in-residence at the Lorraine Hansberry
Theatre, he wrote several world premieres for that company, including
AIR GUITAR (a rock opera) and WE ALMOST MADE IT TO THE SUPER
BOWL (a tragicomedy about racism in the N F L). His works have been
produced or workshopped by some of the top regional theatres in the
country, including the Negro Ensemble Company, The Kennedy Center,
The GROUP Theater, Inner City Cultural Center, Los Angeles Theater
Center, The Hartford Stage Company, Jomandi Productions, St Louis Black
Repertory Company, Crossroads Theater Company, Inner Ear, Oakland
Ensemble Theater Company, The Mark Taper Forum, Karamu House, The
Arena Players, Trinity Repertory Company, San Diego Repertory Theater,
and Woolly Mammoth Theatre Company.

His most recent plays are A PREFACE TO THE ALIEN GARDEN,
MOONDUST, EROTIC JUSTICE, THE NEIGHBOR'S DOG IS ALWAYS
BARKING, HATEMACHINE, WILL HE BOP OR WILL HE DROP? and the
romantic comedy MOON IN GEMINI. These latter plays have come to be
known as the EROTIC JUSTICE PLAY CYCLE. Many of Alexander's early
plays have been printed in various anthologies, and I AIN'T YO' UNCLE is
now available through Dramatic Publishing Company.

Alexander has made numerous recordings as a spoken-word artist with
the alternative performance art band the Black Planet Collective. He is
the recipient of numerous writing awards and fellowships and recently
co-edited *Colored Contradictions: An Anthology of Contemporary African-
American Plays* with Harry Elam, a drama professor at Stanford University.
Colored Contradictions, published by Penguin Press U S A in the fall of 1996,
includes works by Alexander, Suzan-Lori Parks, Cheryl West, Rhodessa
Jones, Keith Antar Mason, Pomo Afro Homos, Shay Youngblood, Talvin
Wilks, Kia Corthron, and many others. A 1975 graduate of Oberlin College,
Alexander also holds an M F A in theater (playwriting) from the University
of Iowa, where he was a Patricia Roberts Harris Fellow.

Alexander is currently the N E A/T C G resident playwright at Jomandi Productions in Atlanta, Georgia, and an artistic associate at Woolly Mammoth, thanks to a residency made possible by T C G and the Pew Charitable Trust's National Theater Artist Residency Program.

ORIGINAL PRODUCTION

THE LAST ORBIT OF BILLY MARS premiered at Woolly Mammoth on
11 January 1999. The cast and creative contributors were:

WENDELL . . . . .Doug Brown
RITA MAE . . . . .Taunya Martin
MAMA . . . . Beverly Cosham
BILLY MARS . . . . .Craig Wallace

Director . . . . Timothy Douglas
Set design . . . . Tony Cisek
Costume design . . . . Raye Leith
Lighting design . . . . .Lisa Ogonowski
Sound design . . . . .Mark Anduss
Properties . . . . .Elsie Jones
Stage manager . . . . .John "Scooter" Krattenmaker

THE LAST ORBIT OF BILLY MARS *Show Sponsors*
Imani Drayton-Hill and Robert Hill
Rick Gore
Peter Miller and Sara Cormeny

CHARACTERS & SETTING

RITA MAE, *a thirty-three-year-old woman with a vulnerable, childlike quality. She is bisexual, with a greater preference for women than men.*

MAMA, *a mother to the universe. Confined to a bed for the duration of the play. A stroke victim. Wants to be put in a rest home.*

WENDELL, RITA MAE's *older brother. A forty-one-year-old struggling musician. A saxophone player who cannot stand up without the use of a crutch. He uses a table leg for a crutch.*

BILLY MARS, *a man possessed by nervous energy. Driven to pursue* RITA MAE *to the ends of the earth. A musician with the soul of a poet. An orphan in his early thirties.*

All of the characters are African-American.

Setting: The play is set in the present. In a lower middle-class neighborhood in St Louis that is a little too close to the highway. The sound of cars on the highway in the background is a constant reminder of where we are.

"Lord, make me so uncomfortable that I will do the very thing I fear."

Ruby Dee

ACT ONE

Scene One

(At rise: lights come up on the Megan home. WENDELL is seated downstage right, taking apart and cleaning his saxophone; the table leg he uses for a cane lies next to him on the floor. We hear the roar of the highway in the background throughout the entirety of the play.)

WENDELL: Rita Mae—close that window. How can a man think with all that highway noise?!!

RITA MAE: No.

WENDELL: Come on, Rita Mae.

RITA MAE: I'm not closing it. It's burning up in here.

MAMA: Rita Mae, baby—when you gonna change my diaper? I asked you thirty minutes ago to change my diaper. I'm gonna get a rash if you don't—

RITA MAE: I got to go to the store, Mama—to get some more Depends.

MAMA: I told you to go last night—I told you to go last night.

RITA MAE: If Wendell would stay home somet—

WENDELL: I'm home right now. You can go to the store right now—but shut that window 'fore you go!

RITA MAE: Why can't you watch Mama, just one night? So I can have some fun—

WENDELL: You know my band gigs seven nights a week—seven nights a week.

RITA MAE: It ain't fair.

WENDELL: Fair? Fair? Whoever said life was fair. Now close that window! Don't make me have to get up.

RITA MAE: Get your Rusty Dusty butt up out of that chair. The exercise might just do your ass some good.

MAMA: Don't you be cussing up in my—

RITA MAE: Shut up, Mama—

MAMA: Who you telling to shut up?

RITA MAE: I'm telling you to shut up!

MAMA: You went out to California and came back a heathen with a demon in you. Your soul is cursed—your soul is cursed. Cursing in my house. Disrespecting my house.

RITA MAE: My house! My house!

WENDELL: Mama, make her shut the window.

MAMA: You stay out of it, Boo Boo.

WENDELL: Don't be calling me Boo Boo. I'm forty-one years old. Don't be calling me Boo Boo.

RITA MAE: Boo Boo—Boo Boo—

WENDELL: Don't be calling me that—

RITA MAE: *(Overlap)* Boo Boo—Boo Boo!

WENDELL *(Overlap)* Don't be calling me—

MAMA: *(Overlap)* Shut up!

RITA MAE: *(Overlap)* Boo Boo—Boo Boo!

WENDELL: *(Overlap)* Don't be—

MAMA: I curse the day you both were born—SHUT UP!

(Silence)

WENDELL: *(After a beat)* Come on, Rita Mae—close that window.

RITA MAE: You want that window closed. Get up and close it yourself.

(WENDELL puts his horn down and fumbles around, searching for his cane. He finds it, struggles up from his chair, and goes toward the window with a severe limp, leaning heavily on his cane.)

WENDELL: *(As he struggles to the window)* How can a musician of my status concentrate with all that highway noise competing for my ear? Daddy was a fool to buy this house.

MAMA: Your daddy was not a fool. A little crazy—but he was not a fool.

RITA MAE: He was a fool for letting white folks drive him crazy.

WENDELL: He had to be a fool to buy this house. *(Slams the window shut and slowly returns to his chair)*

MAMA: This was the only house they'd let a colored man buy back then—

WENDELL: A house with a freeway for a fucking front yard.

MAMA: Boy—if I could get up—

WENDELL: But you can't, can ya?— Look at this house. It's a joke. We ain't never gonna sell it. Who'd want it? What was Daddy thinking? He sho wasn't thinking 'bout my future. The future never entered his mind.

MAMA: Quit trashing your daddy and go and get something of your own. Everything you got came from him, and now you think you so high and mighty you can criticize. You ain't perfect.

WENDELL: Never said I was perfect. I've got a gimp leg that reminds me I ain't perfect. You think I'd be hanging around this here town if my leg had been normal? I'd left this place long time ago.

MAMA: What's stopping you from going now? Ain't nobody stopping you.

WENDELL: The ladies won't let me go.

MAMA: What ladies you got?

WENDELL: Plenty, Mama—more than I can handle—

MAMA: Say what? How come your ladies don't be calling here?

WENDELL: 'Cause they know to find me at the club.

MAMA: Find you at the club.

WENDELL: That's what I said.

MAMA: Rita Mae—do you believe this nigger?

RITA MAE: Mama—watch your mouth.

MAMA: Why?

RITA MAE: You said "nigger," Mama—

MAMA: "Nigger" ain't no bad word—

RITA MAE: I never heard you say that word—

MAMA: That's because I never felt like saying it before—until now! When I look at that fool son of mine, hobbling 'round here without a woman—I see a nigger...a nigger without a woman.

WENDELL: I got's plenty women, Mama...

MAMA: Stop lying, boy—

WENDELL: You don't know what I be having. You ain't with me 24-7. At the club...I've got plenty women. They be waiting for me to get there. When I'm done playing—they be waiting on me hand and foot. It be a whole room full of women just waiting on me.

MAMA: How come you never brought none home to see your mama?

WENDELL: I don't bring none of them 'round here, because it might depress them if I brought them 'round here. It might scare them off—if they really saw how I was living. They just wouldn't understand why a grown man would stay here. They wouldn't understand—my loyalty to you...my devotion to you. How could I explain to them that I could never forsake my mama by leaving my mama.

MAMA: Oh, so you ashamed of us. Is that it? This broke-leg negro think he better than us. Ain't that nothing?

RITA MAE: Mama! Why you always picking on him?

MAMA: Rita Mae—if you don't shut up! I swear I'm gonna do something to shut you up.

RITA MAE: And what you gonna do, laying there looking like last week's passed-over leftovers?

MAMA: I wouldn't be looking so bad if you'd hurry and change my diaper.

RITA MAE: How am I gonna change you if I'm out of diapers? Huh? Can you tell me that?

MAMA: You ain't gotta get salty about it. Just go on to the store and get some—

RITA MAE: And leave you with him?

MAMA: Well now, I done told you whatchu need to do with me.

RITA MAE: I'm not listening to you, Mama.

MAMA: Your life is passing you by.

RITA MAE: My life is fine, Mama.

MAMA: You need to put me in a rest home so you can rest your mind.

RITA MAE: You wouldn't last three months—

MAMA: Try me. I'm a lot stronger than you give me credit for. Your life is passing you by, Rita Mae...passing you by like like all dem cars flying down the highway—never looking back, not even slowing down to give this place a second thought. Why did you come back here?

RITA MAE: You know why I came back—

MAMA: Coming back here was the dumbest thing you ever did.

RITA MAE: (Crosses to the window) I made a promise to myself a long time ago, that I would never abandon you, Mama. You're too good for anybody's rest home.

(RITA MAE opens the window at the same time WENDELL plops back down in his chair.)

WENDELL: Damn it—Rita Mae—whatchu go and do that for?

RITA MAE: You got this place feeling like an oven. I can't breathe...no one can breathe—

WENDELL: I can't think for all that traffic.

RITA MAE: Ain't you got used to it by now?

WENDELL: No!

RITA MAE: *(Screams)* Well, get used to it—'cause the fucking window is staying open!

WENDELL: *(Struggling to get up)* That's what you think.

RITA MAE: Stop wasting your time, boy. I'm just gonna open it again.

WENDELL: So. I'll just close it again.

RITA MAE: I hate you, Wendell...you're so repetitive.

WENDELL: Why did you come back?

RITA MAE: You already know why I came back.

WENDELL: I can imagine—it got a little hectic.

RITA MAE: A little hectic?

WENDELL: —when you're keeping so many secrets—

RITA MAE: I got tired of them spying on me...

WENDELL: —bottled up inside—

RITA MAE: always spying on me...

WENDELL: —waiting to explode—

RITA MAE: Watching my every move. Monitoring all my friends. They would not leave me alone.

WENDELL: Must've been hard to keep from cracking up...

RITA MAE: They kept on prying and prying until they got the nerve to start lying on me. They out and out lied on me. And I thought she was my friend.

WENDELL: Even harder to know who to trust.

RITA MAE: I thought she was my friend. *(A beat)*

WENDELL: *(Slowly crosses to the window.)* Too much traffic noise—can drive a man crazy. Can't recall the last time I slept a full night. Some say they can't tell the difference between the purr of the ocean and the random abstract release of muffler sounds, and crying transmissions. I hear the sickness under the hood of every car that passes by here. Traffic noise is man-made chaos that goes against nature—the way God intended. When crickets chirp at night...their singing is a testament to nature...the universal order of things. Everyone, everything has its place in this world. Chaos is born from one not knowing one's place. And I only need to take half a sideways glance at you to know you in a place where you don't belong—

RITA MAE: But I was born here....

WENDELL: 'Cause you from here, don't make it home.

RITA MAE: If this don't feel like home and that didn't feel like home—then where is home?

MAMA: Home is where you can fart and not have to apologize to no one.

WENDELL: Please—Rita Mae...don't make me walk all the way over there. Please close the window for me.

RITA MAE: No!

WENDELL: I'll watch Mama for ya. I promise to do my fair share. Is that what you want? Do you want me to watch Mama so you can skip on down to the local lesbo bar—

RITA MAE: I'm warning you—

WENDELL: Throw away your bra at the door. Give a flip to the doorman— or whatever that thing was standing at the door carding people.

RITA MAE: I'm warning you, Wendell—

WENDELL: Is that what they learned ya in L A? How to be rude to people. How to be deceitful? How to lie to God?!

RITA MAE: Growing up so close to the freeway—I was programmed for freeway living. See—when you got a freeway for a front yard—there's no sense of community...I mean—you can't cross the street and say hello to your neighbor. You can't wave or talk idly about the weather or compliment him on the roses in his rose garden. You can't talk—say hello to the mailman without shouting, your voice trailing off with the traffic blowing by. If someone says something you didn't quite hear, you smile politely, pretend you heard it, and change the subject to something else. L A was a place to go if you a had a fear of intimacy...a fear of getting to know your neighbor—marking time alone in your car, sitting on the freeway, breathing in the fumes of civilization. You turn off your air conditioner, roll down your window. Suddenly—you don't feel so cut off. And so you start to sing a little tune to yourself at first, but then you start singing louder and louder to anyone and everyone. So what if you only know half the words and can't decide what key you're in. You're just glad to be alive and be in L A in the middle of this mass of humanity and machinery clogging up the freeway. And so you sing. You sing and sing, until the little white men in little white coats come and take you away— or you sing until the traffic starts to move—whichever happens first.

WENDELL: You didn't miss me none—did you?

RITA MAE: I did think about you. In fact—I thought about you and Ma a lot.

WENDELL: You never thought about Pops?

RITA MAE: Never thought about him. Well—I take that back—maybe I did think about him a bit. There was this guy I was seeing once—

WENDELL: You had a feller—

RITA MAE: For a hot minute—he reminded me of Pops—

MAMA: How come you never told no one?!

RITA MAE: You still wake, Mama?

MAMA: And I'm still waiting on you to change my diaper too.

WENDELL: So this feller you were seeing—what was he like?

RITA MAE: Billy Mars—Billy was the kind of fellow who made a girl feel all gooey inside. He kinda had Daddy's way of standing with his feet set wide apart. I can't say for sure, what got my skirt to blow up. Never felt that way about a man before—plenty women did that to me—but no man. I mean—he was kinda plain to look at. But he had a way of looking at you—that made you feel like you were all alone in the universe with just him—and that you—were the center of his universe—that you were the sun, the moon, every star in the sky and that life began and ended with you. He would say,

BILLY MARS: (V O) In the beginning—there was Rita Mae—

RITA MAE: In the beginning there was Rita Mae—oh—he would send shivers up my spine every time he came near, whispering those words, proclaiming his love for me in a way I knew I could trust it.

WENDELL: (At the window) You don't want me to close this window—getting me all hot and bothered.

MAMA: A fly on your arm can get you off—

RITA MAE: Billy Mars understood the need for human touch.

MAMA: Now dat do sound like yo' daddy.

RITA MAE: He was never in a hurry. Such a patient man. Never rushing his advances. He was just polite that way. Never in a hurry to jump yo' bones and never in a hurry to leave your side when he was done. Never met a more generous and grateful lover. Never met a man who loved afterplay as much as he loved foreplay. But Billy said laying there afterward was really the best part—

MAMA: Your heart is racing fast. You just want to slow your heart down—so you can catch your breath—

RITA MAE: A fan is blowing inside your mind—

MAMA: His sweet smell is all over you.

RITA MAE: Your woman-juice scent is all over him....

MAMA: Yo' skin is clingin' to his skin—oily, sweaty—

RITA MAE: Goosebumps rise on your back—

MAMA: You bury your head in his chest....

RITA MAE: Everything you touch comes alive.

MAMA: He has nailed you to the bed and you can't get up.

RITA MAE: He lays on top of you fast asleep. Breathing hard, like a newborn baby, put to sleep after a feeding. He sleeps so innocently. You cannot believe that this is the same man who just a few minutes ago was playing with a handful of your breast, while thrusting his way inside of you... boring a hole into you...seeing right through you to the deepest parts of your being. But in your mind a fan is blowing. Cooling you off, when your engine is running hot. It comes on JUST TO FUCK WITH YOU. Do I dare stick my finger in the fan? Do I dare stick my finger in the fan! What's wrong, honey! Nothing's wrong! No, everything's wrong! Who has time to fake an orgasm when you're busy faking like nothing's wrong! As you tell yourself, please don't stick my hand in the fan! Please don't stick my hand in the fan, and you cry inside yourself hoping, these unhappy thoughts flee your head. But the fan comes back on—keeping you from giving all of yourself to the man laying inside of you.

MAMA: His taste is on your lips. His smell lives on you.

RITA MAE: He lives in you.

MAMA: You can never let him go.

RITA MAE: But he will go. It's his nature to come and go.

MAMA: And it's your nature to make him stay—

RITA MAE: No! It's my nature to let him go!

MAMA: There you go, committing another crime against nature—

RITA MAE: My way of living ain't hurtin' nobody. I'm not committing crimes against nature—I'm expanding it. I think deep down inside every woman is looking for a man who can make love to her like he was a lesbian.

WENDELL: What's that suppose to mean?

RITA MAE: My darling brother Wendell—please use your imagination.

MAMA: He ain't got none—

RITA MAE: No imagination. Po' chile.

WENDELL: When I dream—it's always in black and white—like an old B movie or a gangster flick.

RITA MAE: Ever any romance?

WENDELL: Never any romance.

RITA MAE: How boring.

WENDELL: No, no—my dreams be slamming—action packed and all that. They just be in black and white, and they always end the same way.

RITA MAE: How?

WENDELL: With somebody getting killed.

RITA MAE: So you're just as hostile in your sleep—

WENDELL: I'm a gentle giant—

MAMA: Without a woman—

WENDELL: I got's plenty women—

MAMA: In your dreams—

RITA MAE: Not even in his dreams...didn't you hear? He dreams in black and white. Now what kinda girl is going to show up in those kinda low-budget dreams.

WENDELL: I know one thing—my women will testify—I make love like a real man—not nobody's lesbo!

RITA MAE: And how does a *real* man make love?

WENDELL: You know—I be licking it like a stamp—then sticking it like a champ. I don't be playin' 'round. My ladies get the real-deal Holyfield full-service treatment when they come to me.

RITA MAE: Do you ever talk to your women—

WENDELL: They got "talk shows" for talking. If you're looking for sensitivity, then go somewhere else. But if you come to me—you won't be asking, "Where's the beef?" You gonna leave here walking different from how you walked in.

RITA MAE: You think you all that—

WENDELL: Baby girl—I'm all that and a six-pack of beer. You see—I know how it's hanging.

MAMA: Too bad God didn't give you a little less dick and a little more sense—maybe you would've settled by now.

WENDELL: Maybe I ain't no settler—Ma! *(Slams the window shut.)* Whatchu saying—I shoulda settled like you and Pops? Is this the shit? Is this the American dream—everybody's searching for—a wife—two kids and a fucked-up house by the freeway?

MAMA: At least it's something—

WENDELL: This ain't nothing. You think it's something 'cause you ain't been nowhere—

MAMA: And where have you been? At least your sister left here and been out there on her own. But you—you like that tree in the backyard. Diseased...and never going nowhere.

WENDELL: Whatchu want from me, Mama? Grandchildren? Is that what this is about?

MAMA: I just want you to act like you motivated to do something with your life. That's all. I mean I look at you and I wonder what did I do to fail my children? What did I do to make them so afraid to face life—

WENDELL: Ain't nobody 'fraid of nothing—

MAMA: Then how come you don't go anywhere—

WENDELL: 'Cause there's nothing out there, Mama. I don't have to go far to see there's nothing out there in this world for me. I ain't got to go through all the changes you and Pops went through.

MAMA: Yep. You just like that tree. You stopped growing a long time ago. And you've got the nerve to call yourself a *real* man.

RITA MAE: Leave him alone, Ma.

WENDELL: Don't be taking up for me.

RITA MAE: Both of y'all need to chill.

MAMA: Maybe I failed ya—when I stopped making y'all go to church.

RITA MAE: Give it a rest—Ma!

MAMA: Or maybe it was that idiot box that killed your imagination!

RITA MAE: Ma!!!

MAMA: Yeah. That's how I failed you—by letting you watch too much T V? I know—I shoulda breast fed you longer—

RITA MAE: Wendell—will you watch Ma for me—I need to go to the store—*(Grabbing her purse and car keys)* Please, Wendell—watch Ma for me—I gotta get Ma some diapers—so I'm leaving you in charge now, Wendell—you're the man of the house. Now don't let no one in. Okay? *(After a beat—slowly exits)*

WENDELL: *(To himself)* No. You're the man of the house—Rita Mae—

(Slow fade to black)

(End of scene)

Scene Two

(At rise: RITA MAE *is standing next to* MAMA, *near the end of completing her sponge bath. A big bunk-size bag of generic-brand disposable diapers sits on the floor, in view, near the bed.* WENDELL *is finishing putting together his horn during his first few lines.)*

WENDELL: The highway never sleeps. You'd think in a place like St Louis— people wouldn't have so many places to go. But someone is always on that highway. Day and night. Don't make a difference. Yeah—it slows down at night—but one car is always out there—going somewhere, and just as soon as that one car drives out of the picture, here comes another car's headlights...here comes the noise of another car, then another car, and I want to scream for the moving picture to stop moving, and I want to stop the soundtrack. I want to stop it all, so I can hear the crickets singing and I know they are singing we shall overcome all this mess.

*(*WENDELL *starts playing the scale, terribly off-key. It is clear from the way he holds the horn and moves his fingers, he is arthritic.)*

MAMA: Mothers, hide your children—Wendell is playing again.

RITA MAE: Don't be so mean, Ma—he's just a little tone-deaf.

MAMA: A little tone-deaf? He's the worst horn player God put breath in. He couldn't carry a tune if you put it in a knapsack and flung it over his back.

RITA MAE: Ma—you got to hold still—so I can fasten this diaper. It keeps coming loose—

MAMA: I told you not to ever get those cheap generic kind again. They leak! Depends never leak!

RITA MAE: Ma—I got to economize—

*(*WENDELL *stops playing and puts his horn in its case, then he realizes the table leg he uses for a cane is on the other side of the room.)*

WENDELL: Hey! Who moved my crutch?

RITA MAE: You mean that table leg—

MAMA: Perfect piece of firewood—gone to waste—

WENDELL: Rita Mae—fetch it for me.

RITA MAE: You just gonna have to wait 'til I'm done with Mama.

WENDELL: *(Crawling toward the table leg)* Damn it, Rita Mae—you'se making me late. You just like fucking with me. Don't you? You like making me late.

RITA MAE: And where you going?

WENDELL: I'm going to the club. Where you think? My band gigs seven nights a week—seven nights a week. *(Reaches the cane and stands. Moves his horn by the front door and puts on his winter coat)*

RITA MAE: Yeah, whatever.

WENDELL: Why did you move my crutch?

RITA MAE: Why you accusing me?

WENDELL: I know Mama didn't move it.

RITA MAE: Keep it off the floor and out of the way—'cause the next time I trip over it—I will turn it into firewood!

WENDELL: You ain't doing jack.

RITA MAE: Come on and double dare me.

WENDELL: Butch!

RITA MAE: Punk!

WENDELL: Bitch!

RITA MAE: Faggot!

MAMA: Hey!

WENDELL: Don't make me have to use this cane!

RITA MAE: Come on—bring it! You couldn't whup me when we was kids, and you can't whup me now!

WENDELL: You're lucky my public is awaiting me. I don't have any time to waste on some sexually confused baddilac like you. Ma—if anybody calls—tell them to call down to the club. You got that?

MAMA: Do I look like I'll be answering any phones?

WENDELL: Peace. I'm out of here—

RITA MAE: See ya later, Boo Boo!

(WENDELL starts to leave but stops.)

WENDELL: I am forty-one years old—

RITA MAE: But you act like you're fifteen. *(Mocking him)* Yo, Ma—Peace... and I'm out! *(Scratches her crotch and limps around trying to be cool.)*

WENDELL: Fuck you, Rita Mae!

MAMA: *(Overlap)* Whatd'I—

RITA MAE: *(Overlap)* Fuck you too, Boo Boo!

WENDELL: My name is Wendell Megan. The name means something 'round here. I'm the top horn blower 'round these parts—the highest-paid session man around. So don't fuck with me. Don't try to downgrade my status by calling me Boo Boo or anything else. You refer to me by my given name or don't refer to me at all. Is that clear?

RITA MAE: Nigger—I ain't 'fraid of you.

WENDELL: I ain't asking you to be 'fraid of me. I'm asking you to respect me.

RITA MAE: Well, I don't—and I don't think there's anything you can do to win my respect either.

WENDELL: *(Raises the table leg)* God-dammit!!!

MAMA: Thought you had somewhere to go, boy. I guess you best be on yo' way!

WENDELL: This ain't over! *(He exits.)*

MAMA: I told you 'bout aggravating him.

RITA MAE: He don't scare me none. He's barking loud just to hear himself bark. He ain't ever gonna do shit, 'cause he's cowardly that way. Ain't in his nature to do nothing but talk. Just like most men—full of talk. No backbone whatsoever. Where do you suppose he goes each night, Ma?

MAMA: I don't know and I don't care. Just as long as its away from here.

RITA MAE: I think he's goin' to a fag bar, Ma—

MAMA: You just saying that—'cause you that way.

RITA MAE: Boo Boo's in the closet, and I'm gonna out him if it's the last thing I do.

MAMA: I don't want you stirring up trouble—

RITA MAE: Oh, it's no trouble at all, Ma.

MAMA: You're evil, Rita Mae—

RITA MAE: Boo needs to be brought down off his high horse. And it's my job to bring him down a peg or two.

MAMA: Why is it your job?

RITA MAE: The nigger needs to know his place.

MAMA: But why is it your job to teach him?

RITA MAE: Somebody's got to do it. It might as well be me!

MAMA: But why?

RITA MAE: 'Cause he's a creep and he needs to know it!!

MAMA: But you'll destroy him and he ain't worth it. Besides, he ain't the enemy.

RITA MAE: He ain't on our side either—

MAMA: He's harmless. He's lost—in a world of his own.

RITA MAE: He's sick, Ma—and his sickness is contagious. It needs to be eliminated before it spreads.

(Pause/a beat)

MAMA: Rita Mae—

RITA MAE: What, Mama?

MAMA: What's it like to be with another woman? I mean—how do y'all do it?!

RITA MAE: What?!

MAMA: Don't you miss penetration? I know I miss it—

RITA MAE: Ma—why are we having this conversation?

MAMA: We're two grown-up gals—we can talk—

RITA MAE: Well—I don't want to talk about this—with you!

MAMA: But I'm yo' ma—

RITA MAE: That's why we can't talk—not about this.

MAMA: I miss your daddy—

RITA MAE: I miss him too.

MAMA: You know we was all set to come out to visit ya.

RITA MAE: I know, Ma—I remember.

MAMA: Then you know—he suddenly took sick. One week in the hospital and he's gone. Never been sick a day in his life. Your father's heart was set on seeing you.

RITA MAE: Guess it wasn't meant to be—

(BILLY MARS *enters, he peers through the window for several beats.* MAMA *and* RITA MAE *just watch him, watching them.)*

MAMA: You hear that...somebody out there. Who dat coming up on my porch?

RITA MAE: *(Going to the window)* It's a man.

MAMA: Go fetch my shotgun, so I can pump some fear in him.

RITA MAE: How you gonna shoot somebody when you can't even give yourself a bath....

MAMA: But I can still shoot a nigger. My senses tell me where to aim. You know I got your daddy to marry me with a shotgun. Guess you can say it was a shotgun wedding—

RITA MAE: How many times you gonna tell me?

MAMA: 'Til I get tired of telling it.

BILLY: *(Hollers)* Rita Mae!

MAMA: Do you know this boy, Rita Mae? He sho seems to know you.

BILLY: Rita Mae, you come out here now! I have come for you.

MAMA: Hey, stop all that yapping—fool!

RITA MAE: Shhhhh—mama—don't say nothing. Maybe he'll just go away.

MAMA: What's he doing out there?

RITA MAE: He's just looking—

MAMA: What's he looking at?

RITA MAE: He's looking at us.

MAMA: Why?

RITA MAE: I guess 'cause he's got nothing better to do.

MAMA: Whatchu say his name is?

RITA MAE: Billy Mars, mama...Billy Mars.

MAMA: You mean the one you was in love with—

RITA MAE: I never said that—

MAMA: Don't leave him out there shivering in the cold. Invite him in.

RITA MAE: Are you crazy?! That's the last thing I intend to do.

BILLY: Rita Mae! Come out here! I know you're in there!

(RITA MAE turns off the lamp next to MAMA and all other lights.)

MAMA: Whatchu doing?!

RITA MAE: I don't want him to see us.

MAMA: Are you in some kind of trouble?!

RITA MAE: No.

MAMA: Is he some kind of stalker weirdo?

RITA MAE: There's nothing wrong with him. I just don't want to see him. *(She latches the window closed.)*

MAMA: But why not, sugar?

RITA MAE: I got my reasons.

MAMA: He didn't beat you—did he?

RITA MAE: No, Ma—he was very kind to me—too kind to me.

MAMA: Then why don't you let him in?

RITA MAE: 'Cause I don't deserve him—

BILLY: *(Overlap)* Rita Mae!!!

MAMA: I don't know who's more foolish—you...or your brother.

BILLY: Please—Rita Mae—I just wanna talk.

(Several beats of quiet)

MAMA: What's he doing now?

RITA MAE: He's just standing there—Mama.

MAMA: What's he doing standing there?

RITA MAE: He's just looking—

MAMA: What's he looking at?

RITA MAE: He's looking at us—Mama!

BILLY: This is the last time I'm coming for ya, Rita Mae. Now either you come with me this time or just forget about seeing me again.

MAMA: Sounds like true love to me.

RITA MAE: Or pure hell.

MAMA: Whatchu so 'fraid of, girl?

RITA MAE: I'm afraid of breaking that fool's heart.

MAMA: Evidently—he ain't afraid of getting it broke. Now—why don't you at least show some appreciation for his long journey by going out and talking to him.

RITA MAE: And what'chu gonna do?

MAMA: I'm gonna go to sleep if you put my bed back in place.

(RITA MAE lowers the head of the bed.)

RITA MAE: You call for me if you need anything.

MAMA: You tellin' me somethin' I already know!

(RITA MAE pulls a blanket up over her mother. Then crosses over to the front door. The lights fade on MAMA and get brighter on BILLY. RITA MAE opens the front door but keeps the screen door latched.)

BILLY: Rita Mae—Why didn't you answer my letters?

RITA MAE: I knew you was coming—

BILLY: Then you know why I'm here.

RITA MAE: Why do you torture yourself, Billy?

BILLY: I guess it's my burden. So what's your answer?

RITA MAE: You know my answer. Same as it was in L A. Nothing's changed—so why don'tchu hop in yo' pickup and turn right on around.

BILLY: Ain't nothing there to go back to—Rita Mae—

RITA MAE: Billy Mars—

BILLY: Rita Mae—what's stopping you? Don't you wanna be happy? I know I do.

RITA MAE: Billy Mars. I don't know a thang about you. I don't know your mama—I don't know your daddy. I don't know where you're from or how you came to be or why you love me. And I sure don't know why on Earth I should go back to L A with you. Nor do I know why I should stay here. All I do know is that I'm staying. Now—go away, Billy Mars.

BILLY: Look—your mother can stay with us in L A if you'd just come back.

RITA MAE: My staying here—has got nothing to do with my mama. I just don't want to be in L A anymore. Now—Billy—you're a good man...a sweet man...a special man. You'll find the right girl. A girl you can depend on, as much as she can depend on you. You know—in a pinch—you cannot depend on me. I cannot marry you and promise to be faithful. I cannot promise you—I won't leave you for another girl—

BILLY: I know that, Rita—

RITA MAE: *(Overlap)* Nor can I promise to honor and worship and all that other bullshit—

BILLY: *(Overlap)* I already know that and I ain't asking for none of that. I'm just asking you to come back to L A. Things are empty there—without you.

RITA MAE: No. I can't come back—

BILLY: I don't care if you have a dozen female lovers—just as long as I'm your only man—

RITA MAE: That's what you say now—

BILLY: I mean it, Rita—

RITA MAE: I don't trust you. I don't believe you—And if you are telling the truth—

BILLY: I am—

RITA MAE: Then that's no good either. Every time I had an indiscretion and you looked the other way—my debt to you would mount up. Your holier-than-thou sacrifices, which would seem small at first—would just grow and grow—like a mountain of debt in front of me. Now you and I both know, this doesn't sound like the makings of a healthy relationship. Does it?

BILLY: No—it doesn't, Rita Mae—

RITA MAE: So then—there's nothing else to talk about, is there.

BILLY: I guess there isn't. Guess—I better go then.

RITA MAE: *(Beat)* You want some coffee before you go?

BILLY: No. But I would like to use the bathroom.

RITA MAE: Sure.

(She unlatches the screen door, and BILLY *enters the living room.)*

BILLY: Sure is cozy in here. Didn't realize how cold it was.

RITA MAE: The bathroom's this way.

BILLY: I've made a fool of myself—haven't I?

RITA MAE: I wouldn't say that—

BILLY: My coming here was stupid—

RITA MAE: No, Billy. It was sweet. It's just that—I was the wrong girl.

BILLY: You sure seemed like the right one—when we were together.

RITA MAE: What we had was special. But it's over.

BILLY: I guess that's been the hardest thing for me to accept. I never had a family. You were the only person I ever considered family. I guess that's why I wanted to marry you. I wish there was a way we could be together without one feeling they owed the other one something. I mean, I just want to love you.

RITA MAE: The bathroom's this way, Billy—

BILLY: See—I ain't one of those men—who needs to be in CONTROL— so—you having a thing for—something I can't control—it don't bother me none. I won't trip—'cause I don't need control—the way others do.

RITA MAE: I thought you had to go to the bathroom, but here you are trying to smooth talk—fast talk me.

BILLY: Uh-unh...I won't try to fast talk you. I wanna slow talk some sense into you. Now, I came here to tell you I love you—Rita Mae.

RITA MAE: I know you do—

BILLY: Now, before I met you—I thought I'd never settle down. Or want to. But you don't know the power you have over me. You took me out there to the outer limits, with all those hot-oil massages and feeding me mangos while giving me a bath. You pampered me when we made love—

RITA MAE: You pampered me too—

BILLY: After being with you—I ain't no good for no other woman. Not after trying to fill your hunger. You have a hunger worse than my own. I never encountered a more insatiable woman than you—in this life. The things you thought of—the things you got me to do—the things you made me do. Sometimes I felt out of control—

RITA MAE: You were out of control.

BILLY: We were out of control.

RITA MAE: That's why it was no good.

BILLY: You remember that walk-up flat you had in Silverlake?

RITA MAE: God—did I hate taking groceries up those steps.

BILLY: I remember waking up there in your bed one morning, after we had did it about five times the night before—and I woke up—still hard—still erect. So we did it again. And then you showered and left for work—leaving me there in a daze...in a stupor...I laid there like I was on drugs. The room was still spinning in your wake. So I stumbled out of bed, washed up quick and tumbled into my clothes, split yo' pad and hopped in my car—ready to make it on back to Venice Beach. But that day, when I got in the car—still in a stupor from making love to you—I could not find my way home. I drove around the city in circles...lost for hours, like I was tripping on Magic Mushrooms—but I was just tripping on you. Now I knew every back road— every short cut there was from my pad to yours—I mean, I used to drive a cab in L A. But that day—I could not find my way home. The streets I thought I owned, didn't look familiar—you changed how I looked at it, and every street I drove down led back to your place. I stopped trying to get home that day. I made myself park under a tree, 'cross the street from where you lived, and I went to sleep. I just slept there, until you reappeared—to show me my way back home.

RITA MAE: I remember that. You cried in my arms that day.

BILLY: That day—I never wanted to leave your side again. You took a part of me with you when you left. A part of me I'm dying to get back.

RITA MAE: Yeah—sometimes I miss the sex too—

BILLY: The sex ain't the only thing I'm missing. It's you, Rita Mae—it's you.

RITA MAE: Billy—you'll find another.

BILLY: But I'll never find another like you. There's a stone in my heart with your name on it.

RITA MAE: Billy—you'se the corniest mo'fucka I've ever met.

BILLY: You know who made me that way.

RITA MAE: I guess that's why I love you. You cool and all that—but you ain't too cool to be corny sometimes. Most guys stay clear of them cornfields—but you go straight there.

(RITA MAE *sits, centerstage, as* BILLY *begins to slowly walk circles around her for the remainder of the play. He starts walking very loose, very wide orbits around her at first, but the more he talks, the tighter and tighter the circles around her become.*)

BILLY: You see—I have been hungry—for a long time—for a long time— I have been hungry. And you fed me—the first time you said hello to me... you fed me...you were so kind. L A is not a kind city—and I took to you— like bees to honey, I took to you—you were the brightest constellation to ever come into my orbit. The minute you came into my orbit—I knew you had been sent to me. You see, Rita Mae—you and I, we have history between us. We have enough history for several lifetimes. My spirit is incomplete without you in my orbit. (*Puts his hand on her shoulder*) You knew...I would come for you. Tell me that's not true.

RITA MAE: I knew you would come disguised as a gentleman caller.

BILLY: And you know I ain't no gentleman.

(BILLY *moves his hands across her shoulders. She relaxes for a moment then tenses back up.*)

BILLY: Don't be so uptight. I'm not here to hurt you.

RITA MAE: You just want to tie me down.

BILLY: I already said—I don't want to possess you. I just wanna live within your reach. (*He aggressively begins to kiss the back of her neck and slowly unzips the back of her dress—whereupon he begins kissing her shoulder blades.*) I am chasing you through a forest of desire—a passion forest—a burning forest with trees all aflame. I'm a wolf—nipping at your heels. You wanna run—

RITA MAE: I wanna run—

BILLY: But you can't git away. You run—but each blade of grass sings out your name—giving you away—

RITA MAE: I keep running. I see a big fan in front of me and I wanna run through that fan. I wanna be sliced and diced.

(RITA MAE'*s dress falls to the floor. She is in a sheer slip, with nothing else underneath, as* BILLY *fondles her.*)

RITA MAE: I wanna turn that fan off—but I can't. It looks so inviting to all my fingers. I wanna stick my hand in the fan—I wanna donate a limb. Maybe you'll stop loving me if I had a nub for a hand. Maybe then you'll crawl back to where you crawled from and you'll leave me the fuck alone.

BILLY: Never.

(BILLY *turns her around and kisses her passionately. Just as* RITA MAE *begins to swoon, she breaks away from* BILLY *and crosses the stage.*)

RITA MAE: I awaken—and find myself on the twenty-ninth floor of some empty building. All the windows are broken out and it is freezing. Birds of every kind flock all around me. The birds keep telling me to jump. First they try to con me into thinking I am BIG BIRD...I am one of them...they try to convince me I can fly. But I know—they want to see me splatter on the ground below—so I jump—from the twenty-ninth floor—just for the sport of it—just for the entertainment and humor of all the birds who were ever kind to me, and I know they get a big kick out of my free fall and an even bigger kick out of seeing me splatter on the ground. Splatt!!

BILLY: What's it gonna be, Rita Mae? You coming with me?

RITA MAE: You know I can't leave my mother.

BILLY: So bring her—

RITA MAE: You don't even know why I left.

BILLY: Yo' ma had a stroke—

RITA MAE: This ain't about my mama either.

BILLY: Then why did you leave?

RITA MAE: You remember the last job I had?

BILLY: At the studio?

RITA MAE: No. At the law firm.

BILLY: You mean—the one out in Burbank?

RITA MAE: That's the one.

BILLY: Yeah. I remember. You weren't there that long.

RITA MAE: The attorney I was working for started coming on to me the second day on the job. I told him I was involved, I couldn't go out with him—but he wouldn't stop fucking with me...so I complained to all the other partners.

BILLY: So what happened?

RITA MAE: You wanna know what happened? They started fucking with me—that's what happened. I mean—I couldn't tell they was fucking with me at first. You see—a week after I filed my complaint—they sent me an assistant. Jill—a sweet, fresh-faced girl from Ohio. So, Jill and I are real cool—covering for each other—bringing each other lunch. And then she did something that totally blew my mind. She had the office throw me a suprise party for my birthday. I mean, after getting off to a shaky start— I was actually feeling accepted. And Jill was like the little sister I never had.

I mean—we were so tight—she even crashed at my pad once—after a night of drinking. It was then that the bottom fell out.

BILLY: What happened? Did you sleep with her?

RITA MAE: No. I never slept with her. She wasn't my type—and I never— I never told her about that part of me. Yet she seemed to know. They all seemed to know.

BILLY: What happened?

RITA MAE: What happened next was straight out of Kafka. Just two days after my birthday party I got this memo from one of the junior partners, about a charge being brought against me. That little bitch Jill had accused me of sexual harassment, and the same committee of partners I had gone to previously with complaints of my own—was set to convene the next day to hear Jill's complaint against me. Well, fate would have it that Jill didn't come to work on the day I got the memo. So I tried to call her—but her phone was disconnected. So on my lunch break—I drove over to where the bitch lived. I buzzed her apartment. Nothing. I just wanted to ask her to her face—how could she do such a thing to me? It was then that I realized, I had been set up.

BILLY: Did you hit on her?

RITA MAE: Billy—I just told you she wasn't my type.

BILLY: Rita Mae—tell me the truth—

RITA MAE: I am telling you the truth—

BILLY: Did anything happen—that could've been interpreted as you hitting on her—LIKE AN INAPPROPRIATE TOUCH.

RITA MAE: Are you listening to me? I just told you it was a setup!! The birthday party! Everything! A setup!!

BILLY: So what happened at the hearing?

RITA MAE: There never was any hearing—

BILLY: Why not?

RITA MAE: I was unable to find my way back to the office after leaving her apartment.

BILLY: Why not?

RITA MAE: I had a nervous breakdown right there on the streets. I mean— I had forgotten where I had parked my car. I mean—I went back to where I thought I had parked my car—but it wasn't there—and I knew it wasn't stolen. You remember the piece of shit I drove—

BILLY: Yeah. Who in their right mind would steal that.

RITA MAE: I was out there for hours—looking for my car, covering the same two blocks over and over again. I mean, it was probably right under my nose, but my mind prevented me from seeing it. So, I went back to Jill's building and rang her bell again. Nothing. So, I sat on the steps of her building—hoping maybe she'd show up. But she never did. Hours went by and she never showed. The next thing I know, it's nighttime. It's dark and I still can't find my car. But I'm hearing this little voice in my head. And the voice tells me to go over the overpass down on my hands and knees and suddenly, a car was right behind me, honking at me. I froze. A woman tried to help me, but I tore away from her and ran, upright, to the end of the overpass. Then this voice told me—I was a cheetah. So I returned to all fours and crawled over to a puddle of water. And I drank, the way a wild animal would drink. I was drinking from the puddle as I heard the sound of people approaching. So once again I jumped to my feet, running, the way a person would run. And I kept running 'til a voice—a little irritating voice told me...this bright shiny B M W was my car. So, I took my old car keys and tried to stick them into this shiny B M W, as the voice in my head started screaming, "Bob Marley and the Wailers, Bob Marley and the Wailers...B M W...over and over again...Bob Marley and the Wailers." But then—the Beemer started talking to me, "You're standing too close. Please stand back from the vehicle, please stand back from the vehicle." I stood there, mesmerized by the talking car. I was still standing there, when the police came and found me.

BILLY: How come you never told me any of this?

RITA MAE: How could I? As soon as they let me out of the hospital I was on a plane to St Louis.

BILLY: How come I never knew about Jill or none of this?

RITA MAE: I wasn't at the firm that long.

BILLY: You were there long enough to have mentioned Jill—if you two were as tight as you say you were.

RITA MAE: Your band was gigging all the time then. I mean, your schedule was so crowded—that we didn't hang as much—

BILLY: We talked on the phone every day. You were my woman. You showed up at the club a lot and at rehearsals. We were hangin'. What are you talkin' about?

RITA MAE: I don't recall it the way you do—

BILLY: How come I'm just hearing 'bout Jill for the first time?

RITA MAE: I just told you why—

BILLY: I think you slept with her.

RITA MAE: Fuck you, Billy!

BILLY: YEAH—you slept with her. Or at least tried to.

RITA MAE: I thought it didn't matter to you. I don't need the same accusations from you—I got from them. Fuck you, Billy. You can leave right now.

BILLY: Yeah. That night y'all got drunk. I'll bet you went for it then.

RITA MAE: I thought you said it didn't matter?!

BILLY: The truth matters—the truth always matters. And I think you had a little crush on Jill—that's what I think. That's why you went over the edge. The girl broke your heart—didn't she?

RITA MAE: Fuck you! You can leave, Billy—leave—

BILLY: I ain't going nowhere. You think I drove all this way to leave without the truth? You had a crush on her. Didn't you?

RITA MAE: Please, Billy—

BILLY: You had a crush on her—didn't you?

RITA MAE: *(A beat)* Yes.

BILLY: That's all I wanted to know—was the truth. Which way is your bathroom?

RITA MAE: *(Points offstage right)* That way.

BILLY: Mind if I use it?

RITA MAE: Go ahead.

BILLY: Thank you.

(BILLY *exits in the direction of the bathroom.*)

(*Sound cue: several beats pass, then we hear a toilet flushing.* BILLY *reenters.*)

RITA MAE: Go back there and wash your hands—

BILLY: How do you know I didn't?

RITA MAE: I didn't hear you run any water. I ain't gonna let you touch me unless you wash your hands.

(BILLY *runs back off. We hear water running. He returns, wiping his hands with a paper towel.*)

RITA MAE: That still don't mean I'm gonna let you touch me.

BILLY: The Jill thing broke your heart—didn't it?

RITA MAE: I just wanna know—how did you know?

BILLY: 'Cause you had kept Jill a secret—the way a man would've—

RITA MAE: The way you would've?

BILLY: Yeah—the way I would've.

RITA MAE: There's no fooling you, huh.

BILLY: Nope. You see the truth—I can handle. As long as everything is up front...nobody's keeping secrets from nobody, then—I can handle it. I don't mind playing second fiddle sometimes, as long as everybody's up front and out in the open.

RITA MAE: But sometimes there's a need for secrets.

BILLY: I never saw much difference between keeping secrets and telling lies—that's why I don't have much use for 'em.

RITA MAE: Sometimes secrets can get the best of ya.

BILLY: Did you hit on her?

RITA MAE: I thought we were done with this?

BILLY: Not until you tell me—

RITA MAE: Yes! I hit on her! Yes! She was gorgeous...the second comin' of Marilyn Monroe. What the fuck do you think? Shit! You woulda wanted some too!

BILLY: That's all I wanted to know.

RITA MAE: Are you happy now? Are you satisfied?

BILLY: I just wanted the truth.

RITA MAE: You just wanted to humiliate me.

BILLY: Do you feel humiliated?

RITA MAE: Yes.

BILLY: Well—you shouldn't. You should feel cleansed. Unburdened by that little secret that stood between us.

RITA MAE: You've got a lot of nerve, telling me how I should feel.

BILLY: You know what yo' problem is? You're too fucking literal.

RITA MAE: (Sits) What else is wrong with me? Go ahead and tell me.

BILLY: Well—your hair. That ain't the way I remember your hair.

RITA MAE: (Screams) And I'm too fucking literal?!

MAMA: (In darkness) What's all dat commotion?!

RITA MAE: Sorry, Ma— We better keep it down.

BILLY: She don't sound sick.

BILLY: So where is brother Boo Boo?

RITA MAE: If Boo hears you calling him that—he's gonna go off—I swear. Billy, there's something I never told you about my brother—

BILLY: As many stories as you told me about Boo Boo, I feel I already know your brother.

RITA MAE: Yeah, but there's something I haven't told you.

BILLY: What?

RITA MAE: There's a lot of pain in this house. A deep pain that hurts like a restless ache. When I first left here, I thought I'd never see this place again. I thought I was gone from here forever. You hear that highway—that angry restless highway.

BILLY: Yeah. I hear it.

RITA MAE: I lost my virginity to that highway. Lost all my innocence. I lost something—right here—I can never get back.

BILLY: Do you want me to hold you?

RITA MAE: Do you wanna hold me?

BILLY: I'm dying to hold you.

RITA MAE: Do you think your holding me can make me forget all the things I need to forget?

BILLY: No. But I can keep you warm—if you come over here.

RITA MAE: No. You come over here.

(BILLY *goes to* RITA MAE *and puts his arms around her.*)

BILLY: You look good.

RITA MAE: And so do you.

BILLY: You wanna jump my bones—don't you?

RITA MAE: You would not believe how horny I am. I haven't been laid since I left L A.

BILLY: I recall passing a Motel Six not far from here.

RITA MAE: You don't have to take me to a cheap motel. We can do it right here.

BILLY: In your mother's house?

RITA MAE: A lot worse things have been done here. Besides, we're two consenting adults—

BILLY: But still—this is your mother's house. And where's your brother?

RITA MAE: (*As she unbuckles* BILLY's *belt*) Who knows and who cares.

(*Lights begin a slow fade.*)

BILLY: *(Taking off his shirt)* I ain't never got none in Missouri before.

RITA MAE: Well, Mr Mars—welcome to the "show me state."

(Black out)

END OF ACT ONE

ACT TWO

Scene One

(At rise: the following morning. We hear rush hour traffic and other highway noise. We find RITA MAE *fast asleep in* BILLY's *arms, on the living room sofa, snuggled under a blanket.* WENDELL *is sitting in a chair, close to them, staring at them as they sleep. His mood is somewhere between nonchalance and outright disgust.* RITA MAE *shifts in* BILLY's *arms, trying to get more comfortable and trying to snuggle closer, with a big smile on her face. Her movement causes* BILLY *to stir. They kiss without opening their eyes, for several long beats, getting more passionate with each beat.* WENDELL *just observes, not letting on that he's there.)*

RITA MAE: Billy...last night I started to tell you something.

BILLY: Shhhh—I got something for you first—

RITA MAE: See—this is why I can't go back to L A with you. I'm trying to tell you something and all you can think about is your erection.

BILLY: Please—

RITA MAE: *(Almost mocking)* Mmmmmmmm—amazing—

BILLY: My Billy Mars' bar is still hard—even after last night.

RITA MAE: *(Fondling him under cover/teasing)* It's the eighth wonder of the world. I've got just the place for that, Mr Mars.

BILLY: Yeah—well, you know me—I always want to be in the place to be.

*(*RITA MAE *gets on top of* BILLY, *simulating intercourse, for a few beats.* WENDELL *lets them get into a groove before he finally speaks.)*

WENDELL: How long are y'all gonna do that? 'Cause I'ma go rustle me up some grits and eggs and I don't want to miss the climax. Y'all want anything?

RITA MAE: *(Startled)* Wendell—how long have you been sitting there? *(Pulls the covers tight over her and* BILLY.*)*

WENDELL: Long enough. You got a lot of nerve, Rita Mae!! A lot of nerve! Polluting this house with yo' lust.

RITA MAE: Are you tellin' me if you had somebody to bring home—you wouldn't bring 'em home?

WENDELL: Not to my Mama's house. You been in L A so long—you've lost all sense of what lines not to cross—'round here. At least you didn't bring no white boy in here. That is a man you're with? I really can't tell—from here—

(BILLY *rises from under the covers and stands in front of* WENDELL *naked.*)

BILLY: Let me introduce myself—

RITA MAE: Billy—put your pants back on.

WENDELL: *(Chuckles)* No—keep 'em off.

RITA MAE: Put yo' pants on, Billy!

WENDELL: If he wants to give me a floor show, let him do it. I love a good show. I got a front row seat and all the time in the world.

RITA MAE: That's enough, Billy!

(BILLY *is taking his sweet time looking for his pants in the heap of clothes on the floor. He is very proud of his body.* WENDELL *is aroused and agitated all at once.*)

WENDELL: I can't believe this man—disrespecting my mama's house like this.

BILLY: And you must be Boo Boo. Well, Boo Boo—I must say say, I've really been looking forward to meeting you.

RITA MAE: Billy—I mean it—put your pants back on!!

(RITA MAE *moves and stands between* BILLY *and* WENDELL. BILLY *finds his pants and finally slips them back on.*)

WENDELL: You've been talkin' to this nigga about me—haven't you, Rita Mae? You told him my name is Boo Boo?! My name is Wendell—do you understand that? You and Ma started that Boo Boo shit. You never heard Pops call me Boo Boo. He always called me Wendell or he called me "Handsome."

RITA MAE: Well, he was lying to you. And you're just as sick as he was if you believed him.

WENDELL: Let's get one thing straight right now, Billy Boy. You can call me Wendell or you can call me "Handsome." But whatever you do—don't ever call me Boo Boo again. Do you hear me?!

(MAMA *is ringing a dinner bell, as a dim light comes up on her in her bed.*)

MAMA: What all dat commotion in there?

RITA MAE: See there—y'all done woke up Mama. She never wakes up this early.

MAMA: Come on, Rita Mae. I need you to change me and feed me—change me and feed me.

RITA MAE: *(Putting on her clothes fast)* I'm coming, Mama. Hold your water. *(Under her breath)* That's right, you can't hold your water.

(As RITA MAE *crosses to* MAMA, WENDELL *and* BILLY *keep staring at each other.* RITA MAE *parts* MAMA's *curtains, letting some light through the blinds. Although the lights get brighter on* RITA MAE *and* MAMA, BILLY *and* WENDELL *will remain the main focus.)*

BILLY: Like—I apologize for calling you Boo Boo. Rita Mae never told me you didn't like being called Boo Boo.

WENDELL: Oh...after you gone—I'ma have a real serious talk with the girl about that.

BILLY: Look, Wendell—Handsome Wendell—just so there are no hard feelings between me and you—let me even out the score by telling you something about me—since you seem upset that I know things about you and you know nothing about me. My name is Billy Mars. A name I gave myself, because I didn't like the John Doe the state of California gave me. John Taylor. Now what could be more plain than John Taylor?

WENDELL: I could tell you was an orphan—

BILLY: How could you tell?

WENDELL: You just look like the kinda nigger left on somebody's doorstep.

BILLY: I was left in a garbage bin.

WENDELL: Disposable...just like my mama's diapers. *(Laughs/beat)* I feel yo' pain, brother man. I see yo' scars and that defeated, downtrodden look in yo' eyes. The look of a born loser. Life has done ya wrong.

BILLY: Man—why you fucking with me?! What's up with that?

WENDELL: You had no business—disrespecting my Mama's house.

BILLY: I thought I already apologized for that.

WENDELL: Oh. You done gone way past the point of all apologies. I'm sorry, just don't cut the mustard—for what you did. I mean—did my sister invite you here? Did she pick up the phone and tell you to—

BILLY: *(Overlap)* I came here on my own. Something just pulled me here.

WENDELL: Something just pulled you here?

BILLY: I just had to see her.

WENDELL: But did you have to fuck her—right here in the front room? *(Beat)* Free will. Yesiree. Free will is a mighty dangerous thing. A mighty dangerous thing, indeed. You came all this way—uninvited. Something pulled you here—so you say. Let me give you some free advice.

BILLY: I don't want your advice.

WENDELL: I'ma give it to you anyway. Get away from here while you can. You seen my sister—now go. Go while you can, 'cause there ain't nothing for you here. Do you hear that highway? You hear it? It's calling to you. You hear it calling to you? Billy! Billy! Well, I hear it even if you don't. Billy boy, brother man—it's telling you to turn around and go back. Go back to where you came from. 'Cause there ain't nothing for you here.

BILLY: I'm not leaving without your sister.

WENDELL: Then you're even dumber than you look.

BILLY: If you want me to be on my way, I'll be on my way, but I was hoping I could hang around, because I love your sister, and who knows, maybe I will be a part of your family one day.

WENDELL: It'll never happen. There's some things 'bout my sister—you'll never understand.

BILLY: Your sister and I don't have no secrets standing between us—the way most couples do.

WENDELL: Y'all a couple? A couple what? A couple lesbos? Yeah—I could tell you was that orphan type, when you was kissing my sister like a lesbo instead of kissing her like a man—a real man. All men gotta little bitch in them out there in Cali, with all that faggot ass sunshine weather. Sissy weather. Grow a lot of fruit in that kinda weather. You ain't got no manhood left—chasing my sister. Dancing to her music. You're having severe fantasies if you think my sister will marry a California raisin fruit salad like you. Shit! She don't even like you—leaving you here with me. Now what you gonna do? You wanna jump bad? Then jump bad! Butchu gotta bring some to get some!

BILLY: I don't want to fight you, Wendell. Now, I've been dying to meet you for a long time. Ever since your sister and I started dating—I was looking forward to coming into your orbit, 'specially after Rita told me you were a musician—a sax player. Well—I'm a musician too. I play the guitar. Rhythm, lead—jazz, funk, rock, the blues—makes me no never mind. So where's the gig?! Rita Mae says you gotta regular spot you're gigging at—down on the riverfront. Let me go with you tonight. Let me sit in. I got my ax out in my ride. What d'ya say? Let me tag along for just tonight. I hear the spot you're gigging at is really hot.

WENDELL: It's a small club and it's always sold out—

BILLY: I'll just hang with you backstage.

WENDELL: Bad idea, Billy Boy. See...there really ain't much of a backstage, therefore—there aren't any backstage passes—and even if they did let you in—they'd dock it from my cut of the door.

BILLY: Then I'll pay—I'll pay to play with you.

WENDELL: No. That's a bad idea, Billy Boy—

BILLY: Come on, man—we may never get this chance again. I taught Keb' Mo' everything he knows about the guitar.

WENDELL: I said no.

BILLY: Come on, man—don't be so uptight.

WENDELL: I'm not being uptight. I just don't need you hanging 'round—ruining things for me.

BILLY: What—you think I wanna squeeze in on your gig? I'm not that kinda cat. I just wanna play, man. Keep my chops tight—ya know what I'm saying? Come on.

WENDELL: You really like pushing yo' luck—don't you? I told you—you don't fit into tonight's plans. It's already sold out—like I said. So, you gonna have to catch me on the rebound—next time you're in town.

BILLY: Damn, that's too bad, man.

WENDELL: Yeah. That's too bad.

BILLY: I was really looking forward to playing with you, man...it really would've been something.

WENDELL: Yeah. It really would've been something.

BILLY: Hey. Why don't I go out to the ride and grab my ax and you and I—we can jam right here.

WENDELL: Oh. Bad idea. We can't jam here—on account of Ma. She can't handle the racket.

BILLY: We could play soft.

WENDELL: What's the point in jamming if you can't play all out? It's just not meant to be—Billy Boy.

BILLY: Guess it's just not meant to be.

WENDELL: So—how long you staying?

BILLY: Maybe a few days. I might go further east or further south from here—before I head back to L A. You ever been out there?

WENDELL: I ain't never been nowhere but here.

BILLY: You've never left St Louis?

WENDELL: Never.

BILLY: If you play as good as Rita Mae says, you'd have an easy time if you'd came to L A getting work as a session man.

WENDELL: I do fine here—

BILLY: But are ya making any money? Can you make any money playing what you play—here?

WENDELL: Boy—don't try to git all up in my Kool Aid, when you don't know the flavor. Now I said—I do just fine here. Billy Boy.

(Lights get a little brighter in MAMA's *room.)*

RITA MAE: Billy—I want you to come in here for a minute.

BILLY: Excuse me, Wendell.

*(*BILLY *tries to cross over to* MAMA's *room, but* WENDELL *grabs his arm, stopping him.)*

WENDELL: Leave now, Billy. Don't go in there. Mama's just gonna wrap you 'round her finger—and then what?

*(*BILLY *pulls away from* WENDELL *and shrugs. He enters* MAMA's *room as the lights fade on* WENDELL.*)*

RITA MAE: Billy—I want you to meet my mother.

BILLY: Hello—Mrs Megan—

MAMA: You call me Mama Megan—

RITA MAE: She's mama to the universe. Every Mother's Day, she gets dozens of Mother's Day cards from people she touched, one way or another—

MAMA: I was a school cook for forty years—fed a lot of chillen who remember me. Step aside, Rita Mae—let me talk to your feller. Come a little closer, son. Let me get a better look at you.

*(*BILLY *moves closer.)*

MAMA: Grrreeeaaaattt Day! My, my, my, you'se a nice looking feller—a lot easier on the eyes than Rita Mae made you out to be. This is the same feller you said you were seeing?

RITA MAE: Yeah, Ma—this is Billy.

BILLY: Yep—the notorious Billy Mars—

MAMA: Now what have you gone and done to call yourself notorious? You haven't robbed or killed nobody—now have ya?

BILLY: I'm notoriously stubborn.

MAMA: So, you kinda sweet on my Rita Mae?

BILLY: Oh I'm way past being sweet on her. I want to marry her and I was hoping to receive your blessing—

MAMA: Well, what did my Rita Mae—tell ya—

BILLY: She told me she'd think about it.

RITA MAE: I told you no!!

BILLY: You said you'd think about it.

RITA MAE: Don't be putting words in my mouth—

MAMA: Well—did you think about it?

RITA MAE: I don't need to think about it. The answer is already no.

MAMA: Now, don't be so hasty. It's not like we've been overwhelmed by gentlemen callers since you came home. Look—Rita Mae—since Billy is here, why don't you run over to the grocery store and pick up a few thangs to fix a nice big breakfast for our guest—

RITA MAE: I'll go to the store, Ma—but I want Billy to go with me—

MAMA: Hush yo' mouth—don't be silly girl. Billy here can keep me company—if you don't mind, Billy—

BILLY: Oh no—I don't mind.

MAMA: Good then—you come on and sit here on the edge of my bed a spell.

RITA MAE: Billy—there's something about my brother that you need to know—

MAMA: Would you hush up with that foolishness and git on to the store?

RITA MAE: Billy—whatever you do—promise me this, don't agitate my brother. Sometimes he has a short fuse.

MAMA: Would you hurry along, girl? Take some money from the cookie jar—

RITA MAE: I know, Mama—

MAMA: Make sho you dress warm now—

RITA MAE: I know, Mama—God, you act like I can't think for myself sometimes. (*Leaves* MAMA's *room and crosses in front of* WENDELL) Who you looking at? (*Goes to money/cookie jar*)

WENDELL: You've got a lot of nerve, you old cow.

RITA MAE: (*Putting on her coat*) You better be nice to my guest.

WENDELL: Why should I be nice to him? You ain't being nice to him. Letting him do you in the front room—was that being nice? Naw. That was being hateful. Slut.

RITA MAE: I'm warning you.

WENDELL: You're always warning me. Don't worry. I'm kinda taking a liking to Billy. He asked to sit in with me tonight at the club and I think I'm gonna let him.

RITA MAE: You're kidding, right?

WENDELL: Nope. I'm really warming up to Billy Boy. Who knows—maybe I'll even let you tag along.

RITA MAE: How come you never asked me to come hear you play before?

WENDELL: Never thought you had no appreciation for my kinda music. You know I be playing that outside shit.

RITA MAE: Yeah. Like you belong outside in the woods somewhere.

WENDELL: Billy Boy told me he wants to marry ya. Does he know about you—being funny and all?

RITA MAE: We don't have no secrets.

WENDELL: Not like me and you. You ever tell him about our little secret? You were about to tell him this morning. But you chickened out.

RITA MAE: That's enough, Wendell.

WENDELL: I want you to tell him I got to you first.

RITA MAE: I'm warning you—leave it alone, Wendell. Back up off me! Don't start no mess with me.

WENDELL: You don't start no mess and there won't be no mess. *(Beat)* Do you love him, Rita Mae?

RITA MAE: That's none of your concern.

WENDELL: Oh, everything around here is my concern, darling.

RITA MAE: Why can't I have something of my own—without you always messing with it?

WENDELL: Do you love that boy?

RITA MAE: Don't make me answer that.

WENDELL: Then don't answer. I already know the answer. If you loved that boy—you wouldn't have let him in here last night. If you love him—make him leave now. Otherwise, it's open season and he's up for grabs. Go ahead. Here's your chance. Make him leave. Tell him to go—now.

(RITA MAE starts toward her MAMA's room but hesitates. She stops herself as WENDELL grabs RITA MAE's hand.)

WENDELL: Just like I thought. You could never love him. How could you love him, *(Points to RITA MAE's head)* when ain't no other man been inside there besides me. Am I lying? Your thoughts belong to me. Even when you sleep—your dreams are mine. *(Beat)* Now, since you going to the store, why don't you bring me a quart of buttermilk? Don't come back here with no sissified low-fat shit. You got that?! *(Beat)* And by the way, Rita Mae, I wanna thank you for bringing Billy Boy—to me.

(WENDELL slowly lets go of RITA MAE's hand. After a beat, she exits.)

(WENDELL *goes into a freeze, as the focus shifts to* MAMA *and* BILLY.)

BILLY: All my life—I've wanted a family. A family that Norman Rockwell would've painted if Norman Rockwell had been black.

MAMA: You believe in that cliché—the American Dream?

BILLY: Yes.

MAMA: I believe in people doing the best they can. Rita Mae is special to me. I had three miscarriages between having Wendell and having Rita Mae. So, when she finally came along—I felt blessed. I wasn't bitter about the babies I didn't have—I felt lucky that two of my children survived. My husband and I put all our energy into providing for them. We wanted more for them—than we wanted for ourselves. We wanted their lives to be better than ours. I think most parents wish that for their children.

BILLY: You did a good job, Mama Megan—

MAMA: Sometimes I wonder...sometimes I look at how my chirren's lives turned out and I wonder if their lives have been cursed...instead of blessed. If they are cursed, I'd make a deal with the devil to lift that curse off of them. Take Rita Mae—for example—she's got a pretty woman's face— but an ugly woman's disposition—

BILLY: She's beautiful inside and out—

MAMA: But she don't believe it—she don't see it—just like she don't see herself being married to you, or any man. You seem like the sensitive type. Am I right?

BILLY: I guess so, Mam—

MAMA: Rita Mae might be incapable of giving you everything you want. I mean—I used to go to bed at night and try to imagine what her big day would be like. I'd try to imagine how she'd look coming down the aisle of the church she grew up in, wearing the same wedding gown I wore. As hard as I tried—I kept turning up nothing. Well, one day I was up there in the attic cleaning it out—Rita Mae was helping me. So I got her to try on my wedding dress. She was 'bout the same size I was the day I got married... built a lot like me. She put on the dress and it fit her to a T. Yet, something was missing. That glow—a woman gets—from putting on a special dress— was missing from her face. It was then that she told me she was gay. I cried, "Lawd—tell me it ain't so—tell me it ain't so." Rita Mae said, "I'm sorry, Mama." I said, "What you got to be sorry about? God is the one who should be sorry. He's the one who made you that way." It was that day that I realized that I could no longer dream my children's dreams for them. They came here with dreams of their own. And I had stop trying to force my dreams onto them. Marrying Rita Mae is your dream. But your dream and her dream might not be the same. Will you still love her if she says no?

BILLY: I'd try to. I'd be hurt—but I'd try to.

MAMA: Then do me this one small favor. Try to love her, even if things don't go your way. Try to love her, anyway. That's how a real man—loves a woman.

BILLY: Thank you, Mama Megan. *(He gently holds her hand for several beats.)*

MAMA: My husband—he wasn't perfect either. He was the type to stray from the house every now and then. But when he came home—oh—he really knew how to stir my coffee. So, I would just try to block it from my mind—that my coffee wasn't the only coffee he was stirring. Otherwise, it woulda never lasted. But it lasted. We were married 38 years before he died. Thirty-eight good years. They weren't perfect, but they were good. And that was enough for me. Life ain't a fairy tale. You learn that fast. Ain't nobody ever comin' on a white horse or any horse. Life is about working hard—you even have to work hard to find a little bit of happiness. But it is out there. Happiness is out there, you just can't give up looking for it.

BILLY: Well, thank you, Mama Megan—for sharing your wisdom with me.

MAMA: When you got two chillen as different as Rita Mae and Wendell— life gives you a little wisdom. Neither one of them could wait to leave this town...one went to L A...the other went to New York. Now how more opposite can you git?

BILLY: Wait—you mean—Wendell went away to New York—

MAMA: The boy studied music at Juilliard—though you could never tell it by his playing.

BILLY: He? Went to Juilliard?

MAMA: Sho did...didn't stay there long. But he was there.

BILLY: But he told me he'd never left St Louis.

MAMA: Well—he lied to you. Probably wasn't the only lie he told ya— either. Look—you can't pay no attention to Wendell—besides—there's a little half-truth in every lie. It's not like he means to lie to ya—he just can't help it. Now Rita Mae—she left here and stayed away for a long time. But Wendell—it was almost like he never left. I know one thing—the Wendell who came back here from New York was not the same Wendell who left here.

BILLY: Thank you for sharing that with me, Mama Megan.

MAMA: Now do me a favor, Billy, and send Wendell in here. I got an itch I can't get to.

BILLY: Let me—

MAMA: Boy—you better get on out of here—as cute as you are, I ain't letting you put your hands on me—'cause you might start something—neither one of us can finish.

BILLY: You are something else, Mama Megan. *(Gently kisses her hand)*

MAMA: And so are you, Billy Mars—so are you.

(BILLY holds her hand for a beat then rises and crosses back over to the living room area. Lights get dim on MAMA, brighter on WENDELL.)

WENDELL: Hey there, boy...my mama is something else. Ain't she? So what's the deal? Are you as smitten with my mama as you are with my Rita Mae?

BILLY: Your mother wants to see you.

WENDELL: You was in there with my mama a mighty long time, boy. What was y'all talkin' 'bout? Was ya talkin' 'bout me?

BILLY: A little bit—

WENDELL: She tell you what a big star I am 'round here? I'm the biggest star out there, boy. My shit is way out. And you gotta be way out to catch up to the shit I'm playing.

BILLY: Your mother wants you...now.

WENDELL: Well, she gonna have to wait. So what all else did she tell you 'bout me?

BILLY: She told me you've been to New York.

WENDELL: I ain't never been to New York. I ain't been nowhere. Why she want to tell you that lie?

BILLY: She said you went to Juilliard—

WENDELL: Juilliard? What's that—

BILLY: The college you went to. The music school—

WENDELL: Never went to college. Never heard of no Ju-Ju-Juilliard.

BILLY: Well—I think you did.

WENDELL: You know—Billy Boy. I was just beginning to take a liking to you—but now—you're wearing on my last nerve—wearing out yo' welcome. I think it's time for you to leave.

BILLY: I can't leave without saying goodbye to Rita Mae.

WENDELL: Boy—your skull is so thick. You—you say something pulled you here. Well, I just wish it would pull you back, pull you right on back to wherever it was you came from. 'Cause you—you're in a place where you don't belong, boy. You're lost. You're a lost boy. Driving your car through a desert of confusion. Driving round and round and round in a circle. Driving all around the truth about the woman you think you love. She don't care no more about you, than a mangy mutt, laying dead on the side of the road somewhere.

BILLY: See—that's where you're wrong. You're dead wrong.

WENDELL: Read my lips. My sister hates men.

BILLY: You don't know Rita Mae like I know Rita Mae.

WENDELL: Oh? I beg to differ.

BILLY: Butchu don't know nothing about her heart. Her capacity for love.

WENDELL: Love is overrated. And what is a heart—but a piece of meat—a muscle—a piece of flesh to be devoured? Do you bake it? Boil it? Season it with pepper? Or do you smoke it—until it's blackened? And to think you came all this way—you drove 'cross country for a lesbian—a card-carrying, Indigo Girls/Ani DiFranco-listening, certified lesbian. That ain't love, man. That's stupid. What the hell were you thinking? Coming here, looking like a wounded animal. A stray dog hit by a car. Do you think my sister can heal you?

BILLY: *(Beat)* She...in L A. When I was with her—who I was...where I came from...it didn't hurt as much.

WENDELL: She can't heal ya. She got wounds of her own—injuries of her own—scars far worse than yours. How do I know? I know everything. Besides—I can smell your blood and hear your blues. And what I hear sounds pathetic.

BILLY: I'm not pathetic.

WENDELL: You're beyond pathetic. Lost in a desert of delusion. Your mouth is dry. And my sister is just a long tall drink you wanna swallow. But you're confused. You don't know vinegar from water, water from wine or wine from sweat. All you know is you're thirsty and you think my lipstick lesbian sister is all you need to quench your thirst. Do you think that fountain between her legs gushes just for you? You don't even have a clue about where she's been or where she's going. Nor do you have a clue about this place—you've come to. Trying to get all up in my Kool Aid.

BILLY: Well, let me take a stab at it and try to guess the flavor. Something pretty fucked up must've happened to you in New York for you to feel the need to tell me a lie. Yeah—let's change the subject back to you and your pain, Wendell. Handsome Wendell. It was your daddy that called you handsome, right? When was that? Was that before or after the bedtime story. Or right before he tucked you in?

WENDELL: You really want to start some shit now. Don'tchu?

(As WENDELL *talks, he slowly walks circles around* BILLY, *limping badly, moving clumsily with his table-leg crutch. But as the scene progresses, at some point his limp will disappear.)*

WENDELL: And why should I have to lie to you? You ain't nobody. Now I said I ain't been to no New York, no Juilliard. Never been nowhere. Never no need to go. I'm the biggest star there is 'round these parts. Why should I leave here where I'm somebody—and go somewhere, where I'm nobody? Does that make any kinda sense to you? I mean in California you could be somebody or you could be nobody. I don't know what you are out there, 'cause I don't know ya. But I know one thing for sure—you're a big nobody here. Don't nobody here know ya, but my sister. So that makes you a nobody—'cause she's nobody. See—if—you die around here, nobody would miss you. My sister will miss ya. Maybe. But she ain't nobody— so nobody will miss ya. And seeing how you'se an orphan—your parents won't miss ya—'cause you ain't got none!!! So nobody will miss you— 'cause you ain't nobody and you came from nowhere.

MAMA: Wendell Megan, what's taking you so long to come see about me?

BILLY: Your mama's calling you—   ·

WENDELL: Mama's always callin' me. I don't pay her no mind and neither should you. 'Specially when she's talkin' 'bout me. Don't believe a word she tells you about me. She's nobody to listen to. She hasn't been playing with a full deck since her stroke—maybe even before that—she wouldn't know the truth from a lie if the truth hit her in the eye.

BILLY: And what about you?

WENDELL: What about me?

BILLY: Would you know the truth if it was staring you in the face?

WENDELL: Would you?

BILLY: Let me go out on a limb here and speculate that something happened in New York that you ashamed of. Am I right? Something dark—so dark— you feel compelled to block it from your mind—delete it from your memory. Tell me if I'm getting warm or not.

WENDELL: If you think that's true—then you way off the mark.

BILLY: Then how about the truth between us? The truth between you and I—is that you hate my guts—and I don't understand why?

WENDELL: You talk down to me like you know me—

BILLY: You talk down to me—

WENDELL: But you don't know me.

BILLY: *(Overlap)* You talk down to me—

WENDELL: *(Overlap)* You don't have a clue about who I am.

BILLY: *(Overlap)* You're the one who's clueless—

WENDELL: *(Overlap)* Sticking your fucking nose in places you don't belong. Because you're fucking my sister—it don't mean you can fuck with me. You got a lotta nerve, Billy Boy—a lot of fucking nerve.

BILLY: Maybe I was fucking with you earlier—in my own little way—

WENDELL: See, see—there you go—

BILLY: But there was no malice behind my fuckin' with you. My fuckin' with you was for my entertainment—which meant my intentions were harmless.

WENDELL: See, see, see—you gotta lotta nerve. New in town and you gonna come to my house and start fucking with me—in my house—

BILLY: Your mama's house—

WENDELL: See? There you go again. Fucking with me!

BILLY: I'm sorry, man—

WENDELL: You sure are sorry—

BILLY: Look, Wendell—man—I just want to be your friend, man. You're my lover's brother and I just want to be close. That's why I asked if I could sit in with you at the club. And I still wanna sit in—if you'd let me.

WENDELL: It's time for you to go, man—time for you to go.

BILLY: Get it thru your thick skull. I ain't going nowhere without saying goodbye to your sister!

WENDELL: That's whatchu think? That's where you're wrong.

(WENDELL, *suddenly, without warning, raises the table leg and brings it down on* BILLY's *head with all his might.* BILLY *slumps to the floor, dazed and confused, but still conscious.* WENDELL *drops the crutch and grabs* BILLY *by the head, smashing* BILLY's *head against the floor, once.*)

BILLY: *(Groggy)* Whatchu doing, man?

WENDELL: *(In a trance)* The same damn thing—somebody did to me. New York is where it started—but this is where it ends.

BILLY: Hey, man—don't—hey, man—what—hey, Wend—why? What— hey, don't! Don't!

(WENDELL *gets behind* BILLY *and rips his pants down. He sticks his tongue in* BILLY's *ear.* WENDELL *slowly simulates raping* BILLY, *sodomizing him.*)

WENDELL: Do you like that? You like that?

BILLY: *(Gasping)* No! No!

WENDELL: How's that?

BILLY: Stop.

WENDELL: Is this whatchu wanted?

BILLY: Stop it!

WENDELL: Is that whatchu wanted? Or is this whatchu wanted?

BILLY: Please stop!

WENDELL: *(Humping)* Do you feel me?! Do you feel me?!

BILLY: Please—stop.

WENDELL: *(Humping)* Too late now. You didn't see this coming. Or did ya? You wanted this right—right? You wanted this.

(As WENDELL becomes more crazed, more demented, his violence grows, and grows, as he slowly bangs BILLY's head against the floor, rendering him unconscious. BILLY dies at some point while WENDELL continues to sodomize him.)

WENDELL: You only wanted to sit in with me to show me up! To embarrass me—make me look bad in my hometown. You wanna come into my club, and blow me off the stage with your playing. You think—I'm gonna let a nobody like you walk into my club and show me up? Fuck you! Suppose I told you there is no club? What would you say then? *(He hovers over BILLY, raping BILLY, in a stylized manner. He is killing BILLY and raping him at the same time.)* Huh?! What would you say then?! There is no club! Is that what you wanted to hear? Is that the truth you were looking for? Yeah, nigger—I'm doing you—I'm fucking you—the way somebody fucked me. Is this the kinda of sitting in you had in mind? You nosey-ass motherfucker. I tried to warn you. But you just wouldn't—you couldn't leave it alone. I told you once—you couldn't play—you couldn't sit in—but naw— You couldn't take no for an answer—now look at you—

MAMA: Wendell! Billy!! What's going on in there?!

WENDELL: Do you like sitting in? Huh, boy? See—I can't control that highway noise out there! But I control everything in here. This was never about you and my sister...this was about you and me from the git, Billy Boy! Yeah—you and me—and my need to control— My sister was just a pawn in the game—thrown in to bring you to me. You see, you and I—we are two old spirits who have a history! I have been in the belly of the beast for so long, I have become the beast. Look at me, Billy Boy—I too am a keeper of secrets—oh, you just don't know what deeds I have done. You see Billy— there's this little bar—this little fag bar down on 13th street, near St Charles... I go there sometimes—looking for orphans—looking for you, Billy Boy— I go there looking for you. I can always spot the orphans, the throw-away boys—the ones no one will miss. They are the ones that are always just a little too eager to please—they are the ones with the trusting eyes—with they hearts on they sleeves. They—the orphan boys—they always—they always act a little too desperate for love to be normal. Their air of desperation gives them away to me. They are just so fucking stupid—they'll leave with almost anyone. Aw—it's so easy. And having money—just a little bit of money—enough to buy a kid a meal—only makes it easier. They're so hungry. Starved. So, I feed them. Then I fuck them. Then I kill them. Then I dispose of them. Under the highway. *(A beat)* Sometimes my playing—gets a bit off-key. It sounds off-key to most people, but it don't sound off-key to me. Discord. Modulation. Minor-chord progression. Do you know what I'm saying—Billy Boy? I tried to warn ya—but you knew this moment was coming, when we first laid eyes on each other, when you got up and strutted your stuff for me. You knew, what you were doing, swinging your stuff for me to see.

(RITA MAE enters with an armful of groceries. She drops the groceries, splattering them all over the floor.)

RITA MAE: Whatchu doing, Wendell?! Whatchu doing?!

(WENDELL is still in a trance, humping BILLY, oblivious to RITA MAE as she retrieves the table leg, and brings it down on her brother, repeatedly, until he falls to the floor.)

MAMA: Rita Mae—what's going on in there?! What's going on?!

(RITA MAE grabs BILLY and holds his body in her arms.)

RITA MAE: Don't die on me, Billy...don't die on me. I did some thinking while I was at the store. I did plenty thinking 'bout everything you asked me, Billy. And my answer is yes, Billy—YES—I'll marry you. I'll do my best to be the kind of wife you deserve. I know all you want is a family of your own. *(Cries)* And I'll do my best to give you that, baby—but you can't die on me. You can't die on me. I know you didn't come all this way just to die on me. Please, God—don't do this to me. I'll hate you, God, if you do this to me—

(As RITA MAE is crying, WENDELL is coming back to his senses, recovering from her blow to his head. She is oblivious to WENDELL as he rises and retrieves his table leg.)

WENDELL: *(In a repeated trance as he rises)* A man must always be in control of his environment—a man must always be in control—

(WENDELL walks perfectly, with no limp at all, as he stands over her with the table leg raised over RITA MAE. He is ready to bring it down on her.)

WENDELL: A man must always be in control of his environment. A man must always be in control of his—

(MAMA enters with a shotgun raised.)

MAMA: You stop it right there, boy!!

(MAMA *fires off a round, killing* WENDELL *instantly.*)

(*Lights do a slow fade to black.*)

CODA

(*A solitary light rises on* MAMA, *with her bed in an upright position. We hear the steady roar of the highway.*)

MAMA: Sometimes the highway noise sounds like running water. Sometimes it sounds like rain, coming down in buckets. The highway is always there if you wanna use it. It knows where it is going—even if you don't. Seemed like I outlived almost everything I gave birth to. Seemed like I've outlived every dream I ever had. Rita Mae is still around, but her spirit is long gone. Her spirit is somewhere with Billy in an unmarked grave. A mother tries to raise a child to be independent, filled with dreams of their own. But if a child is cursed with nightmare, instead of being blessed with dreams, how does the mother guide that child through those nightmares? How can any parent know—everything going on with a child. Can you ever know—if every baby-sitter is safe or every playmate a good influence? Or maybe—it was something you ate when you was pregnant—or maybe your husband is really your first cousin on your mother's side. Or maybe the environment you bring 'em up in makes every song they ever play way off-key. I know I did the best I could with my chillen, and left the rest to the lord...that was what my mama did. So, I'm still trying to figure out where the equation went so wrong. Could it really be too much T V? Or maybe it was the highway—the noise of the highway that drove my son crazy—put him over the edge of reality, never to return again. Maybe it was the noise of the highway—the speed and desperation of the highway. The drive-by—the violence—the carnage, the karma, the bloodshed of the highway, the broken twisted metal—the shredded flesh...the sickness of rush hour...the rubber Garfields in rear windows—the babies on board. The pileups, the letdowns, the ten-wheel big-rig trucks...the sound of it all...the accumulated sound of it all...the demonic music of screeching tires—SUDDEN IMPACT, bringing another heartbeat to a halt.

(*Blackout*)

END OF PLAY

MAN, WOMAN, DINOSAUR

Regina M Porter

ABOUT THE AUTHOR

Regina Porter is a graduate of the Dramatic Writing Program at New York University's Tisch School of the Arts. A native of Savannah, Georgia, she has been commissioned by the Actors Theater of Louisville, the Joseph Papp Public Theater in New York, Playwrights Horizons, and the Women's Project.

Ms Porter's play TRIPPING THROUGH THE CAR HOUSE was the recipient of a 1996 Roger L Stevens Award for Outstanding New Play from the Kennedy Center's Fund for New American Plays. The play, which was workshopped at New York Stage & Film and produced by Woolly Mammoth, received a Helen Hayes nomination for Outstanding New Play and was published in Heinemann's *Scenes for Women, by Women*. Ms Porter has been the recipient of an Edward Albee Fellowship, a Van Lier Fellowship, and a Distinguished Alumni Award from The Dramatic Writing Program at New York University's Tisch School of the Arts, where she was also invited to teach playwriting. Ms Porter lives in New York and is writing a new play for Playwrights Horizons.

ORIGINAL PRODUCTION

MAN, WOMAN, DINOSAUR was originally commissioned by American Playhouse; it was subsequently workshopped by Playwrights Horizons in New York.

MAN, WOMAN, DINOSAUR premiered at Woolly Mammoth on 23 March 1998. The cast and creative contributors were:

VERVE WILLOWS . . . . Rebecca Rice
TOOCHIE WILLOWS . . . . Kevin Jiggetts
BERNADETTE MARSH . . . . Caroline Clay
ALAN MARSH . . . . Vincent Brown
LI'L SAMUEL . . . . Daniel Lee Robertson III

Director . . . . Howard Shalwitz
Set design . . . . .Lewis Folden
Costume design . . . . Robin Stapley
Lighting design . . . . Lisa Ogonowski
Sound design . . . . Mark Anduss
Properties . . . . Joseph Stoltman
Stage manager . . . . Deborah Sullivan

MAN, WOMAN, DINOSAUR *Show Sponsors*
James and Marjorie Akins
Lewis Freeman and Gretta Sandberg
Alan Gilburg and Martha Spice
James and Phyllis Kay
Peter Miller and Sara Cormeny

CHARACTERS & SETTING

VERVE WILLOWS, *mid-fifties*
TOOCHIE WILLOWS, *her son, thirty*
BERNADETTE MARSH, *nurse, thirtyish*
ALAN MARSH, BERNADETTE'*s husband, forties*
LI'L SAMUEL, BERNADETTE'*s son, nine*

Setting: A cottage house on Skidaway Island in Savannah, Georgia

Time: Winter, past and present

ACT ONE

Scene One

(A Southern house of fine but unrealistic taste. There is more than a sense of mystery here; there is time, encapsulated and unyielding, time best defined by the numerous ceramic dinosaurs that grace the house and enhance its surreal environment. A two-story house, the bottom half consists of a kitchen and parlor. In the parlor, there is a fireplace and a large arched window. Upstairs, there is a small workroom in which dinosaurs are made.)

(VERVE WILLOWS sits in a wheelchair before the parlor window sipping tea.)

VERVE: Toochie! *(Pause)* Toochie!

(TOOCHIE WILLOWS enters.)

VERVE: Toochie! *(She spins around angrily.)* Godammit! Godammit! Didn't you hear me calling you?

TOOCHIE: No, Ma'am.

VERVE: Toochie, I called you God knows how many times and you say you didn't hear?

TOOCHIE: I was sleeping.

VERVE: You sleep hard.

TOOCHIE: I know it, Ma'am.

VERVE: Entirely too hard.

TOOCHIE: That's what comes of being tired.

VERVE: Well, if I were you, I wouldn't sleep so hard. People who sleep hard don't often wake—and that's a bad thing.

TOOCHIE: I can see how it would be. Especially for me.

VERVE: Only for you? What about me now, Toochie? I'd be left a childless mother. *(Turns to the window)* He's beating her again, Toochie. Mr Dillwood is beating his wife again. What do you suppose she did this time? What do you suppose he thinks she did? Had to be nothing. If ever there was a woman who mastered the art of nothingness, it's that Mrs Dillwood. And so, he beats her. *(Sips tea)* It makes me cringe to sit here. But I can't seem to look away. It's there for us to see. Out in the open. Designed for us to see...I swear she likes it. Something in my mind tells me she's one of those masochistic individuals. The world is full of masochistic people. Why can't she be just one more? She has to be something. What, with the way she takes it. He knocks her down. She stands back up. He knocks her down again. Constantly. Endlessly. How many blows can one woman stand?

TOOCHIE: He's a doctor. Maybe he knows.

VERVE: Very good, Toochie. Maybe that's the reason he hasn't killed her yet. Maybe he stops just short of that fatal blow. *(Pause)* Poor Mrs Dillwood. A doctor's wife ought to at least have shades. *(Sips tea)* Toochie?

TOOCHIE: Yes, Ma'am?

VERVE: Mr Dillwood's beating his—

TOOCHIE: I know.

VERVE: You were watching?

TOOCHIE: No, Ma'am.

VERVE: Then how do you know?

TOOCHIE: Because you've been talking about it.

VERVE: Are you sure you weren't watching?

TOOCHIE: I don't have to watch with you always talking about it.

VERVE: Not just once?

TOOCHIE: Don't seem quite right—looking in other people's windows.

VERVE: You are a stick-in-the-mud if ever there was one.

TOOCHIE: One day, you're gonna see something you won't wanna see.

VERVE: A real stick.

TOOCHIE: Then you'll be sorry.

VERVE: To think! The son of Verve Willows!

(VERVE hands TOOCHIE the empty teacup.)

TOOCHIE: What would you be liking for breakfast this morning?

VERVE: What do you have to offer?

TOOCHIE: Ham. I know you don't care too much for it. That it's not all too good for your diet. But I got a craving for it. And it's lean. So, how about a ham and cheese omelette?

VERVE: I don't like ham omelettes.

TOOCHIE: Not even if they got cheese?

VERVE: Toochie, I don't like ham.

TOOCHIE: But this is special ham. This is butcher's ham. This ain't that super-market salt junk.

VERVE: Ham is ham.

TOOCHIE: Listen, I don't feel like cooking two different breakfasts this morning. I been up in the workroom all night. Why can't we have ham and cheese omelettes just this once?

(VERVE *tosses him a meaningful look.*)

VERVE: Put a little something in my tea.

TOOCHIE: What?

VERVE: If you're going to subject me to eating omelettes with ham and cheese, the least you could do is put a little something in my tea.

TOOCHIE: Ma'am, you know as well as I do that you've put heaven and hell in that cup already. Why not put earth?

(TOOCHIE *pours liquor in* VERVE's *teacup and hands it to her.*)

VERVE: I don't like your tone, Toochie. Lately, I don't like your tone at all. You're getting smug is what. Smug and shitty like. Or should I say, *particularly* shitty with me? But this wheelchair is not forever. Enjoy it while you can. One day I'll be up and about again. And when I am, I'm going to whip your ass like only a good mother can. *(She turns back to the window.)* Mr Dillwood's gone. Mrs Dillwood's lying in a fetal position on the bed— so he must be gone. She always balls up like that after he's beaten her— like she's trying to shrivel her way back into the womb. What else can she be trying to do? When I was a teacher, I'd see sixteen-year-old boys get mad and ball up like that. Ball up so small you wouldn't believe, and talk like infants. But I've never seen an adult become as fetally small as Mrs Dillwood. I wouldn't be at all surprised if she talks baby talk too.

TOOCHIE: Why don't you just go over there and ask her!

VERVE: What?

TOOCHIE: I said, maybe if you went over there and asked her, you wouldn't have to wonder so much.

VERVE: I'm afraid it's hardly the kind of thing you ask a stranger.

TOOCHIE: She's no stranger. She's our neighbor.

VERVE: You don't go over to a neighbor's house and ask, "Do you talk baby talk when you ball up into a fetal position after your husband's kicked the shit out of you?" It's a sure-fire way to make enemies.

(TOOCHIE *places the omelettes on the table. He sits down to eat.* VERVE *hurls the teacup at him and shatters one of dinosaurs.*)

VERVE: What were you going to do? Sit there and eat while my omelette grew cold?

(TOOCHIE *moves over to broken dinosaur.*)

TOOCHIE: *Tyrannosaurus rexes* don't grow on trees, Ma'am.

(VERVE *wheels over to the table.*)

VERVE: Amazing. The level of cholesterol in eggs. Imagine. There are people who eat as many as two to three eggs a day. It's sickening. One person who's been eating two to three eggs a day for, say, fifteen years of his life. (*She tastes the omelette.*) This omelette is good.

TOOCHIE: Thank you.

(*He starts to move upstairs with his plate.*)

VERVE: Where are you going?

TOOCHIE: To eat in my room.

VERVE: I'd rather you stay down here. (*Pause*) Stay down here and keep me company.

TOOCHIE: I don't think so.

VERVE: I didn't mean to break it, Toochie.

TOOCHIE: (*Seething*) Yes, Ma'am.

VERVE: It's just sometimes—sometimes you get on my last nerve.

TOOCHIE: And you don't get on mine?

VERVE: What was that, Toochie?

TOOCHIE: I said don't worry about it, Ma'am. I'll make another one. (*He returns to table.*)

VERVE: This wheelchair is to blame. If ever I get out of this wheelchair, I'll be a new woman.

TOOCHIE: I know you will, Ma'am.

VERVE: A brand new woman.

TOOCHIE: Yes, Ma'am.

VERVE: Because I understand with you being a grown man and all, I understand that you've just about worn yourself out taking care of me.

TOOCHIE: Now that you mention it, I had been thinking....

VERVE: About what, Toochie?

TOOCHIE: It's going on close to a year now since Sir passed. I could use a little help about the place.

VERVE: What kind of help did you have in mind?

TOOCHIE: House help. Maid help. I don't know. Nurse help?

VERVE: *Ingrate!*

TOOCHIE: Now, Ma'am.

VERVE: Don't you, "Now, Ma'am" me. After all I've done for you. You're so lazy.

TOOCHIE: Not lazy, Ma'am. Tired.

VERVE: Leave it to a son to abandon his mother.

TOOCHIE: Forget it, Ma'am. Forget I mentioned it. It was just a thought.

VERVE: A silly thought.

TOOCHIE: Yes: a silly thought.

VERVE: But nevertheless, one you would like to make real?

(TOOCHIE picks at his food.)

TOOCHIE: Food's getting cold, Ma'am.

(VERVE wheels over to the telephone.)

VERVE: Alright, Mr Abandon Your Mother Who Loves You, Scum, let's make your thought real.

(Lights fade.)

Scene Two

(TOOCHIE places a new dinosaur on the shelf. VERVE sleeps before the parlor window. The doorbell rings. Lights come up on BERNADETTE MARSH.)

BERNADETTE: Hello, I'm Bernadette Marsh. Does a Mrs Willows live here?

TOOCHIE: Sure does.

(He points to VERVE snoring in the wheelchair and turns to exit.)

BERNADETTE: Wait a minute. She looks to be sleeping. What do I do?

(TOOCHIE nudges VERVE.)

TOOCHIE: Ma'am? *(Pause)* Ma'am? *(Louder)* Ma'am?

(VERVE wakes with a start.)

VERVE: What in the hell is the matter with you? Did you have to yell like that?

TOOCHIE: You yell at me all the time.

VERVE: That's because you're an ass. And an ass must be yelled at for it to find itself.

TOOCHIE: Well, Ma'am, just so you know, the ass and you have got a guest.

(TOOCHIE *exits.* VERVE *turns to* BERNADETTE.)

BERNADETTE: I'm Bernadette Marsh.

VERVE: Sit down, Ms Marsh.

BERNADETTE: Thank you.

VERVE: Can I offer you a beverage of some kind?

BERNADETTE: No, thank you.

VERVE: Perhaps a swig of Jim Beam? I'm going to have a swig.

BERNADETTE: I don't think so....

VERVE: *(Pouring drink)* Can't say I didn't offer.

(VERVE *moves closer to* BERNADETTE.)

VERVE: Well, Bernadette, I'm sorry our meeting couldn't have been under more pleasant circumstances. But I suppose this is good. You're getting to see a little of the real picture here. The shit hasn't hit the fan, but it sure is flying.

BERNADETTE: Beg pardon?

VERVE: My son. Toochie. He's reached the point where he's no damn good. Simply no damn good. *(Pours another drink)* I suppose the ad outlined everything for you. Gave you an idea of what I'm looking for?

BERNADETTE: A live-in nurse.

VERVE: Nurse. Maid. Jack-of-all-trades. *(Then)* I'm even talking windows. Do you do windows?

BERNADETTE: I can clean good windows. Yes.

VERVE: And cook a mean pot?

BERNADETTE: That too.

VERVE: Can you lift an old woman off a toilet and into a tub? Can you do that?

BERNADETTE: There's nothing domestic I can't do.

VERVE: Good. There is something to be said for confidence in the young. I respect confidence in the young. And you, you are young, aren't you?

BERNADETTE: Thirty years old.

VERVE: A mere babe compared to me.

BERNADETTE: I prefer to think of myself as an almost–middle-aged woman.

VERVE: Babe. Middle-aged woman. Whatever. This hardly strikes me as the kind of thing the average person of your generation would want to do.

BERNADETTE: Well, I ain't the average person of my generation.

VERVE: What makes you so different?

BERNADETTE: I've had more experience. I know more 'bout life.

VERVE: Are you telling me I should hire you?

BERNADETTE: Need. I'm telling you I need for you to hire me. I'm also telling you I'll more than get the job done.

VERVE: Did you bring references?

BERNADETTE: *(Pulls an envelope from her purse)* Yes, Ma'am. I did.

(VERVE looks over BERNADETTE's resume.)

VERVE: You've moved around quite a bit.

BERNADETTE: It's been tough going on the work front, and that's the truth.

VERVE: Why's that?

BERNADETTE: Employers, like employees, got to go where the money is, and they don't always have the resources to take their help with 'em.

(VERVE returns the resume to BERNADETTE.)

VERVE: Well, eight dollars an hour's the best I can do for you here. And it's not negotiable.

BERNADETTE: I'll take it.

(VERVE holds out her hand.)

VERVE: Congratulations, Ms Marsh. The job is yours.

(BERNADETTE shakes her hand.)

VERVE: Your room is upstairs. First room to your right.

(BERNADETTE picks up her suitcase and starts upstairs. She stops, as she glances at something out the window.)

VERVE: What in the hell...? *(She moves to window.)* Oh, it's only Mrs Dillwood. My neighbor. Mrs Dillwood. I feel sorry for her. In time, you'll feel sorry for her too. You think her standing in front of that mirror nude is something? It's absolutely nothing. Mrs Dillwood likes to pass the time that way.

BERNADETTE: Really?

(BERNADETTE moves upstairs.)

VERVE: Just you wait, Bernadette. Mrs Dillwood gets bored enough, she gets to taking out those cigarettes of hers and lighting them one right after the other. She lights them one right after the other and puts them out on her arms. And do you think she cries? Not a whimper. Not a sigh. Not Mrs Dillwood. She's immune. It takes a certain caliber of woman to be so gracefully immune. *(Then)* Bernadette?

(TOOCHIE enters.)

TOOCHIE: Ma'am?

VERVE: I didn't call you. I called Bernadette.

TOOCHIE: I know that. But we need to talk. We need to talk right now.

VERVE: What about, Toochie?

TOOCHIE: Ma'am, I'm a man.

VERVE: When did this notion pop into your head, Toochie?

TOOCHIE: And I've got pride the way a man's supposed to have it.

VERVE: Don't belabor the point.

TOOCHIE: You can yell at me all you want when we're alone, but with other people around—

(VERVE looks at him.)

VERVE: I got you.

TOOCHIE: Just remember that, Ma'am.

VERVE: I'll remember it. Now, go check on Bernadette. See if she needs help with anything.

(TOOCHIE goes upstairs. He taps on BERNADETTE's bedroom door. BERNADETTE steps into the hallway.)

BERNADETTE: Yes?

TOOCHIE: Ma'am sent me up here to see what you're doing?

BERNADETTE: I'm not doing nothing. Just trying to put my clothes in the drawer. Can I do that? Can I put my clothes in the drawer?

TOOCHIE: You can do anything you want.

BERNADETTE: That's good to know.

TOOCHIE: Which you probably need new light bulbs for that room. I better set about finding you some.

BERNADETTE: That would be nice.

TOOCHIE: I'll find you at least two. Sir used to say that room ate up light like crazy.

BERNADETTE: Sir?

TOOCHIE: Sir's my father.

BERNADETTE: Where is he now?

TOOCHIE: In Foxborough Cemetery.

BERNADETTE: Sorry to hear it. *(Then)* He didn't die in this room or nothing, did he? I can't be sleeping in a room where nobody died.

TOOCHIE: He died in a hospital.

BERNADETTE: Good.

(TOOCHIE looks at her.)

BERNADETTE: I don't mean good good. I mean it's nice to know I won't have to worry about ghosts or nothing. Spirits or nothing.

TOOCHIE: Oh.

(He exits. BERNADETTE moves downstairs.)

BERNADETTE: Mrs Willows?

VERVE: Yes?

BERNADETTE: That man,Toochie. He told me you sent him to check on me?

VERVE: Yes. I did.

BERNADETTE: You want me to do something for you? Now, as in the moment?

VERVE: No.

BERNADETTE: Then, if it's alright with you, I'd like to get myself settled and not feel under inspection.

VERVE: I only sent my son up to see if you needed help with anything. Hypersensitivity is not necessary.

BERNADETTE: Believe me. I don't want to get off on a bad foot or nothing. I don't want to sound all rude. It's just, well, I caught this bus out here. All the way out here. It was a long ride too. A long, country-type ride. And that bus, it was just bumping and grinding. Seemed to hit every rock along the paveless roads. Hurt my pussy like you wouldn't believe. Hurt it so, it got me all mean and agitated. Got me in a foul mood. Now maybe— just maybe—this job will soothe that foulness, but I ain't been here long enough to know if that's the case yet. I just barely got my clothes out of the suitcase.

VERVE: Take your clothes out of the suitcase. By all means.

BERNADETTE: Thank you.

(She exits. VERVE waits a beat and calls TOOCHIE.)

VERVE: Toochie!

(TOOCHIE *enters, holding two light bulbs.*)

VERVE: Why did you tell that girl I sent you upstairs to check on her?

TOOCHIE: Cause you did.

VERVE: Still, Toochie, you had no right to tell her that. That makes her think we were trying to spy on her. People don't like to be spied on.

TOOCHIE: That sounds funny coming from you.

VERVE: Don't be a smart-ass.

TOOCHIE: I can't seem to help myself, Ma'am. You bring it out in me.

VERVE: I tell you what I should've done. I should've checked her references. She could be as crazy as a loon.

TOOCHIE: She's not crazy.

VERVE: How do you know?

TOOCHIE: You've been telling me I'm crazy long enough for me to be able to spot it in others. *(Pause)* I'd say she's more lost than anything.

(VERVE *studies* TOOCHIE.)

VERVE: I bet you'd like to help her find herself, wouldn't you? (TOOCHIE *doesn't respond.*) Got naughty-boy thoughts whirling in your head, don't you, Toochie? *(Roaring with laughter)* Well, dream on!

TOOCHIE: You got a cruel heart, Ma'am. Why does your heart got to be so cruel?

VERVE: I can't seem to help myself, Toochie. You bring it out in me.

(Lights fade.)

Scene Three

(It is late at night. BERNADETTE *is in the parlor, caught in a cleaning frenzy.)*

BERNADETTE: Don't make sense. Don't make no kind of sense whatsoever. All this dust and dirt. What right a house got having so much dust and dirt!

(TOOCHIE *enters in his pajamas.*)

TOOCHIE: Could you keep it down?

BERNADETTE: Keep what down?

TOOCHIE: You're talking too loud.

(BERNADETTE *holds up her hand.*)

BERNADETTE: *This.*

TOOCHIE: It's only dust.

BERNADETTE: Ain't no such thing as only dust. Dust is serious. Dust is deadly. Dust can send a person with allergies to an early grave.

TOOCHIE: Do you have allergies?

(She shrugs and continues cleaning.)

BERNADETTE: What kind of people are y'all, anyway? Don't y'all care what other folks say when they come to your house? Don't y'all care 'bout them seeing it all kind of ways?

TOOCHIE: Nobody comes to our house.

BERNADETTE: And such nice furniture too. Going. Going. Gone. To the dust!

(TOOCHIE moves in the kitchen.)

BERNADETTE: We're gonna have to lift up this rug. We're gonna have to lift it up and take it out of here into the backyard. Take it so I can beat some of the dust off it and let it air out. Can't even think about vacuuming it 'til I let it air out. *(Looking at him)* That is, of course, if it's alright with you? *(TOOCHIE doesn't respond.)* Are you listening to me?

TOOCHIE: *It's three o'clock in the morning.*

BERNADETTE: So?

TOOCHIE: The rest of the world is sleeping. Why aren't you?

BERNADETTE: Because I got work to do. Things to clean. I can't be thinking 'bout sleep. What with all the things I got to clean.

(TOOCHIE puts milk in a pan and heats it on the stove.)

TOOCHIE: Go ahead. Go right ahead.

BERNADETTE: I can't clean with you watching me. I got a thing about people watching me.

TOOCHIE: Nurse Woman—

BERNADETTE: My name is *not* Nurse Woman. My name is Bernadette.

(He pours heated milk into a cup.)

TOOCHIE: Drink this, Bernadette.

BERNADETTE: What is it?

TOOCHIE: Hot milk.

BERNADETTE: I don't like hot milk.

TOOCHIE: It'll put you to sleep.

BERNADETTE: I don't recall saying I was sleepy either.

TOOCHIE: You don't have to say you're sleepy. Your eyes, they're fire-engine red. Then too, you're fussing about everything under the sun.

(BERNADETTE *takes the teacup.* TOOCHIE *sips heartily. She hesitates.*)

BERNADETTE: Like I said. I'm not exactly partial to milk in any way, shape or form. Tends to upset my stomach in the worst way.

TOOCHIE: This milk won't. It comes without lactose.

BERNADETTE: What's that?

TOOCHIE: I don't know. But according to Ma'am, milk with lactose doesn't set well in black people's stomachs. So we buy our milk without it.

(BERNADETTEs *drinks.*)

BERNADETTE: Doesn't taste half bad. Course, that doesn't mean a solitary thing. I can drink it now and in five minutes be running to the bathroom left and right. *(Sitting)* But it's really not half bad. *(Pause)* Thank you.

TOOCHIE: You're welcome. *(Pause)* I know what it can be like when sleep won't come. When it's craved. But just won't come. It's hardly a pleasant thing.

BERNADETTE: I'll say. *(She rises to wash his cup.)*

TOOCHIE: You can save it until the morning.

BERNADETTE: Don't go being too nice to your employee. She might take you for granted. Besides, it is morning. And if I look tired, you look wickedly so.

TOOCHIE: I am.

BERNADETTE: I suppose I woke you?

TOOCHIE: Well, you do have the kind of voice that carries across a crowded room.

BERNADETTE: You trying to say I got a big mouth?

TOOCHIE: Well, I... No... I mean, yes. *(Pause)* You know what I mean.

BERNADETTE: That's okay. My husband's all the time saying I got a big mouth.

TOOCHIE: You married?

BERNADETTE: Dead. My husband's dead.

TOOCHIE: People will do that. They will die.

BERNADETTE: The way you say it, it's rather funny. The way I know it, it's almost sad.

TOOCHIE: My father died.

BERNADETTE: You told me.

TOOCHIE: I was close to him.

BERNADETTE: I gathered.

TOOCHIE: He was a complicated man.

BERNADETTE: So?

TOOCHIE: I don't know. I just felt the need to add that. *(Pause)*

BERNADETTE: How long has he been dead?

TOOCHIE: Just about a year now.

BERNADETTE: You and Mrs Willows all that's left?

TOOCHIE: Yep.

BERNADETTE: Y'all two get along more like cat and dog than mother and son. Least from what I've seen.

TOOCHIE: We have our days.

BERNADETTE: I bet.

TOOCHIE: We do.

BERNADETTE: I'm sure.

TOOCHIE: Why're you saying it like that?

BERNADETTE: Like what?

TOOCHIE: I don't know. Mocking like.

BERNADETTE: Cause you're a stranger, and sometimes, when I make small talk with a stranger, I say things mocking like.

TOOCHIE: Wouldn't it be easier to just be nice?

BERNADETTE: Why should I bother being nice—when I can be myself instead. *(Rising)* Now, if you'll excuse me.

TOOCHIE: I guess I've agitated you. You're the easiest woman in the world to agitate.

BERNADETTE: You give yourself too much credit. It ain't hardly you. It's your milk. Lactose or no lactose, it's hit my stomach. And, by God, it rubs me wrong.

(She exits. Lights fade.)

Scene Four

(The following morning. Lights on VERVE and BERNADETTE)

VERVE: There is nothing worse than beginning a new day. New days are stitched in monotony. That's a new day summed up. Monotony. Nothing. But.

BERNADETTE: What would you be liking for breakfast this morning?

VERVE: When I was a child, it was different. There was something exciting about the coming of a new day. Maybe because I didn't know what was ahead. Children like not knowing what's ahead. You might even say they thrive on it. Who ever thinks of becoming an adult? I am intrigued at how we all become adults.

BERNADETTE: I checked the pantry. You got the whole world foodwise in your pantry. So, it's really up to you. Just tell me what you want.

VERVE: A two-way conversation would be nice.

BERNADETTE: Well, Mrs Willows, what do you want me to say? You come out here first thing this morning talking 'bout monotony, childhood, and such. Like any of it matters. Only thing that matters is what is. And right now, that's the breakfast I'm gonna fix you.

VERVE: Prepare me a fruit salad.

BERNADETTE: And the man upstairs? D'you suppose he'll be liking the same?

VERVE: Toochie has an open stomach. You cook it; he'll eat it.

BERNADETTE: That's not what I'm asking you, though. No point in fixing something he doesn't really like. I kind of want to put something together that he'd like.

VERVE: Ham and bacon. He's crazy for ham and bacon.

BERNADETTE: Alright. I can manage that. *(She begins to prepare breakfast.)*

VERVE: We won't hear a peep out of anyone on Bergen Street today. Not even the Dillwoods. It's Sunday, and they've gone to church. On Sunday, everyone on Bergen Street goes to church. They don't believe in God. But still, they go to church. *(Pause)* There is a fine one two blocks away. St Paul's Episcopal Church. Everyone on Bergen Street's Episcopalian. Even Toochie and I are Episcopalian. Bergen Street's only black Episcopalians. Not that we ever go. The good Reverend calls us often. But we don't go. And really, why should we? What can he possibly tell us about life that we don't already know. And death? Well, let him die and return Lazaras anew, then we'll go. To hear a dead man's wisdom, Toochie and I will certainly go.

BERNADETTE: What would you be liking with your fruit salad?

VERVE: Tea—with a swig of brandy.

BERNADETTE: I used to go to church myself. Where I was raised, church was the right thing to do. On Sunday, the place to be.

VERVE: Oh yes?

BERNADETTE: Can't say I ever got anything out of it, though. Most of the time I just went to see the old women catch the Holy Ghost. I loved to watch them catch the Holy Ghost.

VERVE: What called you there the rest of the time?

BERNADETTE: Men. *(Pause)* Didn't know a girl who wouldn't slip into her nylons on Sunday without the thought of finding a good man. Of course, the finding's easy. It's the loving the one you find that's the problem.

(TOOCHIE enters.)

TOOCHIE: Morning.

BERNADETTE: Morning—for the second time. Sit on down at the table. I got your breakfast coming up.

(TOOCHIE sits.)

BERNADETTE: Will you be liking tea like Mrs Willows?

TOOCHIE: Water.

(BERNADETTE places food on the table. She unfolds a napkin and places it on VERVE's lap.)

VERVE: Thank you, Bernadette.

TOOCHIE: This looks real good.

BERNADETTE: Well, go ahead and eat yourself, fool, 'cause there's more where that came from. Same applies to you too, Mrs Willows.

TOOCHIE: Aren't you gonna have anything?

BERNADETTE: Oh, no. I've got plenty to do about the place. I'm fine.

TOOCHIE: You sure?

VERVE: Toochie, don't pester the girl. She says she's fine.

TOOCHIE: I'm not pestering her. It's called being polite.

BERNADETTE: Believe me—I raided the refrigerator earlier. I'm a long way from hungry.

VERVE: You did?

BERNADETTE: Well, not raided raided. I just helped myself to some toast and cheese. I didn't think you'd mind? *(She looks at VERVE.)* I guess you do mind?

VERVE: Well...

TOOCHIE: If you make a list of things you like, the next time I go to the market I'll get it for you.

BERNADETTE: I wouldn't want to put you out the way.

TOOCHIE: You wouldn't be.

BERNADETTE: Are you sure?

TOOCHIE: Positive.

BERNADETTE: I'd certainly appreciate it.

TOOCHIE: Consider it done.

BERNADETTE: Well, I'm glad, then. I guess I should also thank you for last night. It's true. That milk made me sick as a dog, but the thought was really nice. Last night.

(TOOCHIE *smiles at her.*)

TOOCHIE: Oh, it was nothing.

BERNADETTE: For me. It was something. A little thing. But something all the same.

TOOCHIE: I feel good hearing that. You don't know how good I feel hearing that.

(VERVE *puts down her fork.*)

VERVE: Why don't you two just go fuck. It would be easier on my digestive track.

TOOCHIE: Watch your language, Ma'am.

VERVE: My sweet, baby-faced Toochie could do with a good fuck.

(TOOCHIE *rises.*)

TOOCHIE: I said, watch your language.

VERVE: Fuck. Fuck. Fuck.

(TOOCHIE *exits.*)

BERNADETTE: Mrs Willows, that was plain uncalled-for. *(Pause)* There was no need to embarrass him like that. I get the feeling you're embarrassing him all the time.

VERVE: And what if I do?

BERNADETTE: A little tender loving care would serve him better.

VERVE: The world is overflowing with people who need tender loving care. The world is inundated with people who need tender loving care.

BERNADETTE: True. But most of them aren't lucky enough to find someone to give it to'em. Me, I'll give it to'em.

VERVE: Is that right?

BERNADETTE: He's not bad-looking. I ain't been at it in a while. It sure is right. *(She removes her apron.)*

VERVE: Young lady, get a hold of yourself.

BERNADETTE: I got a perfect hold of myself. *(Smiles)* Was a time before I married, when I could rouse a man to the highest heights. Make things so he'd forget he was a man for a while and think he was a bird and such. An eagle of some kind. I was in touch with myself then. I liked myself. I just got to learn to like myself again.

(BERNADETTE moves upstairs in pursuit of TOOCHIE.)

BERNADETTE: Toochie?

(Lights fade on VERVE and rise on TOOCHIE's workroom. He stands at his work table. BERNADETTE enters.)

BERNADETTE: Why do you let her talk to you like that?

TOOCHIE: She's...cantankerous. No harm done.

BERNADETTE: There's all the harm in the world.

TOOCHIE: Ma'am's my mother.

BERNADETTE: She's your enemy too.

TOOCHIE: How can my mother be my enemy?

BERNADETTE: Sometimes, your family will do you the most harm. They know they can get away with it.

TOOCHIE: It's none of your business either way.

BERNADETTE: I know. And it's not like I'm the type that usually cares about other folks' goings on. I'm a for me, myself, and I person. And yet, here I am....

TOOCHIE: Feeling sorry for me?

BERNADETTE: Worrying that you'll feel sorry for yourself. I know how it can be when a person gets to feeling sorry for herself.

TOOCHIE: Himself.

BERNADETTE: Well... *(She eyes the room.)* So, you been making dinosaurs all your life?

TOOCHIE: First, my father. Then me.

(She reaches to pick up one of the dinosaurs. TOOCHIE places a firm hand over hers.)

TOOCHIE: Why don't you look at some of the others? These, they're personal.

(She continues walking about the room.)

BERNADETTE: Well, this dinosaur stuff. It's great. It's different. *(Pause)* Of course, depending on how much you do it, it could also be boring.

TOOCHIE: There you go again. With that mocking tone.

BERNADETTE: I guess you do other things too?

TOOCHIE: Here and there.

BERNADETTE: Some of the best things are done here and now.

TOOCHIE: You mean like sex and all that?

BERNADETTE: Yes. Like sex and all that.

TOOCHIE: You playing me for the fool?

BERNADETTE: I'm trying to get a message across to you, but you ain't listening.

TOOCHIE: That's cause you're doing it in a roundabout way. You're doing it in a maybe/maybe not way.

BERNADETTE: You really think I'd be up here risking embarrassment if this was a maybe not?

(BERNADETTE's eyes fall on a radio. She crosses and turns it on.)

BERNADETTE: You dance?

TOOCHIE: No.

BERNADETTE: Well, I do.

(She dances by herself. TOOCHIE can't take his eyes off her. He rises, hesitates, reaches out to touch her.)

TOOCHIE: Soft. You're soft....

(BERNADETTE laughs. They slow drag.)

BERNADETTE: I like you.

TOOCHIE: Yeah?

BERNADETTE: What do you think of me?

TOOCHIE: I think you're a woman. In my mother's house.

(BERNADETTE stops dancing and leans against his work table. She reclines on top of it.)

BERNADETTE: Not just that, Toochie. I'm a woman. In your mother's house. In your room. On your work table. *(She pulls him to her.)* I've made my move, honey. You make yours.

(TOOCHIE kisses her. Lights fade.)

Scene Five

(VERVE has pillaged the parlor. Dinosaurs are broken and paper is strewn about. VERVE dangles from her wheelchair in a drunken stupor. Schubert plays in the background.)

VERVE: I listen to music. Though I cannot dance. Classical music. As sad as my legs are old. *(Touching them)* My legs. *(Squeezing them)* My legs. *(Dropping hands dejectedly)* Shrivelled like vienna sausage. These legs...

(TOOCHIE enters.)

TOOCHIE: Ma'am?

VERVE: And here goes Toochie. Son of mine. Are you an eagle yet? You still look like a man to me. A mere man. *(Pours a drink)* What a disappointing metamorphosis.

(TOOCHIE turns off the music. He moves back to her.)

TOOCHIE: Look at you.

(He lifts her up properly in the chair.)

VERVE: I liked it better the other way.

(TOOCHIE moves into kitchen. He returns with paper towels and wipes VERVE's legs.)

TOOCHIE: You know your bladder can't stand all this alcohol.

VERVE: I've peed myself.

TOOCHIE: I know.

VERVE: I'm all wet.

TOOCHIE: I know.

VERVE: Not very ladylike, is it?

TOOCHIE: Tearing up the house ain't either.

(She pours another drink. He takes it from her.)

TOOCHIE: I don't think so.

VERVE: Where's your girlfriend?

TOOCHIE: I hadn't known her long enough to use that word yet.

VERVE: Oh, but you will; you like her.

TOOCHIE: Can't deny that.

VERVE: I don't even have to ask if you screwed her. I can smell that you screwed her.

TOOCHIE: You don't smell nothing, Ma'am. I took a bath before I came down here. I wouldn't not take a bath before coming down here.

VERVE: Oh, you're just like your father. Just like Sir. Fucking women in my house. Next, you'll be eating pussy too. A cuntsman to rival your father.

TOOCHIE: *Christ.*

(BERNADETTE *appears at the top of the stairs.*)

BERNADETTE: Toochie?

TOOCHIE: Yeah?

(BERNADETTE *comes downstairs, holding a crate of dinosaurs.*)

BERNADETTE: Are these the ones we're taking to the flea market?

VERVE: Make her go back upstairs. I don't want her to see me like this.

TOOCHIE: You should've thought about that before you put the bottle to your mouth.

BERNADETTE: What's wrong?

TOOCHIE: Ma'am's had a little too much to drink.

BERNADETTE: You call this a little? (*She lowers the crate.*) And as nice as I had the place looking!

(VERVE *peers out the window.*)

VERVE: (*Sing-songy*) Mr Dillwood is a handsome man. A very, very handsome man. I love to watch him knot his tie. He knots a most becoming tie. A doctor needs a perfect tie.

BERNADETTE: I better put some coffee on.

VERVE: I swear right now, he's thinking fast. That mind of his is whirling fast. A knot tied slow. But thoughts go fast. (*Looks at* TOOCHIE) Better fast than slow, I say. Nothing worse than slow I say. If thoughts must go, go fast I say.

(BERNADETTE *crosses to* VERVE.)

BERNADETTE: I'm fixing you a nice, hot pot of coffee, y'hear me, Mrs Willows?

VERVE: I don't want any coffee.

TOOCHIE: How about a nice, hot bubble bath, Ma'am?

VERVE: That sounds agreeable.

BERNADETTE: That's a good idea. A nice, hot bubble bath. I'll set it for you right now.

VERVE: Toochie will give me my bath.

BERNADETTE: Oh, we don't want to bother Mr Toochie. He needs his energy for the flea market. I'll fix your bath. It's my job.

VERVE: Don't touch me, Bernadette. *(Then)* Bernadette, if you touch me, I will scream.

(BERNADETTE *starts for* VERVE, *and* VERVE *screams.)*

TOOCHIE: I'll give you your bath.

(VERVE *stops screaming.)*

BERNADETTE: You should've let her kept on. She would've tired herself out.

TOOCHIE: Would you let me deal with her my way?

VERVE: That's right. You let Toochie deal with me—his way.

(Lights fade.)

Scene Six

(The flea market. TOOCHIE *is at his booth, hawking his wares.* BERNADETTE *stands alongside him.)*

TOOCHIE: I've got dinosaurs to sell. Like you wouldn't believe. Dinosaurs. Come over here and see for yourself. *(He holds up a dinosaur.)* This is *Mamenchisaurus.* He's little here, but in real life he was nearly seventy-two feet long. Can you imagine something as big as seventy-two feet long walking this earth? *(He gives the dinosaur to* BERNADETTE.*)* Probably not. But you can imagine what you hold in your hands. A nice little replica to hold in your hands.

(TOOCHIE *pushes a button on the Mamenchisaurus. We hear music.)*

BERNADETTE: It's a music box!

TOOCHIE: That's right, folks. I've got music in my dinosaurs. Everything from *Don Giovanni* to James Brown. *(He picks up a Stegosaurus.)* I've even got dinosaur bread boxes. *Tyrannosaurus rexes* that serve as Bubble Yum Bubble Gum machines. A penny in the tail and a piece of bubble gum pops out the mouth. And if regular old plates have become a bore, look at this: *(He holds up a plate with dinosaur etchings.)* You can eat from your plate and educate yourself at the same time. Have you ever been to a fine restaurant, had your silverware fall on the floor and had to kneel down and try to find it—only you couldn't, because underneath your table it was completely dark? Well, with this glow-in-the-dark dinosaur silverware, those days are gone forever.

(He picks up another dinosaur.) And if you shy away from things that draw attention to themselves, these plain ceramic dinosaurs will also do. They fit nicely on coffee tables and in bedrooms. You can appreciate them and almost forget they're there. That is, until one of your neighbors comes over and asks you where you got it from. And when you tell them, you don't have to cuss under your breath, thinking they're copycatting your style. Because Toochie Willows won't make no two dinosaurs alike. Every *Diploducus* has a different pair of eyes. Every *Chasmosaurus'* armor is carved a different way. Every *Pterosaurus* has his own personal wings to fly. *(Smiles)* What it all amounts to, folks, is buying yourself a unique thing. Everybody ought to at least have one unique thing. And twenty-five dollars is a reasonable price to pay.

(Lights fade.)

Scene Seven

(The same day. VERVE *is freshly bathed and sober. A knock is heard at the front door.* VERVE *moves to open it. Lights on* ALAN MARSH *and* LI'L SAMUEL. ALAN *carries a duffle bag and a shovel on his back. Both he and* LI'L SAMUEL *are dirty, ragged, and tired.)*

VERVE: Can I help you?

ALAN: I'm looking for Bernadette Marsh.

VERVE: She's not in.

ALAN: You expecting her back?

*(*VERVE *looks him up and down.)*

VERVE: Maybe.

ALAN: Well, if it's alright with you, I'd like to wait 'til she comes back. *(Pause)* I'm her husband, you see....

VERVE: Do come in.

(He enters with LI'L SAMUEL.*)*

ALAN: I hate to inconvenience you.

VERVE: Sit down, Mr Marsh.

ALAN: Alan. Call me Alan.

VERVE: Verve Willows here.

(They shake hands.)

ALAN: Bernadette, I don't suppose she told you none 'bout me? Don't suppose I been the topic of her conversation?

VERVE: I can't say that you have.

ALAN: Well, so it goes. *(Pause)* This is our son, Li'l Samuel. Go ahead and say hello to the woman, boy.

LI'L SAMUEL: Hello.

VERVE: Hello, Samuel. Would you like some ice cream? Can I treat you to some ice cream?

LI'L SAMUEL: No, thank you.

VERVE: And you, Mr Marsh? Would you like a drink?

ALAN: Oh, a drink right now would be real good.

(She pours a drink.)

VERVE: Can you take one-twenty proof?

ALAN: I can take anything you got. In my tiredness, it'll ease me on.

(She hands him the drink. It trembles in his hand.)

ALAN: This is what a woman can do to a man.... *(He drinks the liquor greedily.)*

VERVE: Easy, Mr Marsh. The trick is to go easy.

(ALAN coughs. LI'L SAMUEL pats him on the back.)

ALAN: Easy? Did you say easy? *(Holds out his hands.)* Tell it to my hands. *(Looks at them)* They done gone all awry on me. I'll never be able to dig a good grave again.

VERVE: You're a gravedigger?

ALAN: Best in all of Swainsboro. Dig for the black and the white alike. Ask just about anybody and they'll tell you, can't nobody dig a grave like Alan Marsh. *(Smiles)* Then again, not many people'd want to. Ain't exactly a glamourous job or nothing. But somebody's got to do it, 'cause as sure as folks live, they gonna die. And somebody's got to be there to bury them right. *Me.* I bury 'em right. *(He pours another drink.)*

LI'L SAMUEL: Daddy. Don't.

ALAN: I'm all right, boy. *(To VERVE)* He's worrying that I drink too much. Lately, I been really at it. I could drink you out of house and home.

VERVE: Go right ahead. There's more where that came from. Plenty.

(He rises to eye the house.)

ALAN: I can see where the place got that cleaned-by-Bernadette look. She's a cleaning fool. A loving and a cleaning fool.

VERVE: I'll say.

ALAN: That's how 'bout we came together. Her, cleaning stairs at Johnson Funeral Home. I landed sight of her scrubbing those stairs clean. Scrubbing like I'd never seen. She had this—this aversion in the face of dirt. Just moved me so. *(A smile of recollection.)* Right then and there, something happened. Seemed like all the years of whoring in me just whimpered out. That gotta-have-a-woman dog in me plumb whimpered out. And she was the one I wanted. The one I had to have. Course, want's a funny thing. Folks almost never want and think at the same time, 'cause if I'd been thinking, maybe it would've occurred to me that cleaners and gravediggers don't make for much love-wise. They're forever judging each other love-wise.

VERVE: Well, I'm touched by your depth of emotion for your wife. I really am. But you do have your son here to show for your relationship. He's a beautiful result of your relationship.

ALAN: Don't mean a thing.

VERVE: Don't say that.

ALAN: Oh, don't get me wrong now. I got all the love in the world for this boy. Me and him real tight. But all my love ain't enough. Just you look at him. Look in his eyes. They'll tell you Daddy's doing an okay job. Daddy gets him along. But it's Mama he needs. Daddy can't hold a light to Mama. *(He notices* VERVE'*s empty glass and pours her another drink.)* I just don't understand her doing it. Can't understand her upping and going when there's a child to consider.

VERVE: Perhaps she did it because there was a child to consider.

ALAN: How now?

VERVE: May I give you some advice, Mr Marsh? Would you take some advice from a shrivelled-up old woman?

ALAN: You ain't shrivelled. There's a radiance in you.

VERVE: *(Flustered)* Yes. Well. Maybe. *(Then)* I would like to tell you to kill her. My life would be easier if you killed her. But that would be somehow unjust of me. So, I'll give you some genuine advice to leave her alone. Find yourself another woman to raise Samuel and leave this one alone.

(He looks at her.)

ALAN: How you gonna love somebody and leave 'em alone? Something in that word love won't let you leave 'em alone. You courted somebody. They done laid out this plush red carpet, so that everything's all nice and comfy underneath your feet. You got all this crazy luxury that can just go on forever. Then—just like that—your red carpet maker goes and takes your carpet away. Things ain't like they used to be. Things ain't so nice and comfy no more. You're standing on a hardwood floor, and it's full of splinters. Seems you can't hardly walk, what with the splinters thrashing at your toes. Now, don't you know you're gonna long for that same red carpet? Don't you know before you even think 'bout buying another one, you're gonna try to get back the one you already had?

VERVE: Even if it's taken?

ALAN: Come again?

VERVE: I don't know much about love. I stopped loving my husband a long time ago. He stopped loving me. But I can tell you a thing or two about lust. And for the past day or so, your wife and my son have been lusting it up on Bergen Street.

(ALAN *bolts out of his chair.*)

ALAN: What?

VERVE: You take it easy now.... Don't go seeing red—especially not in regard to my son.

ALAN: Your son? I don't care about your son. It ain't his fault. The fault's with Bernadette. She's got the goods that make a man want. (*He stands in a deep study.*)

VERVE: Mr Marsh, what's in your head?

ALAN: I'm thinking 'bout L'il Samuel here. I'm thinking 'bout me dragging him from place to place in search of that whore. We been living like animals for weeks now. In search of that whore. (*Then*) It ain't no life for a kid. I've sunk so low, I'm powerless. (*Picks up the bottle.*) Except for this....

LI'L SAMUEL: You ain't powerless, Daddy. You're a big man.

ALAN: I'm a nobody, and you on the road to becoming a nobody too. (*He starts for the front door.*)

LI'L SAMUEL: Daddy?

ALAN: You stay put now.

VERVE: Mr Marsh, you can't just leave.

(ALAN *takes a rabbit's foot talisman out of his pocket and places it around* LI'L SAMUEL's *neck.*)

ALAN: This boy...he knows my heart. (*He turns to exit.*)

VERVE: And *what* do I tell Bernadette?

ALAN: Tell her I look forward to the day when I can dig her grave, 'cause I'm bound to do a half-assed job.

(ALAN *exits. Lights fade as he stands outside, casing the* WILLOWS' *house.*)

(*Blackout*)

END OF ACT ONE

ACT TWO

Scene Eight

(Later the same evening. The first image we see is that of ALAN *perched on the* WILLOWS's *rooftop. He performs a ritual with dirt, turtle shells and broken glass, muttering as he does so. It begins to rain and he laughs. Lights on* TOOCHIE *and* BERNADETTE *as they return from the flea market.)*

BERNADETTE: In all my days, I never seen folks go as fool as they did over your dinosaurs. They were near fool. They were!

TOOCHIE: You think today was something? Oh, Bernadette, today was nothing. You should've seen way back when we had our store. *Sir's Dinosaurs*, it was called. Right in the heart of River Street. People all over the country would order from our catalog, come in and buy. Pay prices you wouldn't believe. Prices sometimes I still can't believe. That's how come I learned to make dinosaurs.

BERNADETTE: Well, you certainly make 'em good, honey. And you talk like a real salesman too.

TOOCHIE: I'm also tired like a real salesman.

BERNADETTE: Why don't you go on and get a little shut-eye? I'll check in on Mrs Willow. She's probably got a hangover that just won't quit.

*(*VERVE *enters.)*

VERVE: I've been drinking so long, I don't get hangovers. *(Smiles)* But I'm moved by your concern. As I was by your desire to make an eagle out of my son. *(Moving closer still)* Although I must confess, a serious something baffles me....

BERNADETTE: And what might that be, Mrs Willows?

VERVE: I don't know how you can begin to like my son when you don't even want your own. *(Calls* LI'L SAMUEL*)* Come out here, young man.

*(*LI'L SAMUEL *enters. Pause.)*

BERNADETTE: Now, look, what's happened here.... *(She scans the room with a ready guard.)* Alan? Alan Marsh?! Don't make me yell and cause all this noise. Come on out of the woodwork so we can tussle face to face. I wanna gab with you, man, face to face!

VERVE: Your husband is gone.

BERNADETTE: *Where's* he gone?

VERVE: He didn't say. I didn't ask.

BERNADETTE: *(Trembling)* Now, if only I could breathe. This here's the kind of thing that makes it near impossible to breathe.

VERVE: Aren't you going to even say hello to your son? Doesn't he rate one hello?

BERNADETTE: Hello, Li'l Samuel.

LI'L SAMUEL: Hey, Mama.

(BERNADETTE *crosses over to* LI'L SAMUEL. *Gently, she turns him around.*)

BERNADETTE: You've grown....

TOOCHIE: Is there something I should know?

VERVE: There's shitloads. Imbecile that you are.

TOOCHIE: Shut up, Ma'am.

VERVE: Moron that you are.

TOOCHIE: I said shut up.

VERVE: Would be like you to fall in love with a married woman. And a gravedigger's wife at that.

TOOCHIE: What is she talking about, Bernadette?

(A beat)

BERNADETTE: I'm married, Toochie.

TOOCHIE: As in husband?

BERNADETTE: Yes.

TOOCHIE: As in whole other life?

BERNADETTE: *(Nods)* Yes...

(TOOCHIE *lets this register. He turns to* VERVE.)

TOOCHIE: Take the boy out of the room. He oughtn't to be here.

VERVE: You can't handle her alone. You're not savvy enough—

TOOCHIE: Ma'am.

(VERVE *exits with* LI'L SAMUEL. TOOCHIE *looks at* BERNADETTE.)

TOOCHIE: Well...I guess this is what's called news to come home to... in a major way. *(Pause)* How long you been married?

BERNADETTE: Nine years.

TOOCHIE: That's solid. That's a rock. *That's a child.*

BERNADETTE: My husband and me...You ever seen two people on the same
road, but moving more and more in different directions? Since day one,
me and Alan been like that. Walking along the same road, but moving
more and more in different directions. And it's not like I didn't tell him
that. It's not like he didn't know. His pride wouldn't *let* him know.

TOOCHIE: I don't suppose it crossed your mind to get a divorce?

BERNADETTE: *(Defensive)* It took nine years before it crossed my mind to run.
Don't stand there asking me 'bout divorce.

(TOOCHIE *begins to pace.*)

TOOCHIE: For the past few days, I've been seeing one side of you. One side
I took for nice. But now this whole other life's come walking through my
door. Me, I've all the time lived with Ma'am. I've all the time had this life
that's one and the same. I can't go from second to second adjusting myself
to change.

BERNADETTE: Mrs Willows don't change 'cause she's a drunk woman.
You don't change 'cause you're a man living with a drunk woman.
You've got your own shackles to deal with. I broke out of mine.

(TOOCHIE *starts for his workroom.*)

TOOCHIE: To hell with you, Bernadette.

BERNADETTE: Then it's settled. I'll clear out of here tomorrow morning—
first thing.

(TOOCHIE *exits.* BERNADETTE *is alone on stage. She finds a broom and sweeps.
Her sweeping becomes almost frantic. Its frantic nature coincides with the rain
outside, which comes down in torrents now.* BERNADETTE *crosses to the front
door and opens it.*)

BERNADETTE: Alan Marsh? You just had to go and muck it up, didn't you?
Had to go and mess with my life again....Well, you listen to me and you
listen good: I'm not coming back, you hear? *I'm not coming back.*

(BERNADETTE *retreats inside the house.* LI'L SAMUEL *comes downstairs. A beat*)

LI'L SAMUEL: Mama?

(BERNADETTE *jumps.*)

BERNADETTE: Yes, Li'l Samuel?

LI'L SAMUEL: I missed you.

BERNADETTE: Did you, baby?

(LI'L SAMUEL *steps toward her.*)

LI'L SAMUEL: Daddy missed you too.

BERNADETTE: Li'l Samuel, please don't come out here pleading your father's case to me.

LI'L SAMUEL: He missed you too. *(Pause)* When we gonna be a family again?

(BERNADETTE stiffens. She grabs LI'L SAMUEL by the arm and wipes dirt off him compulsively.)

BERNADETTE: You're dirty. You're filthy. You know I can't stand filth!

(LI'L SAMUEL backs away.)

LI'L SAMUEL: Mama—

BERNADETTE: *(Softens)* Wait, Li'l Samuel—baby—*wait*. Mama didn't mean that. A bath. Mama just want to give you a bath....

(Lights fade.)

Scene Nine

(The following morning. ALAN sleeps on the WILLOWS's rooftop. TOOCHIE enters, holding a crate of dinosaurs. VERVE sits smugly at the kitchen table.)

VERVE: Breakfast is heating in the oven.

(TOOCHIE puts down the crate and stares at VERVE.)

VERVE: We've got fried bacon. Honeyed ham. Buttermilk biscuits made from scratch. I put one in my mouth and it evaporated away. It was just that good. And those grits! Those aren't ordinary grits. Bernadette has yellowed them with cheddar. Goes perfect with eggs, sunny-side up. In fact, everything about breakfast this morning is perfectly sunny-side up. *(Pause)* I've got to give it to the country gal. She's a clever one. Trying to retrieve the heart through the sensitive stomach. But we won't fall for it, will we, Toochie? We won't fall for it at all.

(BERNADETTE enters with her suitcase. She wears the outfit she wore when she first appeared at the WILLOWS's front door.)

BERNADETTE: Mrs Willows, I'll be needing that money you owe me.

VERVE: Surely you don't expect me to pay you after all the trouble you've caused?

BERNADETTE: I worked, didn't I?

VERVE: In the horizontal sense, perhaps.

BERNADETTE: Look, I'm leaving this house a lot cleaner than I found it.

(Begrudgingly, VERVE digs into her money pouch and gives BERNADETTE her salary.)

VERVE: Good riddance.

(BERNADETTE *counts the money before putting it away.*)

BERNADETTE: You owe me more than this, but I won't sweat the knickels and dimes.

(BERNADETTE *pockets the money.* VERVE *wheels over to the window and stares out.* TOOCHIE, *whose eyes have remained glued to his plate, takes out his wallet.*)

TOOCHIE: How much more do we owe you?

BERNADETTE: About five dollars.

(TOOCHIE *gives her the money.*)

TOOCHIE: Where will you go?

BERNADETTE: Somewhere in town.

TOOCHIE: What will you do?

BERNADETTE: Manage. I've got industry in me.

TOOCHIE: You've also got a little boy who needs a roof over his head.

BERNADETTE: That's not for you to worry about, now is it? (*Crossing to the foot of the stairs and calling out*) Li'l Samuel, shake a leg! We got to bus to catch in ten minutes! Li'l Samuel?!

(BERNADETTE *moves up the stairs to get* LI'L SAMUEL.)

VERVE: Toochie, you really ought to come over here. Mrs Dillwood's outside in pink skimpy underwear. She's wearing pink skimpy underwear and a black bra. I can't help but question her clarity of mind. No woman thinking straight would mix underwear that way. Certainly, not one of her class. Color coordination is the be-all and end-all with women of her class. (*Then*) And here comes Mr Dillwood. He's holding a towel. He's trying to cover her with his towel. But she's running away. She's skipping away. With scissors in one hand and Lady Guinivere tulips in the other, Mrs Dillwood is skipping away.

(TOOCHIE *rises.*)

TOOCHIE: Ma'am?

VERVE: Yes?

TOOCHIE: Bernadette is leaving us.

VERVE: Bravo!

TOOCHIE: She's leaving us, but I don't want her to go.

VERVE: Yes, you do.

TOOCHIE: No, Ma'am.

VERVE: Take it from your mother. I know you do.

TOOCHIE: But I don't know it, Ma'am.

VERVE: That's because she's pulled the wool over your eyes.

TOOCHIE: *(Shakes his head)* No, Ma'am.

VERVE: Toochie, she's got you all mixed up.

TOOCHIE: Happy...I've been something close to happy with Bernadette here.

VERVE: Well, I've been miserable!

TOOCHIE: You're always miserable, Ma'am. What else is new?

VERVE: Before, we were miserable together...

TOOCHIE: Maybe—*maybe*—I don't want that life no more.

VERVE: Toochie, I really don't care what you want. *(Then)* Pour me a drink.

TOOCHIE: No.

VERVE: Toochie, pour me a goddamn drink!

(TOOCHIE crosses to the liquor cabinet and begins to remove the liquor.)

TOOCHIE: There isn't going to be any more drinking in this house.

VERVE: Now, you hold on a minute—

TOOCHIE: I just tried to tell you something important, and it flew over your head.

VERVE: I've been drinking alcohol all my life. I've been addicted to alcohol all my life. It is my one good thing. Who are you to come between me and my one good thing?

(TOOCHIE drops the liquor bottles and starts for VERVE.)

TOOCHIE: Your son. *Your stupid, idiot, jackass, moron—son.*

(VERVE gives him wide berth.)

VERVE: Don't you raise your *hand against me!*

TOOCHIE: I'm sick of you—witch.

VERVE: Not as sick as I am of this wheelchair. I didn't *ask* to be in this wheelchair.

TOOCHIE: No, Ma'am, you just drank yourself there, and *you're gonna be there for the rest of your life.*

(BERNADETTE appears in the hallway. She has overheard their exchange. TOOCHIE turns to her.)

TOOCHIE: Bernadette—

BERNADETTE: Please don't involve me in y'all's mess.

TOOCHIE: It's your mess too.

BERNADETTE: No, Toochie, I don't think so.

TOOCHIE: *(With quiet force)* Listen to me: This is your home. You live here. *(Reaches to hold her)* I want you to make this place comfortable for you—and your boy. And if Ma'am gets to asking for English Breakfast tea, you make sure English Breakfast is all that's in it.

(TOOCHIE exits. ALAN descends the rooftop and follows him. BERNADETTE clears the liquor cabinet quietly.)

BERNADETTE: Well, Mrs Willows?

(BERNADETTE drags the trashcan offstage. LI'L SAMUEL enters. A beat.)

VERVE: She's outside throwing away my sense of being. My goddamn Jim Beam. That's what happens when you get up in age like me. Strangers dillydally into your house, turn your son against you, and throw your liquor in the trash.

LI'L SAMUEL: I'm hungry.

VERVE: So?

LI'L SAMUEL: I'm hungry and want to eat.

VERVE: The world is full of hungry people who want to eat. The world is inundated with hungry people who want to eat. What makes you so special?

LI'L SAMUEL: I don't know.

(LI'L SAMUEL stares at her plate. She pushes it toward him.)

VERVE: How old are you...?

LI'L SAMUEL: Nine.

VERVE: Well, it's hard to be nine. It's no fun being nine. There's a big difference between being eight and being nine.

LI'L SAMUEL: How d'you know?

VERVE: Because I used to teach emotionally disturbed children. I'd get them when they were eight and there was still a chance for ideals. You know what ideals are?

(He shakes his head, no.)

VERVE: Perfect things—images—goals you'd eventually like to make real. But by the time they turned nine, most of them didn't want to hear about ideals. They were either moving toward them or turned away. Disillusioned—*fucked up*—turned away!

LI'L SAMUEL: You're yelling at me.

VERVE: I yell at everyone.

LI'L SAMUEL: My daddy told me not to let folk go yelling at me.

VERVE: Your daddy isn't here now. *He's gone and left you.*

(LI'L SAMUEL *lowers his head.* BERNADETTE *enters.)*

BERNADETTE: Li'l Samuel, go on back to bed and get your rest.

LI'L SAMUEL: I thought we was leaving.

BERNADETTE: Not yet.

LI'L SAMUEL: When then?

BERNADETTE: There's been a change in plans.

LI'L SAMUEL: I'm still hungry.

(BERNADETTE *puts more food on* LI'L SAMUEL's *plate.)*

BERNADETTE: I don't want you in Mrs Willows's hair now. Eat in your room.

VERVE: Let him keep me company.

(LI'L SAMUEL *resumes eating.)*

BERNADETTE: Has your daddy been feeding you right, Li'l Samuel? You act like you haven't seen food in days.

LI'L SAMUEL: Daddy fed me alright.

BERNADETTE: What's alright?

LI'L SAMUEL: He gave me popcorn and potato chips. He gave me burgers and fries.

BERNADETTE: That's real alright, Li'l Samuel. That's healthy *alright.*

LI'L SAMUEL: I liked it just fine!

BERNADETTE: Watch your tone. Don't go showing off in front of Mrs Willows.

(VERVE *leans closer to* LI'L SAMUEL.)

VERVE: See what I mean? They dillydally, they do. And throw your being in the trash. *(Then)* What's that you have around your neck there? Is that a rabbit's foot?

LI'L SAMUEL: Two. I got two rabbits' feet sewn together.

VERVE: Does that bring double good luck?

LI'L SAMUEL: More like stronger good luck.

(LI'L SAMUEL *removes the talisman from around his neck and shows it to* VERVE.)

LI'L SAMUEL: These feet here come from relative rabbits. They come from rabbits that was kin that Daddy caught out in the wild. See how one foot's all bigger than the other? See how it's got that bigger shape? That's 'cause it was a big rabbit. A Mama rabbit. Now this other one here, it's all small. This other one here wasn't nothing but a bunny. That same Mama rabbit's bunny.

VERVE: How interesting.

BERNADETTE: My husband uses nature to do his bidding. A rabbit's foot to bring him a little good luck. A chicken's heart to turn somebody else's good luck bad. Of course, the chicken heart and all, that's small time for Alan. Strictly small time. When he sets his mind to it, he goes to nature big. He caught hold of me that way.

(LI'L SAMUEL *stops eating.*)

BERNADETTE: Well, go on. Eat your food.

LI'L SAMUEL: I ain't hungry no more.

BERNADETTE: You were eating like a maniac fool a minute ago.

LI'L SAMUEL: *(Pushing his plate away)* I said I ain't hungry.

BERNADETTE: It's his Daddy. He can't stand for me to talk about his no-good daddy.

(LI'L SAMUEL *rises.*)

LI'L SAMUEL: *He's better than you.*

VERVE: Tell her, young man!

(BERNADETTE *yanks the talisman away from* LI'L SAMUEL. *A beat*)

BERNADETTE: I was eighteen. The youngest of four girls. All my mama ever seemed to spit out was girls: girls who married; girls who worked; girls who died young. And there goes me. The country, my place to be. My thing to know. Food to cook. Clothes to wash. Enough chores to make anyone grow old young. That didn't fit into my permanent plan. I had bigger things in mind. Away-type things. Then comes grave-digging Mr Marsh. Setting his mind on me. Setting his life on me. I called him fool. I laughed him fool. Said out and out I wanted better. Even when folks about town got to telling me that I oughtn't to put him off that way, I shrugged them off and kept straight ahead, working, saving, to get away and do better. He came one night. Like a Zorro, rooty bad. And dragged me out of my own house. On a tombstone—naked—for three nights I laid. Tied and gagged—I laid. You ever seen a graveyard at night? Or the spirits there? You did, you'd know shouldn't nobody be dead. It's sad and lonely dead. All they talk about is loneliness. And lost love: *the dead. (Then)* I'd see old women, antebellum white. They'd slither their way out of the black dirt, holding on to the shreds of their crinoline skirts like it was still a fine thing and not the patches of nothing it really was. They'd come to me with their dainty, skeleton smiles and say, "Young lady, you've got to love that man." I'd see relatives of mine, cousins from slavery times, their hands and feet bound with shackles that rang like bells every time they moved. They didn't like my situation much. But in chains and shackles, what could they do—except tell me to love that man? The worst were the children. Infants. Babies. Cut short from life. They'd crawl around the graveyard on their hands and knees. Searching for a mother on their hands and knees. A few would find their way to me. Sidle on top of me, wanting milk not in my breast to give. And when they realized I was all empty, they'd cry like you wouldn't believe. But it made perfect sense to me. Love. They too were telling me I had to love that man. *(Pause)* On the third day, your Daddy came. He fucked me. He washed me. He fed me figs and cheese. *And God help me... I loved that man.*

(BERNADETTE *tosses the talisman into the fire.* LI'L SAMUEL *rushes to the fireplace. His small hands reach into flame. Lights fade)*

Scene Ten

(Lights on the flea market. TOOCHIE *hawks his wares.)*

TOOCHIE: I've got dinosaurs to sell. Like you wouldn't believe. Dinosaurs. Come over here and see for yourself. *(Holds up a dinosaur)* This is *Triceratops*. Bedecked with brow horns scary real. He might not seem all too imposing here, but in real life he was a plant-eater of the fiercest kind. Look into his eyes. They're bursting rich with color. *(He peers into* Triceratops's *eyes.)* That's right, folks. I got color in my dinosaurs. Kaleidoscopic images to change and redefine. And if this object of imagery strikes you as somehow trite, if you believe in having your dollars better spent—get a load of this: *(He holds up another dinosaur.)* Remember the last time you and your family camped out in the wild? And you, trying to relive vintage Boy Scout days, got this notion in your head that you could start a fire? Only—days later— to reach your destiny's site. Skin, mosquito-bitten red. Children, whining for color T V, and you, down on your knees rubbing branches together like a pathetic fool? *(He opens the mouth of the dinosaur and removes a match.)* Well, next time you'll go better prepared! *(He runs the match along the tail of the dinosaur and creates a small spark.)* That's right, folks. I got fire in my dinosaurs. To warm you on the coldest nights and keep predatory creatures at bay. Of course, it won't come for free. These are rough times, so it can't come for free. Surely, twenty-five dollars is a reasonable price to pay?

*(*ALAN *steps forward.)*

ALAN: I'll pay you five dollars. For this one. Five.

TOOCHIE: I'm afraid that won't do.

ALAN: It's all I got.

TOOCHIE: I'm sorry.

ALAN: It's all I got.

TOOCHIE: There's labor involved here. There's toil. I have to make a profit.

ALAN: Mister, it's for my son. *(Pause)* Do you know what it's like to have a son?

(TOOCHIE studies ALAN.)

TOOCHIE: No...but I know what it's like to have a father. I had some father.

ALAN: Maybe, you halfway understand then?

TOOCHIE: Well...

(TOOCHIE turns his attention back to his dinosaurs.)

ALAN: Was he there for you?

TOOCHIE: What?

ALAN: Your father? Was he there? *(Then)* It's the ones who ain't around that sons harp on the most.

TOOCHIE: Of course, he was there for me. Of course, Sir was.... *(He picks up a dinosaur and gives it to ALAN.)* Ten. I can't do you better than that.

(ALAN reaches inside his pocket and comes up with dirt and heavy change. He begins a slow count.)

ALAN: I really appreciate this, mister.

TOOCHIE: Toochie Willows is the name.

ALAN: As in the son of Verve Willows?

TOOCHIE: That's right. You know Ma'am?

ALAN: I've heard her name abouts.

TOOCHIE: Well, take a card. Send some customers my way, and next time I'll cut you an even better break.

(ALAN continues to look at TOOCHIE.)

TOOCHIE: Is something wrong?

ALAN: Yes... No... How old are you?

TOOCHIE: I don't know. How old do I need to be? *(Then)* I'm thirty.

ALAN: I was thirty years old. Once. A long time ago.

(ALAN pays TOOCHIE. and walks in circles about his booth. TOOCHIE resumes hawking his wares.)

TOOCHIE: I've got dinosaurs to sell. Like you wouldn't believe—dinosaurs. Come over here and see.... *(Stops)* You're making me dizzy walking in circles like that. Maybe, you want to sit down.

ALAN: Next to you?

TOOCHIE: Whatever gets your goat.

ALAN: Son, you don't want me sitting next to you....

(ALAN finishes his bottle of whiskey. He leans against TOOCHIE's booth, sways, stops, and retches up vomit. TOOCHIE hesitates before crossing to help him.)

TOOCHIE: Man, I knew you weren't feeling well when I first landed sight of you. *(He hands ALAN a handkerchief.)* You got a home?

(ALAN shakes his head: yes; no.)

TOOCHIE: Let's get you home....

(Lights fade.)

Scene Eleven

(The same evening. The WILLOWS's house. Lights on TOOCHIE and ALAN. TOOCHIE doodles on a napkin.)

ALAN: I haven't had rump roast like this since God knows when. I haven't had beef this tender in.... *(He digs into his plate of food.)*

TOOCHIE: Well, I'm only sorry our cook wasn't here to fix it for you. My cooking skills can't hold a light to Bernadette's.

ALAN: Bernadette...

TOOCHIE: Drink your coffee.

ALAN: *Bernadette.*

TOOCHIE: It'll sober you up quick.

(TOOCHIE pours ALAN coffee.)

ALAN: I could really use some whiskey to wash my food down. Where you store your whiskey 'round here? *(He rises and crosses to the liquor cabinet, which is empty.)*

TOOCHIE: We don't keep alcohol in the house.

ALAN: Big house like this—no alcohol? *(Whistles)* Well, well, well—that puts me in a real fix!

TOOCHIE: How's about some water?

ALAN: I'm better off with this coffee shit. *(He returns to his seat and drinks the coffee half-heartedly. There is a pause.)*

TOOCHIE: You don't have to be quiet and all. You can talk if you'd like.

ALAN: Maybe I don't got nothing to say.

TOOCHIE: Okay. I'll say a thing or two then.... I come home. There's no Bernadette. No Ma'am. There's not even a note or nothing. And it's not like Ma'am to leave the house. She's been almost ten years in this same house. But I'll keep drawing. I'll keep drawing to put it out of my mind.

ALAN: You lucky you can put things out of your mind. Some folk can't. Some things just eat at some folk and make'em crazy. Me...a man who couldn't even stand the taste of alcohol.

TOOCHIE: But you can now?

ALAN: Damn straight. *(Then)* Keeps the bitterness out! *(Leaning over and eyeing* TOOCHIE's *drawing.)* That looks like me?

TOOCHIE: Yep. (ALAN *reaches over and tears the napkin to pieces.)*

ALAN: Don't go drawing me. I don't believe in folk drawing me.

TOOCHIE: *(Smiles)* You're superstitious.

ALAN: Only fools ain't.

*(*TOOCHIE *rises and finds himself a plate.)*

TOOCHIE: I think I'll have some rump roast too. It's kind of nice to sit and eat with another man. Sir and I used to stay up late at night, eat all kind of heavy meals and talk.

ALAN: About what?

TOOCHIE: Mostly Ma'am. How he wished things had turned out different with Ma'am. It's heartbreaking the way people want things to turn out different. They seldom do.

ALAN: Depends on the people. *(He rises again.)* This is a nice setup you got here. You must do well for yourself?

TOOCHIE: Alright. I do alright.

ALAN: I bet you're really something with the girls.

TOOCHIE: Oh, I don't know about all that.

ALAN: Come on, Willows. Don't bullshit a bullshitter. Young buck like you. Got that sweet kind of face women go crazy for. Drop their panties and go plumb fool for. *(Winks)* The ones that still wear panties, that is.

*(*TOOCHIE *smiles despite himself and slaps his knee.)*

TOOCHIE: The ones that still wear panties. That's Sir quality. That's good!

ALAN: Now, me, I got a mean face, you know? I got a liability face, you know? The kind that women see and go, "Oh, shit. Steer clear of him. I know what he's about."

(TOOCHIE *stops laughing.*)

TOOCHIE: What are you about?

ALAN: The truth.

TOOCHIE: Which truth?

ALAN: I didn't know it came in varieties.

TOOCHIE: People use it different ways.

ALAN: Well, I'm the *only* truth, Willows. Husband and wife. 'Til death do us part. That little ditty... (*Whistles*) No white castles here. No Prince Charming here. No birds in the sky. *No sky period.* I'm a man. *A real man.* All I know is dirt. It's shaped my world and bound my dreams, so that every time I touch a woman she knows she's just another filly on the road to becoming dust. Know what I mean?

TOOCHIE: Not really.

ALAN: Well, you just hold that thought—*while I pee.*

TOOCHIE: I'll show you to the restroom—

(ALAN *exits.* TOOCHIE *rises and opens the duffle bag alongside* ALAN's *chair. He searches through it quickly. His eyes fall on a shovel.* TOOCHIE *grabs the shovel and starts upstairs. Lights come up on* ALAN *as he enters* TOOCHIE's *workroom.*)

ALAN: What things do we got ourselves here?

(TOOCHIE *steps into the workroom.* ALAN *stands before the shelf holding one of Sir's dinosaurs.*)

TOOCHIE: Those ones my father made. Before I was even born, those things, he made....

ALAN: You got some gift with your hands, Mister.

TOOCHIE: Thank you.

(ALAN *places Sir's dinosaur back on the shelf.*)

ALAN: This room is like another world. I can feel myself caught up in another world.

TOOCHIE: Can't you just see yourself walking through a jungle with a club, with a spear—with a club *and* spear? Doing almost anything to survive— in a time when it was near impossible for a man to stay alive?

ALAN: Easy. I can see that easy.

TOOCHIE: I'm sure you can, Mr Marsh. It is Alan Marsh, isn't it?

(ALAN *turns around and smiles at* TOOCHIE.)

ALAN: You're playing a dangerous game, boy.

TOOCHIE: Maybe. *(Then)* Possibly. *(Then)* Hardly.

(ALAN *notices the shovel.*)

ALAN: Why you gripping my shovel like that?

TOOCHIE: I don't know.

ALAN: Tch, tch, tch. *(Then)* I think you do know. *(Then)* Give it here.

TOOCHIE: I'm going to have to ask you to leave.

ALAN: Willows, we both know I'm not leaving here 'til I get what I came for.

TOOCHIE: *Who* you came for.

ALAN: Same difference.

TOOCHIE: Do you beat Bernadette?

ALAN: I'd say that's more of my business.

TOOCHIE: Well, you go on and come back here later, and you can hear it from her mouth that you're finished.

(ALAN *steps toward* TOOCHIE.)

ALAN: Do you know who I am, boy?

TOOCHIE: A drunk like Ma'am.

ALAN: This *drunk* could snap your neck like a twig.

TOOCHIE: I don't want any trouble.

ALAN: Won't be no trouble you don't cause no trouble.

(TOOCHIE *steps back.*)

TOOCHIE: Stay back.

ALAN: Make up your mind, Willows. You want me to stay back or go?

TOOCHIE: I want you to stay back *and* go.

ALAN: You seem kind of confused there. You sure?

TOOCHIE: Fuck you, Mr Marsh.

ALAN: That's *some way* to talk, boy.

TOOCHIE: Leave—*now*.

ALAN: Considering you're putting it to my wife. Socking it to my wife!

TOOCHIE: Your wife doesn't love you anymore.

ALAN: Bullshit.

TOOCHIE: I doubt she loved you to begin with.

ALAN: *Nine years. I gave nine years to that woman.*

TOOCHIE: Those years—they're gone.

ALAN: You can't take everything that belongs to me and tell me it's gone. What if I was to take something that belonged to you—a little something even? *(He backs toward the shelf containing Sir's dinosaurs.)* Aren't these the ones your father made? Ain't part of his life somewhere in these things he made? Now, what if I was to just...if I was to—

TOOCHIE: Put it down.

(ALAN picks up a single dinosaur and lets it drop to the floor.)

TOOCHIE: *I'm warning you.*

(ALAN picks up another dinosaur and drops it in the same easy manner. He reaches for yet another one, and TOOCHIE moves to stop him. The two men struggle. TOOCHIE tightens his grip on the shovel and lands the better blows. Blackout.)

Scene Twelve

(It is much later the same evening. Lights up on BERNADETTE, LI'L SAMUEL, and VERVE. LI'L SAMUEL's hand is in an arm sling. BERNADETTE removes his coat.)

VERVE: I thought for sure Samuel would tell the doctor.

BERNADETTE: How's your hand?

LI'L SAMUEL: Okay.

BERNADETTE: Just let me know if you feel any pain. We've got a ton of painkillers to ease your every pain.

(LI'L SAMUEL stares at his mother.)

BERNADETTE: Don' look at me that way, Li'l Samuel....

LI'L SAMUEL: Say you're sorry?

BERNADETTE: I'll fix you a cup of hot milk.

LI'L SAMUEL: Are you sorry?

BERNADETTE: *(Nods)* Li'l Samuel, you know I am. *(Pause)* Come on... I'll tuck you in.

(BERNADETTE starts upstairs with LI'L SAMUEL.)

VERVE: Maybe, you want to put Samuel in my room tonight?

BERNADETTE: I beg pardon?

VERVE: I have a hunch he'll sleep better there.

BERNADETTE: Mrs Willows, do you think I would intentionally hurt my own child?

VERVE: *(Shakes her head)* No, but you run from hot to cold too quick.

BERNADETTE: And you don't?

VERVE: Let's not argue. It's been a long evening, Bernadette.

(BERNADETTE relents and leads LI'L SAMUEL to VERVE's room. VERVE moves to the parlor window. She begins to draw the blinds but spots something that sends her rearing back in her wheelchair.)

VERVE: What in the hell is going on out there?

(A beat later, TOOCHIE enters. He is covered with dirt, and out of breath. He makes a beeline for his room and is startled by VERVE.)

TOOCHIE: Ma'am.

VERVE: Toochie....What were you doing in the Dillwood's yard? *(Then)* What were you doing out there?

TOOCHIE: I killed him, Ma'am.

VERVE: Mr Dillwood?

TOOCHIE: What would I want to kill Mr Dillwood for? I don't even know him that well. *(Then)* Alan Marsh. He's the one.

VERVE: Toochie, no...

(TOOCHIE attempts to get past VERVE.)

TOOCHIE: Didn't listen. Wouldn't listen. Came back here giving me shit.

VERVE: Are you sure he's dead?

TOOCHIE: *(Ranting)* Who needs it. I certainly don't need it. *(Stares at his hands)* But my hands...Ma'am... What am I gonna do with these hands?

VERVE: Sit down, Toochie. No—don't sit. You got blood on you. Stand.

(VERVE wheels over to TOOCHIE and wipes the blood off his trembling hands.)

TOOCHIE: What are we gonna do?

VERVE: *(Thinking aloud)* We'll call the police. That's what we'll do. We'll tell them he broke in. We'll tell him you panicked—

(TOOCHIE backs away.)

TOOCHIE: Jail?

VERVE: No jail, Toochie.

TOOCHIE: I ain't going to jail.

VERVE: They'll believe us. He's trash, Toochie. You come from a good family.

(TOOCHIE retreats to his workroom. VERVE starts for the telephone but stops short. She wheels around the living room trying to gather herself. A beat later, BERNADETTE enters.)

BERNADETTE: I'm gonna put some milk on. You want anything while I'm at it?

VERVE: Strength!

BERNADETTE: I'm afraid that's not in the cupboard, Mrs Willows. That's not in the cupboard at all. *(She pours milk into a saucepan and sets it on the stove.)*

VERVE: Under the kitchen sink—behind the pipe—you'll find a tin can with some money in it. Bring it to me, Bernadette.

BERNADETTE: Now?

VERVE: *Now.*

(BERNADETTE finds the tin can and gives it to VERVE. VERVE opens it and takes the money out. TOOCHIE returns, wearing a coat. He sees BERNADETTE and turns his back.)

BERNADETTE: Sit on down, Toochie. I just put some milk on.

VERVE: *Strength!*

(TOOCHIE continues to stand.)

BERNADETTE: What are you doing with all that dirt on you?

TOOCHIE: I don't know....

(He crosses to the window and peers out of it. BERNADETTE watches him.)

VERVE: Toochie's gone and killed your husband.

(BERNADETTE sits down.)

BERNADETTE: Now, look what's happened here. I didn't want no bloodshed here. *(Pause)* Alan...poor fool... *(Then)* Where is he?

TOOCHIE: Dillwoods' yard.

BERNADETTE: What were you thinking?

VERVE: Leave him be.

BERNADETTE: Oh, Toochie...

(TOOCHIE moves past BERNADETTE.)

TOOCHIE: Goodbye, Mama.

(VERVE attempts to hold onto TOOCHIE. He reaches over and kisses. He exits.)

VERVE: Toochie!

(BERNADETTE looks at VERVE. A beat)

BERNADETTE: Do you want me to go after him? *(Pause)* Just say the word, Mrs Willows—and I'll go.

*(*VERVE *hands* BERNADETTE *the tin can full of money.)*

VERVE: Would you, please?

*(*BERNADETTE *hesitates.)*

BERNADETTE: Take care of Li'l Samuel. He's a good boy....

(She exits. A long pause.)

VERVE: He called me Mama.

*(*LI'L SAMUEL *enters.)*

LI'L SAMUEL: I can't sleep....

VERVE: *(Softly)* Toochie called me Mama.

*(*LI'L SAMUEL *crosses to the stove.)*

LI'L SAMUEL: Most all the milk's boiled out of the pan. *(He struggles with his bandaged hand to pour the milk into a cup. He sits at the kitchen table.)* Is she gone?

VERVE: Yes.

LI'L SAMUEL: Are we here by our lonesomes?

VERVE: *Yes.*

LI'L SAMUEL: Ain't lonesome a terrible thing?

*(*VERVE *regards* LI'L SAMUEL *with interest.)*

VERVE: Drink the milk, Samuel. It just might make you strong....

*(*LI'L SAMUEL *lifts the cup to his mouth. Lights fade.)*

END OF PLAY

THE PSYCHIC LIFE
OF SAVAGES

Amy Freed

ABOUT THE AUTHOR

Amy Freed's play FREEDOMLAND was a Pulitzer finalist in 1998, with productions at South Coast Rep, Woolly Mammoth, and Playwrights Horizons. THE PSYCHIC LIFE OF SAVAGES was the 1995 recipient of the Joseph Kesselring Award, a national award presented each year by the New York Arts Club to an outstanding new play. Previous winners have included Tony Kushner, Anna Deveare Smith, and Nicky Silver. PSYCHIC LIFE was also named the winner of the prestigious Charles MacArthur Award for Outstanding New Play at the annual Helen Hayes Awards in Washington, DC. The play had an extended run after a successful premiere at Woolly Mammoth. An earlier version of the play was first developed and performed in San Francisco under the title POETOMACHIA, where it was recognized by the Bay Area Critic's Circle and awarded an Outstanding Achievement Award for an Original Script. In its earlier version, it was also a finalist for the Susan Smith Blackburn Prize in 1994.

Freed's other plays include the critically acclaimed STILL WARM, a black comedy about the rise and fall of a famous anchorwoman. It was produced at San Francisco's Climate Theater in 1991. Freed was selected that year by the California Arts Council to receive a Playwriting Fellowship.

CLAUSTROPHILIA, a one-act play about Edgar Allen Poe and his child bride, was originally commissioned by the San Francisco Theater Project. Subsequently produced by Climate Theater (along with the premiere of her one act THE GHOUL OF AMHERST) and directed by the author, it was highly acclaimed and received two Drama-Logue Awards.

A native New Yorker and former actress, Freed lives in San Francisco. She has worked as an acting teacher and director for the various training programs of the American Conservatory Theater, VITA Shakespeare Festival, and California Shakespeare Festival, as well as conducting playwriting workshops for A C T and S F State University. She has a B F A from Southern Methodist University, and a M F A from American Conservatory Theater.

ORIGINAL PRODUCTION

THE PSYCHIC LIFE OF SAVAGES premiered at Woolly Mammoth on 10 April 1995. The cast and creative contributors were:

TED MAGUS .... John Lescault
DR ROBERT STONER .... Will Marchetti
ANNE BITTENHAND .... Naomi Jacobson
SYLVIA FLUELLEN .... Cynthia Bassham
RADIO INTERVIEWER/TITO/STUDENT .... Paul Takacs
REBECCA/STUDENT/KIT-KAT .... Anna Belknap
EMILY/VERA .... Deb Gottesman

Director .... Howard Shalwitz
Set design .... Dan Conway
Costume design .... Howard Vincent Kurtz
Lighting design .... Daniel Schrader
Sound design .... Neil McFadden
Properties .... Tessa Dunning
Stage manager .... Sarah M Delia

THE PSYCHIC LIFE OF SAVAGES *Show Sponsors*
Ronald and Anne Abramson

DISCLAIMER

This play is a work of dramatic fiction inspired in the loosest sense by the lives and writings of several major poets. The persons, events, and relationships described are imaginary and not intended to be in any way factual or biographical. All poems are my invention.

Amy Freed

CHARACTERS

SYLVIA FLUELLEN, *a young American poet*
TED MAGUS, *a young English poet*
ANNE BITTENHAND, *an American poet in her forties*
DR ROBERT STONER, *a man in his sixties, the American Poet Laureate*
EMILY, *the ghost of Emily Dickinson*
VERA, DR STONER's *wife, played by the actor playing* EMILY
TITO, ANNE's *husband*
RADIO INTERVIEWER, *played by the actor playing* TITO
KIT-KAT, ANNE's *daughter*
REBECCA, *a young mental patient, played by the actor playing* KIT-KAT
FEMALE COLLEGE STUDENTS/PARTY GUESTS, *played by the actors playing* TITO
and KIT-KAT

ACT ONE

Scene One

(A radio station)

(TED MAGUS, DR ROBERT STONER, *and* INTERVIEWER *are on the air.)*

INTERVIEWER: Welcome to *Potshots.* I'm interviewing Britain's Ted Magus and our own American Poet Laureate, Dr Robert Stoner, here at Wardwell College. Mr Magus, you say, in your introduction to *Songs of the Fen,* "Bark and bleat. Reach into your own darkness and remember how to howl. Ask the beasts. Ask the birds." What does that mean?

TED: Call to a hawk in a foul black wind, and have him scream his answer to you. I have.

INTERVIEWER: What are you suggesting—?

TED: I'm sure Dr Stoner would share my belief that the poet is the shaman, chosen to heal our soul-sick society—

STONER: I couldn't agree less.

TED: Oh, really?

INTERVIEWER: Would you like to say more about that, Dr Stoner?

STONER: No.

INTERVIEWER: Mr Magus. You consistently use nature as metaphor—the hawk, a symbol for freedom and release, the cow for domestic stagnation...

TED: A trout don't think when he leap for the sky.

(Pause)

INTERVIEWER: Let's talk about some of your poetic techniques. Your unique use of rhythm, for example.

TED: Rhythm. It's both awakening and sleep inducing. Trance. The fall-through to the spirit world. I'm very interested in that. Paradox. We are surrounded by paradox. In sleep, we wake. In waking, we sleep. We starve in the midst of plenty. And in fasting, we become full.

STONER: If my aunt had a dick, she'd be my uncle.

TED: Oh, but exactly. Dr Stoner, you're joking, but the joke is, you've actually touched something far truer—

STONER: Oh, please.

INTERVIEWER: You've said a lot, here, Mr Magus, let me pick up on what you said about rhythm. Do you actually attempt to induce a trancelike state in the reader?

TED: Well, there's an instance, in the title poem, for example, where I say—
Skirts of the wind sweep
dry rustle grasses
shuka shucka shucka
There go me glasses
The green bog trembles, a night hunter screeches
I thrust into the darkness—
And think about the leeches.
Deeper and deeper the green muck sucks
And still am I reaching Down. Down. Down.
Goodnight, little peepers, little sleepers, God's sticky creatures.

INTERVIEWER: It seems that there's almost a tribal intensity at the beginning and then it slides imperceptibly towards what's really a hypnotic lullaby near the end.

TED: Exactly.

INTERVIEWER: Extraordinary.

TED: Well, do you know what's even more extraordinary, I came to find out later what I heard in the bog that day was known in ancient Bali as the monkey chant. Identical! It goes—
shak shaka shak
shak shaka shaka shaka shak,
shak shak shak
shak shaka shaka shaka shak...

INTERVIEWER: Fantastic.

TED: Chanted by hags. Women are more connected with the occult.

INTERVIEWER: Which brings us to you, Dr Stoner.

STONER: Why?

INTERVIEWER: You said in a recent interview, Dr Stoner, that you are not convinced of the innocence of the Salem witches.

STONER: There's a lot of room for doubt in my book.

INTERVIEWER: And quite a "book" it's going to be. I doubt any book of poems has been awaited with as much eagerness as your free-verse cycle on the life of Cotton Mather. Will you give us a little teaser?

STONER: Well, there is this one little piece I've begun about the witch-girls. Now, I have the image, the spear is in my hand, as it were, but I'm having trouble with the target. Frankly, I think that what with the damned insulin therapy that maybe my focus is a little off, but well, here goes.
Mather knew—
And for this they hated him, all the dark daughters,
Old Cotton, he was blessed with eyes that see 'round corners
Eyes that through God's hard grace could render even termites translucent.

With those pale and potent eyes
Mather could see the Witch Girls—

And then it goes something—something—something—
I don't know. And that's where I've been stuck with it for years, now.

(Pause)

INTERVIEWER: Interesting. The whole process, I mean—

STONER: I can hear the shrill of a high wind, and a chill, like a damp petticoat. Oh, they're around, all right, and they're probably out to fuck me up.

INTERVIEWER: Who, Dr Stoner?

STONER: The witch-girls, of course.

INTERVIEWER: What?

TED: *(Slowly, as if feeling his way in a trance)* One. Mather sees in a dream. A young witch screams astride the bucking buck from Zanzibar. Her ice-cold teat reminds him of his wife.

STONER: Ha-ha! Not bad, son.

TED: Wait! Wait! I'm getting...

Two. Seen in residue of
Lumpy morning porridge—
Bowl uncleared by slattern daughter,
Does she dance now with the broom—?

STONER: An old witch and a young one
With their mobcaps cast aside
Stand in skanky petticoats
Bare toes sunk in stable muck—
Hold a jar,
It's full of winter wheat—
And something fat and white.
Floating closer, Father Mather sees
His member! Long and hungry—
Too large to be a maggot, with that freckle on the tip!

TED: *(Angry and excited)*
Mather, in a lather, now
Knows the way is stony
But that fire will be the answer,
If he wants his penis back!

STONER: My boy! My boy! My boy!

INTERVIEWER: We've just witnessed an astonishing improvisation between two remarkable poets, it seems to have surprised them as much as it did me, they're embracing now, on the stage floor, much moved, much emotion, and Ted Magus is now drumming in what seems to be a tribute to the senior poet, who has his eyes closed and is covered in sweat. Our time is up and—astonishing program—goodnight, this was *Potshots*, live from Wardwell College.

TED & STONER:
Shak shak shak shak shaka shaka shaka shak!
Shak shak shak shak shaka shaka shaka shak!

Scene Two

(A mental institution)

(ANNE is on phone. REBECCA, a young mental patient, is sitting on the floor, drawing on a large pad.)

ANNE: I'm okay, I'm not okay. I'm okay! Stop yelling at me! Would I be back in the nuthouse again if I knew why I did it! Use your head, Tito! I'm sorry, lover. I can't really make sense of it to you. Because you won't—no, you don't—do you remember that thing I was describing? What happened last week at the hairdresser's, where the tops of the trees started forming into a hostile pattern? I can just tell! For God's sake! *(Pause)* Don't you think I'd rather be home taking the lamb chops out of the oven? Or whatever you cook them in. If I could cook, I mean. It's not a matter of making an effort! I have a time bomb in my brain, and it just—WENT OFF! That's all. *(Pause)* Did my agent call? Well, why didn't you say so? They're taking *Thoughts On My First Bleeding Time*! That's wonderful! Did you tell her where I was? *(Pause)* Listen! My readers do not *care* that I'm a *nut*! My readers *love* that I'm a nut. So tell her. No, baby, not this weekend!

Because, I can't HANDLE it, that's why. Don't you understand that it's a little hard for me to be playing wife and mother for you and our daughter right now? I just feel like the whole world is one big, stinking gas chamber! Don't come up yet!

(She hangs up. Pause. She crosses to REBECCA, who is muttering to herself as she draws. ANNE looks at REBECCA's drawing.)

ANNE: What's that?

REBECCA: My dog.

ANNE: Why does he have so many legs, baby?

REBECCA: *(Upset)* Because his name is Spider!

ANNE: That's just what I thought. Isn't he beautiful!

REBECCA: Hey, Anne. I'm going home for the weekend. *(Stabbing her drawing pad)* I hate it there! *(Hopefully)* Want to come?

ANNE: Oh, baby. I've got a home of my own not to go to.

REBECCA: *(Resuming her savage drawing)* Last time I was home, my mother made a pot roast. And the funniest thing—right as we sat down? It started to bleed. Then it started moving, and she really knew she had done something wrong. She was screaming at it and waving her feelers. Wow.

ANNE: *(Intensely)* Oh, yes. That is very interesting. Yes. *(Thoughtful pause. She lights a cigarette.)*
Breakfast is crawling all over the house—
The toast is coming out of the drain—

(REBECCA begins to draw her.)

ANNE: The cereal is gossiping.
The fried eggs are swimming like devilfish.
I look into the garbage disposal—
That dark stinky navel
And it is saying Mmmm.
It is saying Mmmm. Mmmmm. Mmmm.

ANNE & REBECCA: Mmmm. Mmmm. Mmmm—Mmmm. Mmmm. Mmmm—

(ORDERLY enters with SYLVIA in a wheelchair. She is radiant with malice and rigid with self-loathing. Her arms are covered with bandages. She does not move or speak.)

ANNE: Who's this?

ORDERLY: New roomate. C'mon Rebecca, time's up.

(REBECCA backs out, frightened by SYLVIA's appearance. ORDERLY exits. ANNE sizes up SYLVIA. SYLVIA stares at something invisible. A pause)

SYLVIA: *(A savage private declamation)*
What odd godmother, what withered aunt,
Did you invite—
Mother, O Mother—
to my first birthday party?
Where everyone danced the Hanukkah dance, but me—

Standing alone, all foolish and Unitarian, my tea set filled
With scummy water.
You wept but could not help me.
I have still not the ear for jigging.

(A pause)

ANNE: That's—very good.

SYLVIA: *(Looking at* ANNE *for the first time)* Thank you.

ANNE: What a strange, gritty...somethingness...it has. You're very talented.
(Lighting a cigarette) So what happened to you, Miss Golden Girl?

SYLVIA: *(Rarely looking at* ANNE *and speaking with frightening enunciation)*
I live in a house on campus with some of the other girls. Everyone gathers
in the common room at night, to dry their hair and paint their nails.
Much laughter and vicious, cozy gossip. But whenever I spoke, there
was a potent silence. As if a foreigner had just—farted.

ANNE: I see.

SYLVIA: I tried to blend in. Mother told me to let down my hair. No one
likes a grind. So I wore a mud-pack to dinner in an attempt at henhouse
sisterhood. Mistake! I was the only one. My world flickers around me,
soundless. Faces look like soap bubbles. When I close my eyes, the faces
disappear. I want to keep them closed.

ANNE: *(Pulling her chair closer)* Oh, baby. Death is a big commitment....

SYLVIA: For a while, I thought of leaving school. But that would have killed
Mother. She would have loved that. No. There is no dropping out for a
Golden Goose. So I just said, "No, thank you."

ANNE: Oh, yes! The lovely "no, thank you" moment! Ha!

SYLVIA: Some time back I'd discovered a trick of cutting myself with a
pen knife to get me in the mood for composition. It's how I came to write
"Rose Red at the Big Game" for Seventeen last year. Second prize, maybe
you saw it...?

ANNE: I'm sorry, I...

SYLVIA: So it didn't take much, just a little extra pressure, and—

ANNE: There you were....

SYLVIA: My heart started to beat faster. I was real! An excursion into the
fabled third dimension!

ANNE: Oh, really? For me it's more like—

SYLVIA: At first it was like flying...you really do start seeing—

ANNE: Seeing your *life*! Like pictures in a scrapbook! Oh, I *know*! Mummy and Grandma dressing me in a bunny suit!

SYLVIA: Me, standing in a soggy gym-suit, when I'd wet myself in fear before the teams were chosen...

ANNE: Padding my first bra!

SYLVIA: *(Increasingly excited)* Mother walking me to school on the first day of college...

ANNE: *(Trumps her)* Making love in the back seat of the family Ford...with Daddy!

(ANNE is shocked at this memory—the women turn to stare at each other.)

SYLVIA: *(Turns away again, suddenly composed)* Then something changed. Suddenly I couldn't see. A ringing in my ears. Terrifying, but at the same time so *important*...like I was going—

ANNE: Where?

SYLVIA: I never found out. But I felt I was expected. Then, of course, my *mother* broke down the door. And here I am.

(Pause)

ANNE: Got a fella?

SYLVIA: Flesh disgusts me. My own face sickens me! Encrusted, swollen, greasy in the cracked, yellow mirror over the dormitory sink. Well, hello, Truth! There you are! No wonder it was darkness that seemed more... forgiving.

(Pause)

ANNE: No one special, huh. I'm beginning to get the picture.

SYLVIA: Nobody wants to go out with me. *(She looks away.)*

ANNE: Yes, they do. Oh, sure they do. Why not? Why ever not, Baby-girl?

SYLVIA: My hair is rat-colored, and my lips are smeary and— *(Savagely)* I've never got below an A-.

ANNE: Lip-liner! Peroxide! Blow an exam! C'mon, Baby! Live a little!

SYLVIA: I don't want it! I just want to stay here forever and watch the hair grow on my legs. I love it here.

ANNE: Me too.

(ORDERLY enters, begins to wheel SYLVIA away.)

SYLVIA: Where are we going?

(ORDERLY wheels SYLVIA to shock treatment station.)

Scene Three

(A wing in the psychiatric hospital)

*(*SYLVIA *is receiving electroconvulsive therapy.)*

SYLVIA: *(Ecstatic with electricity)* Yes! Yes! Yes!

(She catapults to a sitting position. Sound of wind in a desert. EMILY *enters—a small, terrible ghost dressed in an elaborate, white, Civil War dress.)*

EMILY: "Convulsion—pleases—for it does not counterfeit."

SYLVIA: Who are you? A hallucination? I did not expect this.

EMILY: Oh, phoo. Let me try again. *(She clears her throat shyly.)*
"The pink and tender earthworm
Waits the rending of the beak—
And cut in half—
It dies again—
A sensate coffee cake!"

SYLVIA: *(Curiosity mingling with terror)* Beak—cake! Can you do that?

EMILY: *(Quivering)* What a pleasure this is. I rarely get to greet a kindred spirit.

SYLVIA: Kindred? You and me? What do we have in common?

EMILY: A certain desire to—scratch the surface? Here, you dropped this.

(She pulls out a big razor blade and offers it to SYLVIA, *who reaches for it tentatively.)*

EMILY: *(Whispering)* I'm so glad you'll be joining me. It's been so lonely being dead. I have no one to talk to, and I've been looking for—*(She primps a little.)*—that Special Anyone for the longest time.

*(*SYLVIA *drops the razor.)*

SYLVIA: Special "Anyone"?

EMILY: *(Shyly)* I've felt him so close, sometimes. But, oh, well, Longing is its own Rapture!

SYLVIA: *(Fighting rising hysteria)* If you are a hallucination, shouldn't you perhaps be gone?

*(*EMILY *smiles at her.)*

EMILY: Rapture. Now there's a word. From the Latin. To seize, pillage, plunder, rape. Mmmm. *(Shouting)* Take me, somebody! I'm not busy!
(Seems to be listening to something) They're playing with me, again.

SYLVIA: *(Afraid to know)* Who?

EMILY: Ooh, that naughty universe! Tell me. *(Coming closer)* What did it feel like?

SYLVIA: No! *(She is convulsed by an electric current.)* Yes! That was a good one! *(Terrified)* I want you out!

EMILY: You won't remember me when you wake up. But I'll remember you!

SYLVIA: Please go away!

EMILY: Not just yet.

SYLVIA: My head is splitting!

EMILY: *(Screams)* How else will anything get in? *(Pause. She is mortified at herself for losing her temper.)* I'm truly sorry. Want to meet my baby? *(She reaches under her dress and pulls out a shriveled, blasted little book.)* Isn't he beautiful? Guess who his father was. *(Lifting her arms)* Lightning!

(SYLVIA convulses.)

EMILY: Poor thing. But I can't take care of him any longer. And I've selected you to be his mother! And now, you can have him! He'll bring you luck.

(EMILY advances with burnt book.)

SYLVIA: No! No! No! Sterility! Madness! Bone-bag! I want real children. I want a man to plunge his stake through my heart so that I can sleep at night!

(EMILY tosses it on SYLVIA's lap.)

SYLVIA: I don't want it! It's a curse!

EMILY: Our duty is to sing. No backsies!

(She disappears, singing a wordless note.)

SYLVIA: *(Convulsing, gratefully)* Yes! Yes! Yes!

Scene Four

(A classroom at Wardwell College, a women's Ivy League school)

(TED MAGUS is conducting a poetry seminar. FEMALE STUDENTS are taking notes. SYLVIA walks into the classroom area, joining the other girls during TED's story.)

TED: Yes. The ending was a nightmare. I wrestled with it for weeks, like Jacob wrestling the angel. Finally, I dreamed it. I saw the slug dying, covered with salt by a vicious housewife. As clear as day, I dreamed him, a big, quivering mass of slop and mucus writhing in the rotted mulch...and I found the final lines..."And bubbling there, I'm left alone, a bitter pool of fragrance, shrinking in the sun."

ALL THE GIRLS: Wow. Oh, that's incredible. I cried when I—

TED: So. What have we learned? Don't be polite. Don't be small. Poetry is not all rose gardens and my cat with last year's dead leaves, you know. We're talking about the dark side. The unmentionable terrors. The unspeakable joys. What are yours? Show me. I know my fears are... shedding tears in public, showing affection for other men...in a physical way, you know, hugging, wrestling, that sort of thing, and—Ha! Dancing!— I mean why—dancing? It terrifies me. My own twisted ideas of manhood, I suppose, as passed down from one generation of small, cramped men to another, when—my God! The blood of our ancestors *thrummed* with the dance. A good jig, a leap under the moonlight—the hunt, the rites of mating or of death—oh come! Let's...tango! Who wants to jump in first?

GIRL ONE: *(Played by female actor. A flirt. Comes up to front of class with notebook. Adjusts her sweater. She giggles.)* Um, okay, I'm a nervous wreck. Okay. Should I say anything about this first? Or just go?

TED: I'm not your judge. I'm not your executioner.

GIRL ONE: Oh, Time, why keep'st thine armies marching on
Destroying flesh and withering with age?
The swelling breasts of happy girlhood droop, and—

TED: Yes, yes. And all that. I can tell you've faithfully studied the form. I commend your hard work. I recommend...a naked swim with a boy you love in a rock quarry in the blaze of a hot afternoon.

GIRL ONE: I'm not sure I understand....

TED: Good, good. That's a start. Who else? Come, come, come.

GIRL TWO: *(Played by male actor. A grind. She comes to front of class with notebook. Very nervous. Adjusts her glasses. Suddenly levels a passionate gaze at* TED*)* The azure Mediterranean
Leaps against the chalky cliff
My skin scorches in the hot Greek sun
I left my sunblock at American Express
Dmitri sticks his hand inside my dress
Why, oh, why do they overload these donkeys so?

(Pause)

TED: Someone else? No one? Oh, come, come. Don't make me talk about dancing, again.

*(*SYLVIA *gets up. Recites)*

SYLVIA: It is again the place of nightmare.
Hot breath surrounds me, rich and reeking.
Brambles tear the skins from my thighs—
As I run, my blood excites.

Oh, rip from me this borrowed hide.
Teach me my skin.

(GIRLS *look at each other.*)

TED: Excellent.

SYLVIA: Omigod. Really? Thank you.

TED: I mean, profoundly—usual...usual, but excellent.

SYLVIA: Excuse me?

TED: You know, girls, it's interesting, that this last being one of the best,
it's also one of the worst. Ha! That feels like the beginning of an insight!
So? What. Class dismissed. Assignment! Assignment! For next week,
I want everyone to go out and—spend a night—on a park bench.
And write a poem about it.

(Pause. Consternation in the class)

TED: *(Thundering)* Or don't. It doesn't really matter, does it?

(Student puts up her hand.)

TED: No, I'm not taking any bloody questions! Just *do* it!

(Students leave. TED *collects papers.* SYLVIA *walks over to him. He looks up.)*

TED: What's up, Miss—Fluellen? is it?

SYLVIA: I have a little bone to pick with you.

TED: Oh? What?

SYLVIA: "Profoundly usual"?

TED: *(Packing up books, not looking at her)* Oh, you know, the Tarzan-Meets-
Rima-the-Bird-Girl fantasy stuff, the typical Junior-year ambivalence about
fellatio, the underlying hatred of your mother. But other than that, it's very
well crafted. One of the best.

SYLVIA: *(Choking with fury)* Tarzan? Rima the Bird Girl? Junior-year
ambivalence about—How dare you? How dare you? You—standing
up there bullying all the girls all week in that filthy black sweater! Well,
how about you! How about your boring male performance anxiety that's
so rippingly evident in "Afternoon of a Slug!" Talk about profoundly usual!

TED: *(Laughs)* Oh, what nonsense.

SYLVIA: Oh, come on! After the evil housewife puts salt on the poor old slug
and you say, "And bubbling there, I'm left alone, a bitter pool of fragrance,
shrinking in the sun...."

TED: Don't be idiotic. "Afternoon of the Slug," my dear girl, is about the
agony of the creator, writhing in the fleshy bondage of his own creation.

An artist must come to terms with agony. The bubbling of a salted slug on a summer morning...

(Pause)

TED: Oh, my God.

SYLVIA: Ha-ha-ha! I'm right, I'm right, I'm right!

TED: I don't believe it.

SYLVIA: I caught you out! I—

TED: Be quiet! I'm thinking. "Short, thick, white-bellied worm, I have not the vertebrate advantage..."

SYLVIA: "Flesh-helmeted, despised—"

TED: Shut up, will you?

SYLVIA: Ha-ha-ha.

TED: *(Mounting concern)* "—the boneless one that will never stiffen—oh, where are you, muscle for my dreams...for my ramping will..." Oh, God. I don't believe it! It is! It's about my dick!

SYLVIA: See, I told you, I was—

TED: I can't believe it. It's so bloody obvious. I sweated blood over "Afternoon of a Slug." It was a death struggle. I pursued that poem like Ahab chasing after Mo—.

(Pause)

SYLVIA: I am so attracted to you.

(TED looks at her.)

TED: Don't fuck with me, Miss Fluellen.

SYLVIA: I'm going to.

TED: I'm death to little girls.

SYLVIA: I'm not a little girl.

TED: And I hate women!

SYLVIA: Not as much as I do!

TED: *(Crossing to her)* I'm trouble. I'm a filthy rucksack of a man in the dung heap of existence. I want a great muck of a woman, not a bright little coed. I need a Big Ugly Woman!—to wake me up. When we have each other in the dead of night, it won't be full of sticky tenderness. It will be with the ancient frenzy of the fire ants that couple and kill.

SYLVIA: You don't frighten me.

TED: Such an all-American girl. Dyed yellow hair, red-painted lips and—

(Grabbing her arms—she gasps and tries to break away.)

TED: —bandages all over your arms. *(He laughs.)*

SYLVIA: Take your hands off me, you sick bastard!

(He releases her easily. She stares at him for a moment, then suddenly pulls him to her for a passionate kiss. He mounts her as she lies back over the desk top. Her head hangs upside down, face toward audience, hair streaming downward. A tableau. TED remains frozen in position as SYLVIA speaks.)

SYLVIA: *(Face front, ferocious, joyful)*
Off! Sticky Mother Pot!
I throw my saddle shoes at your head
And dance barefoot with a goat-footed giant
We are laughing at you, he and I.
My lips are red and my hair fills the forest.
(A metered laugh)
Ha-ha-ha-ha-ha.

Scene Five

(ANNE's house. ANNE is in her bed. She is in a state. Her husband TITO is with her.)

TITO: What can I do? I just don't know what to do for you!

ANNE: Get Dr Dickter on the phone! I want to go back to the bin! I want to go back to the bin!

TITO: Please, baby, no. Shall I call one of your lovers?

ANNE: It doesn't help. Nothing helps.

TITO: *(Reluctant)* Do you want—to have sex with me?

ANNE: *(Anguished)* I might as well masturbate! I mean, c'mon, Tito, we've become the same person! *(Pause)* Oh, I've hurt you, baby, my love. I'm a big mess. Make me a milkshake? I want the big sweet mama I never had. I want it with a straw.

TITO: Chocolate?

ANNE: *(Screams)* Vanilla! Don't you listen?

TITO: All right! *(He leaves.)*

ANNE: *(Sing-song)* Mommy's feeling crazy! Kit-Kat! KIT KAT!!!

(ANNE lights a cigarette, fussing for a moment. KIT KAT enters, apprehensive.)

ANNE: *(Sweetly)* Oh, it's so good to be home again with my Bunny-girl. Let's cuddle up. Give me your hands. Baby Bunny, do you believe that Mother loves you and what happened has nothing to do with you?

KIT-KAT: *(Reluctant)* I guess so.

ANNE: *(Taking her hands)* I'm so sorry, Kit-Kat, that you had to find me like that. Never again. Believe me?

KIT-KAT: I guess so.

ANNE: Do you really, Kitty? 'Cause part of our healing is to say what we really feel. *(Pause)* What is it, Baby?

KIT-KAT: Oh, Mom. It was so gross! I had to clean everything up, all the puke and the pills— and all the kids coming over for my Sweet Sixteen party! Why'd you have to try and kill yourself on my birthday!! You hate me!!!

ANNE: I do not! Shut up, you little bitch! Are you out of your mind? I said I was sorry!

KIT-KAT:	TITO:
	(Entering with milkshake)
Sorry!	For Christ's sake, Anne!

ANNE: Oh, God, Tito—I could die! —this waste of my life—forced early into marriage (that prison routine of pancake breakfasts and chicken pot pies)—scrubbing toilets instead of fighting to save myself, singing idiot songs to an insomniac infant, whose little red face could only reflect my own fury back to me—

TITO: *(Furious)* First of all, we eloped. Secondly, you don't cook, I do. And Kit-Kat has done all the housework! Ever since she moved back from foster care!

ANNE: You are undermining me! Do you give a shit if I survive or not!

TITO:	KIT-KAT:
Of course—	Oh, Mommy, what's wrong!
What did I do?	
Stop crying—	

ANNE: Then support my truth!

TITO: *(Leaving so he won't hit her)* Excuse me. I've got to check the roast.

ANNE: Oh, shit. *(Pause)* Mommy loves you, baby. Forgive me.

KIT-KAT: For what?

ANNE: I'm grudging my blooming baby her day in the spring sun. Look how beautiful you are. I'm sorry I missed that darn party.

KIT-KAT: It's all right, Mom.

ANNE: No, it's not all right! I wanted to give you something my mother never gave me. Trust in yourself. In your body. Listen. You are beautiful. Your vagina is beautiful.

KIT-KAT: Mom, please, you're embarrassing me.

ANNE: Don't be. Everything you are, everything you feel, is right, love. Kitty, are you padding that bra—that can't be YOU—is it? Let Mommy feel— *(Swiping at her)*

KIT-KAT: No!

ANNE: Listen. I know how it is when you're young and your whole taut little body is singing the song of sex. Is there anything you'd like to ask Mommy?

KIT-KAT: I've got to go. Some of the gang is waiting.

ANNE: I want you to never feel ashamed, baby.

KIT-KAT: I'm not.

ANNE: I love you!

KIT-KAT: I know you do.

ANNE: Mommy wrote a new poem, in the hospital. It's going to be in *The Atlantic Monthly*. Isn't that exciting?

KIT-KAT: Cool.

ANNE: Don't you want me to read it to you?

KIT-KAT: *(Exiting)* Yeah, but not right now.

ANNE: All right, my angel. Some other time when you have the time. Jesus. *(Sighs. Reaches for her last cigarette and crumples the empty pack. A silence. Then, as a prayer, or a poem, or something she sees in the curling smoke)*
Jesus—God—Baby—
What would you do with an old crazy lady—
Can you smooth this old piece of worn brown wood—
With your carpenter's hands—
Can you make something out of me?
Anne is finally ready for you, Jesus—
A holy man with holes in his hands—
A man in a white dress with a kind, kind, face—
Sweet old ghost that blesses all our adulteries—
'Cause we are all adults now, aren't we?
Except I'm not, Jesus, God, Baby—
I'm just little Anne
And I need a Big Kind Daddy to help this old girl home.

Scene Six

(STONER's *house*)

(*Preparation for a surprise birthday party is under way.* VERA *is hiding guests.* STONER *comes in with dry cleaning in a plastic bag.*)

STONER: I'm sixty-five years old, and every word I ever wrote is a lie. Fuck everything. (*He rips out the clothes and puts the dry-cleaning bag over his head.*)

EVERYONE: SURPRISE!

STONER: AAAHHH!

EVERYONE: Happy birthday to you, happy birthday to you, happy birthday dear Daddy-Bob, happy birthday to you.

VERA: Honey, blow the candles out and make a wish.

STONER: You blow them out. I don't give a fuck.

VERA: Bob, people came from all over the country for your birthday.

STONER: Why? Oh, I'm so depressed. I'm dead already. Why didn't they just send flowers.

OTHERS: Oh, Daddy-Bob, no. No, that's not true. We love you, Daddy-Bob.

VERA: C'mon. Sweetie. Things aren't so bad. Blow out the candles.

STONER: I went out on the street, and the clouds were jeering faces. A dog pissed on my leg while I waited for a light to change. I was going to be the long-awaited messenger for my time. Arriving bloody, half dead, but bearing the olive branch of hope! All I am is half-dead. I want a scotch on the rocks.

EVERYONE: Noo, noo, noo.

STONER: I keep trying to remember something.

(*Pause*)

VERA: What, honey?

STONER: (*Angry*) Anything, goddammit. I'm hollow. An old shell. I can't finish a sentence anymore, let alone a poem!

(TED *and* SYLVIA *enter.*)

STONER: And here's my young friend Ted—the bold new voice that makes my life's work a pile of shit.

(*Pause*)

TED: Happy birthday, Dr Stoner. So good to see you again.

STONER: Who's the little miss?

TED: This is Sylvia, Dr Stoner—

SYLVIA: *(Brightly to all)* Wife!

STONER: 'Spleasure.

SYLVIA: Dr Stoner, I just can't *wait* for the Cotton Mather poems!

GUEST: Jesus!

STONER: *(Sobbing)* Oh, God, God, God— I wish I was dead!

SYLVIA: What did I say?

SOMEONE ELSE: No, Daddy-Bob. Please—

TED: Now, now, Daddy-Bob, what's all this?

STONER: I find that weeping fills me like a great storm, and all I can do is cry until I can breathe again. Ahh! *(He sobs while everyone waits. Abruptly, he stops.)* That's better. Really, I'm clear, again. Let's have cake! How are you all, all my young friends?

EVERYONE: Oh, we're fine, Daddy-Bob, Martha's play was reviewed in *American Quarterly, The New Yorker* took *Winter in Narragansett*—

(STONER and VERA sit on the couch with cake as guests chatter.)

STONER: *(Howling)* Can't somebody kill me?

(Silence)

SYLVIA: Well, Ted, I don't know about you, but I'm ready to—

STONER: Vera, I want a scotch!

VERA: No, baby, no! And that's final!

GIRL: How about a little—

STONER: Do I look like I want any damn cake?!

(ANNE enters.)

ANNE: *(To VERA)* I don't know if he'll remember me, it's been so long— I was in his workshop ages ago....

VERA: Hello, dear. Hang on to your hat. Do you two know each other?

SYLVIA: Oh, hello.

ANNE: *(Kissing her)* Baby! Mwaa! How well you look! Have you—

(STONER falls to his knees, arms outstretched.)

STONER: *(Sings)*
O Faith, most fragrant oil,
We yield it up to you!

Essence of the lily mild—
The gift of rack and screw!
(Pause) Does anybody know what I'm talking about?

TED: *(Quietly)* Yes, Doctor Stoner, yes.

(He crosses to him. STONER *stays on knees. Looks sideways at* TED*)*

STONER: I once sensed the hard promise of God like distant chords of scary music. I've been sitting on the moon like a good little boy my whole damn life. Trying to be grateful for my fucking lunacy. One of God's special presents. I was promised a message and I've been so patient! Well, I've lain forty years on my right side and all I'm getting is bed sores!

*(*GUEST *snickers.)*

STONER: You think that's fucking funny? We'll talk about it in hell, you and I!

SOMEONE: He's really gone.

TED: Oh, no, he's not.

STONER: *(Gets to his feet. Surveys the room with rising paranoid enthusiasm)* I spy with my little eye! The whole F B I! They're under the bed! They've had my number since my great days on the White House lawn. They don't know I'm too washed up to be a subversive. Come on out, boys, have some fucking cake! *(He crawls under the table, cake plate in hand.)*

VERA: I'm really sorry, everyone. Robert? Oh, please, Bob—

TED: *(Cutting in loudly)* Let's admit what's happening, here. This man is crying out for help. Please. Can we all join together in a ritual of healing?

(Murmurs of assent.)

TED: You need a brother in the lonely walk, Bob-Doctor. We're all here with you. Would you like to hold my hand?

*(*TED *offers his hand to* STONER *under the table.* STONER *considers and then takes it, allowing himself to be led to the living room floor like a dog.)*

TED: Please! Everyone. Join us on the floor. Leave your cake. Robert is in crisis. *(He test-drums on the floor.)* Dum dah dah dum!

MAN: All right!

STONER: *(To* TED*)* Where did we meet? I've forgotten....

TED: On the radio, Doctor Stoner. Last fall? I read from *Songs of the Fen*... we worked on the Mather poem together...

STONER: ...shak shaka shak...?

TED: That's right, that's right! Please, Robert, you must trust me. I'm with you. I hear you. And I understand your torment with the great hard Father. Listen to me. He's not home. He never was. *(Pause)* But the Mother is.

GUESTS: *(Reaction)* Wow. Yes. The Mother is.

STONER: What the fuck are you talking about?

TED: Don't think—! (STONER *starts to respond.*)

TED: Look where it's led you. Don't talk! Words can't heal a heart.

(Some of the guests are nodding, starting to get weepy. They press each other's hands in support.)

TED: Try with me. I know it's hard, I know it doesn't make *sense.* Let's drum for healing, Dr Stoner.... I've seen miracles happen. Let's break a sweat!

VERA: He's on a new medication....I don't know if he should—

MAN: Let's all get naked together! I'll go first!

VERA: No!

TED: *(Drumming softly)* We call for healing...hear us, great Mother!

(Some drum. STONER *is confused. He drums.)*

SYLVIA: *(To party guest)* Take your hand off me—Ted! That man just—

TED: Shhh!

(SYLVIA *goes and stands behind* STONER *in a huff.*)

TED: We're asking for the healing of our friend brother Robert...when the spirit moves you, let him speak through you.

GIRL: I love everyone in this room. Why not? Why shouldn't I? There's no shame in love!

TED: Good! Yes! Dum dah dah dum, dum dah dah dum. I can feel it. We are starting to invoke something. Name the unnameable—put words to the darkness—

STONER: Ahh! Someone's here! An evil spirit...I sense her presence—she's standing next to me with a look of anger and disapproval...she hates me! And I'm only a little boy!

TED: *(Quietly)* For Christ's sake, sit down, Sylvia. *(Beating on floor)* Dum, dah dah...

(SYLVIA *shoots* TED *a furious look and sits down huffily.*)

STONER: Dum dah! Dah! Ahh! Ahh! *(He stands up, suddenly. He's hallucinating.)* Where am I, where am I?

(Response from circle—anguish from VERA, *excitement from group.)*

TED: *(Excited)* What do you see, Robert? Take us with you—

STONER: *(Terrified)* A jungle as green as a lemon! The leaves are sharp and glowing!

TED: The primeval lap of the great Mother!

STONER: *(Horrified)* Insects hanging upside down—with eyes as big as hubcaps! Everything is chewing everything!

TED: Yes! Yes! Accept! Don't be afraid! The great circle of creation! It is the dance of being!

(Motions to the guests. They start to frolic in a pagan fertility circle.)

STONER: Everything is fucking everything!

GUESTS: *(Euphoric)* Yes! Love! Ha-ha! Fuck! I feel love! We love you, Daddy-Bob! Fuck! Fuck! Fuck! There's no shame in love! Hare' fuck!

(VERA puts her face in her hands. SYLVIA watches, repulsed. ANNE watches STONER, distressed. TED has his eyes shut and is pounding on floor.)

TED: It's all right, Robert—there is no death—just love, and the great good light of—!

STONER: The sun! What's wrong with it! It's horrible! Its rays are like ice—it's trying to freeze me! *(Realizing)* I'm Adam! The first man! Oh, poor Adam! I'm so lonely I wish for death, but it hasn't been invented yet!

(He is sobbing. No one knows what to do. The circle falls into disarray, some still dancing, others stop. Suddenly ANNE steps into the center. Assertive, sexual)

ANNE: But love has! It's me, baby, Eve.

(The group hushes.)

STONER: Ahh! Adam's senses thrill. His skin ripples.

ANNE: I'm here for you, baby, my old Adam baby! I'll keep you warm. Come creep into my arms and rest.

STONER: Could you love a bad, bad man like me?

ANNE: Oh, doll, all men are bad. Eve just loves and loves her bad little boy.

(STONER moves into her arms. She holds him. VERA sits in corner quietly.)

TED: Astonishing. Beautiful. She's stepping into his undermyth.

SYLVIA: What?

GIRL: Wow.

SYLVIA: Did you say his "undermyth"?

TED: Be quiet, or leave.

ANNE: It's all right now. Everything is all right now.

STONER: I think I know you. Oh, my, it's not little Annie from my Tuesday night class at Boston College! Look how you've changed!

ANNE: Yeah, I know.

STONER: You used to be a morsel and now you're the whole three layers! Isis! Cleopatra! Betsy Ross! Come with me and be my love, we'll face the dark together, you and I!

ANNE: Oh, you lovely man! But you have your good Vera, and I have my dear, boring, Tito.

STONER: Oh, no, don't send me away now that I've found you. Beautiful Mother! It's you! It's you! Love me! Love me or I'll die!

VERA: I think he might, too. This has happened before. The Air India stewardess, the Jamaican nurse, the lady from the I R S—oh, please, Miss Bittenhand, don't turn him away.

ANNE: Oh, really, I couldn't....

VERA: I'm begging you as a wife. Help him. I can't. Take him with you... he will make you feel so cherished...for a while. *(She exits.)*

GIRL: And to think I almost stayed home tonight.

STONER: Come live with me and be my love.

ANNE: Where would we go, you Great Wonderful Mad Daddy?

VERA: *(Reentering with checkbook)* We have a cabin near Indian Lake. You could be there by tomorrow evening if you—

(She tries to put checkbook in STONER's pocket.)

STONER: Who the hell are you, bothering my love and me? Keep your money, strange woman. We don't need your money.

ANNE: Hey!

(VERA passes checkbook to ANNE behind STONER's back.)

VERA: Bless you, dear, oh, bless you. I thank you and America thanks you. Take good care of him. Call me when he's himself again. Does this put you out very much?

ANNE: Put me out? I don't think so. *(VERA and ANNE embrace.)*

ANNE: C'mon, Papa-Doc.

MAN: *(Quietly)* Daddy-Bob.

ANNE: Let's you and me go play house.

STONER: In Xanadu, did Kublai Khan
A stately pleasure dome decree—

(As he and ANNE exit)

STONER: —my inspiration is coming back to me...my angel, you restore me to myself!

(GUESTS *stand around uncertainly.*)

GIRL: Let's celebrate, anyway. Let's celebrate that we're here, we're alive, we have warm flesh, awake minds, there is love in this room—

TED: *(Smiling at her)* Absolutely—let's all—

VERA: Do you mind! Thank you all for coming, but I think I'd like to be alone, now.

EVERYONE: Goodnight, Mrs Stoner—call me if you just want to talk, shall I stay and help you clean up? Good night, good night, good night—

(GUESTS *leave.*)

TED: Are you going to be—

VERA: No.

TED: Would you like me to—

VERA: No.

SYLVIA: Are you sure that you—

VERA: No.

TED: Well, uh, goodnight, then.

(*He and* SYLVIA *exit.* VERA *sits alone onstage.*)

END OF ACT ONE

ACT TWO

Scene One

(A cabin at Indian Lake)

(ANNE and STONER have just arrived.)

STONER: I'm frightened. Woman. Woman!

ANNE: I'm here, honey.

STONER: I'm really in for it now. Oh, I can feel it coming on. I'm feeling very, very sneaky, and so much smarter than everyone else.

ANNE: But you are!

STONER: No, you don't get it. I'm harboring these little epigrams. Like... this one...occurred to me, just as we came in the door. "Insouciance is dominion's ticket." It means nothing to me yet, but soon it will and then I'll be lost, lost, lost and back in those dreadful arts-and-crafts rooms, making ashtrays and moccasins, the laughingstock of ghosts. Soon, I'll feel those awful giggles come upon me, and I'll be a laughing Jack, a balloon of grotesque euphoria! Oh, I hate my enthusiasms...afterwards. I love them when they're happening, though.

ANNE: You just keep talking to me, and I'll rub your shaggy old head, and I promise you my damndest that we're never going to find out what your little epigram means.

STONER: Annie. How unbearably lovely you are. That is something that I can still see.

ANNE: Want to go to bed?

STONER: You'd let me have at you?

ANNE: I don't see any problem with that.

STONER: I'm blinded, by your goodness. I may die, to gaze upon such beauty. Look at you!

ANNE: Don't look too hard. Let me—

STONER: Sweetness of my heart. Why are you afraid to be seen? The little places where you're crumbling are full of light. Tiny air bubbles are bearing your clay away and replacing you with helio-sycory.

ANNE: And what might that be, Crazy One?

STONER: Divine substance. I love your little sags and bags. It means the beginning is near, my Eternal Salamander, my Sun-Angel.

ANNE: You're nutty as a fruitcake, but I think I'm falling in love. Oh, you move me, you old madman. You're so different then when I first knew you. You were sour and respectable, then. Scary and oh, so learned.

STONER: I was trapped in the lower levels. The horrible sea-bottom of my special lie.

ANNE: You're losing me. Take me with you.

STONER: I was a lie! A false monster built of pretension and the desire to be admired. Why, my greatest poem was a fraud. The poem I once read on the White House lawn, "To a Confederate War Horse, Dead at Chattahoochee." Biggest fraud of my life.

ANNE: Oh, the horse poem? But I loved that! *(Jogging his memory)*
"There you lie...
Dung and honor smeared, inseparable—
In the clotted strands of your tail..."

STONER: *(Slowly)* "—What did you know, Great Beast,
Eater of Oats,
Of men with beards in boardrooms of Washington,
Or of a ringleted girl smacking her pickaninny silly
You carried her on your back,
Old Switcher of Flies—"

ANNE: "—Had you known, would you have run so,
Would you have burst your great heart
Willingly, for the Confederacy,
That harpy in a hoopskirt?"
Look at me, I'm weeping. Lies, or no lies, no one did it like you, sweetheart. You were the king.

STONER: Well, I did do a jolly good job of pirating Walt Whitman. He probably spun his way to China when he heard that one.

ANNE: What do we do now?

STONER: Go to bed and wait.

ANNE: Yes.

STONER: Lie down with me. I can't have at you, really, of course. All that's long gone with those salts and God knows what of Dr Von Seyffertitz, but a little sanity is much sweeter to me now, except for those moments when I'd trade it all for madness. But would you take a nap with me, Sweet Anne? It would mean more than anything else I could think of.

ANNE: You know, it's the funniest thing.

STONER: Yes?

ANNE: I was never one for naps, but, right this minute, that seems like the best idea.

STONER: Crawl in.

Scene Two

(TED and SYLVIA's *place. It is an old restored lighthouse with rough stone interiors and a dominant upstage window. Morning. Sounds of the sea. They sit across a Ouija board, hands on the planchette.)*

SYLVIA: This isn't going to work! I'm a fat, phony fraud!

TED: Shh. Shh. Go on. Ask him again.

SYLVIA: I come to the spirits as a tongueless mute. I seek my voice. What strange grip chokes me and leaves me silent? For many moons now, I have lingered in an aimless malaise. Why cannot I write, Mr Pandora?

TED: Why cannot you speak normally?

SYLVIA: Mr Pandora—there is a force that stifles me. Throttles this songbird so she cannot sing—she that once sang free. Would it be so hard, Mr Pandora, to speak to me and tell me what am I supposed to do? It is I, the true seeker that comes to the spirits in her hour of need. *(Pause)* Oh, just move, you fucker! Tell me something! Anything! Who do I have to fuck to get an idea?

(Planchette starts to move.)

SYLVIA: There! He moves!

TED: Look at him go!

BOTH: Go—t—wait, you're pushing it— *(Spelling it out)* G-O T-O H-E-L-L. *(Pause)*

SYLVIA: *(To the board)* You bastard. He just told me to go to hell. I'm being rejected by the occult. Oh, this is really too much! *(She gets up and crosses away from table.)*

TED: You're overreacting. A certain amount of nonsense just comes up.

SYLVIA: Oh, ho ho. No, no, no, Ted, I wouldn't call this nonsense. It's calculated to wound—Mr Pandora is aiming his advice right for where it hurts. Go to hell. That's been the message of my life. "Go to hell" is what they said when I tried to join the swim team. "Go to hell" is what they thought when I asked them to my birthday party. Oh, yes, they came all right, but only to laugh and sneer, while Mother played the piano and sang, in her peculiar voice, parlor songs from the wrong *century*! Go to hell. I listened to those voices, and finally I *went* to hell, my Sophomore year, when I tried to cut off my head with an ax!

TED: What?

SYLVIA: I couldn't tell you the whole truth. After I slashed my wrists I became afraid I hadn't done the trick. I tried to cut off my head with an old wood-ax!

TED: God!

SYLVIA: *(Suddenly playful)* Fooling! Fooling! Oh, silly, just my wrists. *(Kisses his head)* Mwaah! *(Furious again)* I know all about Hell!

TED: Then fucking write about it! I've got to go. I'm due at the station at two.

SYLVIA: Oh, baby, good luck! I'll be listening! Oh, wait, your manuscript! Silly!

TED: Try and do a little work, huh?

(TED kisses her, grabs manuscript, exits. SYLVIA waves. Goes to table and pulls out her notebook)

SYLVIA: Go to hell. Hell. Hades. The dark underworld from which Demeter, the mother of the earth, returns. Astarte. Inanna. Gaia. Hmm.
"The bee-struck blossom nods,
Heavy in the pregnant honey-scented breeze—
It is waiting for her—
She is coming, she, dressed in a gown of grain—"

(She falls into a stupor, hypnotized by her pencil. EMILY enters through upstage window.)

EMILY: The little maid snug in her cot
The sun poked in his head
And lifting up the coverlet
He saw that she was dead!

SYLVIA: *(Jerking upright—terrified)* Oh, my God! Who are you?

EMILY: The tooth that circles in your soul
And carves its basement out.

SYLVIA: *(Trembling)* Aahhh! That's—not very good!

EMILY: Perpetuity has made me sloppy. Don't think I don't know. Any way—I can't maintain much longer, Everything is pulling at me from Everywhere, and later...or sooner...I've an appointment with—

SYLVIA: What?

EMILY: Oblivion! Ahh! Now there's a word to lift your head to!

(She pantomimes lifting her head off of her shoulders. SYLVIA *screams.)*

SYLVIA: How did you get in here?

EMILY: Oh, no, no, no. I'm not. Here. In that sense. I'm your imaginary friend. You might say. That's the degree before psychotic. That's when *you* become *my* imaginary friend.

SYLVIA: What?

EMILY: Don't worry. That's a ways off yet. Months! *(Laughs)*

SYLVIA: What do you want?

EMILY: Company! A chance to hear your verse—maybe later, a little game of knucklebones— oh, never mind that—look. You seemed stuck. I can help. I really believe in you.

SYLVIA: Oh, no, I don't think that—

*(*EMILY *assaults her, wrestling her to the floor.)*

EMILY: Just spit it out!

SYLVIA: The honey-scented breeze ripples the branch—

EMILY: *(Quivering)* —And everyone was dead.

SYLVIA: Galloping sunrise scatters its tangerine largess—

EMILY: And everyone was lonely and dead.

SYLVIA: *(Desperately)* Long-legged hares clip-clop their legs together— they joy at the meadow's newness—they are bringing her to herself—!

EMILY: *(Beside herself, getting off* SYLVIA, *and raving around the room)* And we tried to get out of our coffins, but we couldn't! Ha-ha-ha! And we tore our nails out, scratching at the ceiling! And we screamed and screamed, but God couldn't hear us! Yes! Yes! Yes! *(Pause)* But that's just me talking!

SYLVIA: Stop it! This is horrible!

EMILY: Horrible! Oh, where I am now is so far past horrible! Horrible was the last report of land—what I wouldn't give for merely horrible—I'd give my eyeTEETH, if I had any!

SYLVIA: Where are you....

EMILY: *(Howling as some undertow sucks her back out through the window)* Where you belong—!!

SYLVIA: Wait—!

EMILY: *(As she disappears from view)* Out! Of! Time!

*(*SYLVIA *mechanically picks up her wooden spoon and mixing bowl.)*

Scene Three

(Afternoon. A radio station)

(TED *is on-air with* INTERVIEWER.)

INTERVIEWER: If you're just joining us, we're chatting with poet Ted Magus. Exciting to have you with us. Ted! How would you describe your direction in these new poems?

TED: Basically what I'm trying to do is rip a new asshole in a dead language.

INTERVIEWER: Umm. That's really interesting that you should say that— because I found that I literally couldn't sit down for hours, after reading some of them. I just had to pace, I was disturbed.

TED: Good for you. That's very good. It means you're open. It means you're more than just a suit with an English degree from some death-mill bullshit university.

INTERVIEWER: Ha! That's interesting.

TED: The Spider.

The light through the window is green with rain.
The dust lies thick upon the sill.
The schoolboy in me becomes unstuck.
I write my initials and then write "Fuck."
A buzzing draws my eye.

A spider is squatting on a fly.
Her eight hairy legs unknot his tie,
He was happy just an hour ago
Dreaming of dog shit!
Now eight hairy legs—
Root—and find—
His green heart's shell,
And his screams become her dinner bell—
As eight hairy legs beat in time.

INTERVIEWER: —God! You know, it's so odd. I'm sweating!

TED: You're a man. You're alive. You're simply a man who's alive.

INTERVIEWER: *(Fighting tears—quietly)* —I'm sorry—God! It's just—

TED: I know. I know. I know.

(The men look into each other's eyes. TED *pats the* INTERVIEWER *on the back.)*

Scene Four

(Evening. TED *and* SYLVIA's *house)*

*(*SYLVIA *is cooking as* TED *enters.)*

TED: Sweetheart, did you hear that! Were you listening? He asked me back for next week. Ha-ha!

SYLVIA: Terrific. Let's eat.

TED: I wasn't nervous at all. I felt calm, like I had a right to be there, just simple. Sharing who I am and what I think. How'd I do? Was it all right?

SYLVIA: Eight legs? Eight hairy legs, you utter fuck? Is that what you think of me?

TED: What?

SYLVIA: You think I don't know that's me?

TED: What I want to know is are you really crazy, or are you just pretending?

SYLVIA: Because if you think that was me, we can just end this here and now. I will not be humiliated on national radio as some kind of big, rubbery, Venus flytrap! Is that what you think I am, some kind of big, rubbery, Venus flytrap?

TED: Actually, you're more medium sized and chalky.

SYLVIA: Medium sized and chalky!! *(Pause)* I deserved that. Oh, Ted. You have a laughter in you that heals my heart. Thank God we found each other. Let's eat. You were wonderful. Absolutely thrilling. I've married a giant. You stimulate me! When I'm with you I feel like I'm teeming with new life, new ideas. I see a bean sprout in a jar, and I hear a villanelle, a cat asleep on a porch step...I still can't seem to get much down on paper, however.

TED: Do we have any beer?

SYLVIA: *(Thoughtfully)* My man wants mead to wash down his meal...the bubbling joy-nectar of the distant spit of bees now dry and dead.

TED: You're a little over the top tonight.

SYLVIA: Over the top! Excuse the shit out of me. I'll subside. *(She is silent.)*

TED: I know what's going on with you.

SYLVIA: Oh, you know what's going on with me. You know what's going on with me.

TED: You're angry because you don't have a dick.

SYLVIA: What?

TED: That's not completely true. You're angry because you don't have a dick, and you can't write. I have a penis, I have a pen. I can piss for yards and yards. You know, I could write poems on a highway divider. I don't wear out Ouija boards and consult fifteen horoscopes before *not* writing all day. I just write down what's on my mind, I guess you could say I'm alive.

SYLVIA: Well—gee, everything's about ready.

TED: Did I hurt your feelings? *(Pause)* Then why are you smiling?

SYLVIA: *(Screams)* Stop yelling at me.

TED: Yes, there! Just, BE there, in—that! place. That hurt place. Breathe from there.

(She starts to cry.)

TED: That's right. It's all right. I'm here. Come here.

(She gets in his lap.)

TED: Better?

(Pause. She nods.)

TED: Sorry. I just sensed you needed to be lanced. Like a boil.

SYLVIA: Honey. Is it tame? Our life, I mean?

TED: No.

SYLVIA: *(Earnestly, sweetly)* Because, if you want something different, just tell me. I can be other things, for you. I mean, I can't be one of your eighteen-year-old students, but then, they can't read your work with any discrimination, with any critical insight. They can't see where it starts to be less than honest, where you're bluffing, where it starts to suck. See, I can.

TED: Give it a rest, huh?

SYLVIA: Let's do something completely unexpected. Let's make love. Right here in the mashed potatoes. Here and now.

TED: *(Surprised. Pleased)* Big silly slut— *(He reaches for her.)*

SYLVIA: I'll just put some newspaper under the dish. *(She gets up.)*

TED: Well, then. That isn't exactly here and now, is it.

SYLVIA: It will be here and now in just a second.

TED: But the here and now you wanted to jump into is dead and gone.

SYLVIA: Oh, don't be so pedantic.

TED: I'm not pedantic! How dare you call me pedantic!

SYLVIA: Well, you're not UN-pedantic, I mean, it's not an insult—

TED: *(Exploding in frustration)* Aggghhhhh!

SYLVIA: What. What's the matter?

TED: Nothing.

SYLVIA: Don't you want to tell me?

TED: I'm going out for a walk.

SYLVIA: You are not! I will not have you walking out on me!

TED: Get out of my way.

SYLVIA: *(Swiping at him)* Noo! You stay here and fight with me man to man!

TED: I can't fight with you man to man!

SYLVIA: Yes, you can. Yes, you can, yes, you can! Do it! I know you want to do it! I dare you. Do it, you bastard!

(She starts pushing him. He grabs her and pins her arms.)

SYLVIA: Ow, stop it, you're hurting me!

(He rushes her and they start to tussle. He bends her back over the table. They have sex. They do not hear each other's fantasies.)

SYLVIA: I cannot SCREAM
You have cut out my tongue
Nazi scientist!

TED: Too young for a stewardess, who can she be?
This red-headed one who wants me—

SYLVIA: My Jew blood sinks into the slate
Hey S S Mister, take my—

SYLVIA & TED: Sister!—Sisters?

TED: My shaggy flanks burn—
For a bottle of beer and a long fuck—

SYLVIA: It is the time of the gouge and pluck
I tremble and curse my luck—

TED: There are no names here—
That way seems truest—

SYLVIA: I am no name to him, just Jewess —

TED: We three, happy, in the long tall grass—
Just me, two jolly sisters,
Balls and ass—!

(He comes. Pause.)

SYLVIA: *(In a terrible level voice.)* He has slit me open
In this place where Jack gutted his sluts—

(TED *gets off of* SYLVIA. *Buttons himself up)*

TED: Baby, I'm so sorry. Look at you. I'm an animal. I don't know my own strength. You have mashed potatoes in your hair. Oh, spinach on your white blouse. Now, that was great.

(Silence)

TED: Baby, what's the matter? I said that was great! I forgot you were my wife!

(Silence)

TED: Oh, get over it. What's the matter? Look, I'm not going to apologize. Oh, baby, say something. Please say something.

SYLVIA: Look what you did to my arm. It's all purple.

TED: Yeah.

SYLVIA: And my skirt's ruined!

TED: I'll buy you a new one. As soon as I get a job.

SYLVIA: Oh. God. I feel—really— *(Pause)* Good! Really good! Ted!

Scene Five

(Outside. One month later)

TED: And this is the wisdom of wolf—
In the beginning was the howl—
In the middle was the owl pellet—
And in the end will be the memory of meals.

STONER: *(Entering)* What the fuck is that supposed to mean?

TED: What does it sound like?

STONER: Nothing!

TED: That's right. Cold freezing nothing...out of which we must invent ourselves from a stone and a fart. Like Wolf.

(TED *and* STONER *are now taking a walk.)*

STONER: That's the most insidious crap I ever heard.

TED: *(Crestfallen)* Oh, really? Do you think so?

STONER: Save it for your students, son. I wrote the book on bullshit.

TED: Ha. Marvelous! Marvelous!

STONER: Ha-ha-ha! You actually snow people with this shit. I like you, young Ted. I want you to call me Bob-Father. I've never invited anyone, before.

TED: Bob-Father! Do you mean it? I never had a proper father. Bob-fath—

STONER: "I walk through the chill New England copses, wearing Vera's hand knit sockses." That's the only verse I've written all year, and I have the feeling that I didn't write that, either. I think maybe I heard it somewhere. You know, this is the very coast where perhaps Mather himself walked, wrestling with his God, and all I hear is the mocking hoot of a distant garbage barge.

TED: *(Excited)* But, that, what you just said, about the mockery of a distant garbage barge! There it is! You're meeting the great emptiness, just as he did! Now, that—is powerful!

STONER: Who do you think I am? Fucking Robert Frost? Meet the great emptiness! That's too damn easy, my boy. You small, sorry men!— (don't be offended—I'm very fond of you, personally)—you small, sorry men! You've gone and pulled God down from the sky to shape Him to your own devices.

TED: Well, He didn't put up much of a fucking fight, did He?

STONER: Aha-ha-ha, aha-ha-ha! You have no idea how funny that is.

TED: What do you mean?

STONER: As if He has to try and fight! He's laughing while he waits, quiet and slack as a pussycat as you do what you want, rewriting him to fit your beast-nature.

TED: I think we'll find instinct a better God than some old man with a beard and a stone tablet.

STONER: You'll have to kill me. We can't both be right.

TED: Oh, not so. Not. So. The world to come embraces contradiction. Why look at you, Old Calvinist like you, you've left your wife again.

STONER: I'm a miserable old bastard. I can't wait to die. Except that I feel all right, just now. And it's true. I am in love, one last time. Isn't a woman just a wonder?

TED: Once a woman throws her legs over your head, you're finished.

STONER: Ah! Aha-ha-ha! You put me in such a good mood, Teddy Bear. It's so refreshing to have changed women. You'd think that sex wears off when you stop having it. But it doesn't. It just keeps getting better.

Scene Six

(Meanwhile. Interior)

(SYLVIA's kitchen. SYLVIA and ANNE are making dinner, rather SYLVIA is. ANNE smokes and nurses her drink.)

ANNE: *(Dreamy)* Baby, if you had it to do over again...would you still use a razor blade?

SYLVIA: I don't know if I could, again. That was almost an accident. I didn't know I'd cut myself 'til I saw blood. Like a gorgeous blossom.

ANNE: Sylvia, I just admire you so much. I could never cut. I'm a big coward. Booze and pills. If I didn't have my kill-me pills, I wouldn't have even tried once.

SYLVIA: I could drown. The great welcoming arms of the sea—.

ANNE: Ha! Virginia! Dazzling.

SYLVIA: Jumping off a bridge, falling in front of a subway car, what else—what else—pass me the spatula? That's a whisk.

ANNE: Swallowing lye? I mean, it's always right under the sink—it's there—oh, no. No.

SYLVIA: Yes! Yes! Yes!

ANNE: God, you're something. I just don't think I have it in me.

SYLVIA: Eating fire, like the daughter of a God?

ANNE: No, I mean—all this—pie crusts—. Look at you go!

SYLVIA: Oh, it's easy. Oh, I know, I know, gas!

ANNE: Gas, yes!

SYLVIA: Jumping?

ANNE: Are you nuts?

SYLVIA: Burning alive?

ANNE: God! —Your whole skin rolling up like a big garage door!

SYLVIA: Intestines roasting before your eyes, like the Indians used to—

ANNE: Oh, Sylvia, Sylvia—we have fun together! The little sister I never had!

SYLVIA: My new dark auntie!

(They hug. SYLVIA breaks off abruptly.)

SYLVIA: That's enough. Oh. I'm sorry. It's just I—

ANNE: You don't have to explain anything to me! Do I need manners! Fuck manners! Mother, impeccably pleasant to the help, and then she went and douched me with carpet cleaner!

SYLVIA: My God, did that really happen?

ANNE: Doctor and I were never totally sure. But if it didn't, I must have felt it necessary to invent. And why? Tell me what you feel and I will never punish you! "Back off, Annie! I don't like to be touched!" Yes! Give me that! What are you working on?

SYLVIA: Perhaps a chanty about a woman lit like a wick by the hot quick flame of a man. Oh, I know one! Gun—blam!

ANNE: No, I couldn't take having my face spattered all over. I mean, it's happening all ready! *(Feeling her chin, anxiously)* I used to have a profile like a Greek coin!

SYLVIA: Oh, no, you look wonderful! For your age!

ANNE: Honey, I don't care. In a way, I mean. Do you know what Daddy-Bob said to me? He told me that decay sets in so that divine love can get in the cracks! Isn't he mad and marvelous? Oh, I still believe in death, more than ever, but I'm becoming much more wholesome. Where did you put that scotch? It's all Stoner, cracked old minister. And we go to all the best parties! Dinner at Allen Ginsberg's next week! Just with him and Peter!

Scene Seven

(Same. TED *and* STONER *approach from outside.)*

STONER: *(Entering)* I'm not going.

*(*TED *enters behind him.)*

TED: Look, Sylvia, we found a horseshoe crab!

SYLVIA: Not on the table. Put him outside.

ANNE: Oh, look at him! Isn't he marvelous! Like a big, ugly, spiky shoe! Can I touch it?

(A moment between TED *and* ANNE*)*

STONER: *(To* ANNE*)* I said I'm not going!

SYLVIA: *(To* TED*)* Porch! Quick march!

ANNE: *(Crossing to* STONER*)* Of course you're going, lover. Ginsberg's the big new thing.

STONER: Well, I'm the big old thing, and I won't go. I hate his work.

TED: *(Getting drinks)* Why, Bob-Father? Don't you think it's remarkable in its power, its anger, and the purity of its vision?

STONER: I think it's a sad day in hell when a big fruit like that provides the defining voice of his generation.

ANNE: Lover, it doesn't matter if he loves ladies, boys, or pussycats. Love is love.

STONER: Men don't matter? Women don't matter? Destroy the principalities of creation themselves?

SYLVIA: But, Doctor Stoner, you write all about adultery and pills and being insane.

STONER: Well, I write that it's a damn shame, too, don't I? I don't put it forth as a new damn religion, do I?

TED: Daddy-Bob, I think you fail to understand something. The old dualities are over. Read Jung! Freud! For instance, the Communists, are they the devil? They think we're the devil! Hysteria! We do it with everything! Take sex!

ANNE: Yes! Please!

TED: The good, clean wisdom of the body, the ecstatic, the defining experience! Dirty *that*, now *that's* pornography!

ANNE:	SYLVIA:
Yes.	Now, I don't know about—

TED: Ah, ah, ah! And is it also coincidence that the people that are the most sexually terrified are the most rabid anti-Communists?

ANNE:	SYLVIA:
Ah. So true!	That's complete nonsen—!

TED: No, no, think about that. It's true, it's true, it's—

STONER: The world is turning. I'm sorry to see it. The destruction of species. This constant intermarriage of Italians and Jews. Ancient identities are being lost. The foundations of manhood and womanhood disappear. And God is no longer speaking to us.

SYLVIA: God never spoke to us!

(Pause)

STONER: Well, that's true. But we always listened anyway. And out of that listening came everything wonderful. But we don't need him anymore.

ANNE: So gloomy! So gloomy! I think we're missing the celebration that is lurking just around the corner! That nothing's really wrong, anymore! Except the really wrong things, of course...

STONER: And you say that as if you've said something simple.

ANNE: Look, it's like...I don't need to write in rhyming couplets. You know how hard I work to find new meters, and once I do, I stick to them, but it's play, not fear, that gives me my structure. And I think that's a damn good metaphor for living.

TED: Play, not fear. I like that. Like marriage. It's a choice, not a jail sentence or a coffin.

SYLVIA: But it's serious play. I mean, we take its limitations seriously. We took an oath, I mean. To care for each other exclusively and eternally. That's not all that playful. It's more like sacred.

TED: Can't the sacred be playful? I mean, look, as long as the impulse is there, then the oath is a true oath. But once it's gone, the truth of the emotion, then who cares if there was any bloody oath or not?

SYLVIA: But if we knew emotion was always there, then there wouldn't be any such thing as an oath. An oath before God is to give you strength for those times when—

TED: When what?

SYLVIA: When the emotion isn't there.

TED: Look, if something's dead, bury it!

SYLVIA: But marriage. It's inevitable that the flesh lose its luster. *Literally*, it does. *You* know about that, Anne, I mean, we were talking about that before. Without some kind of, well, moral commitment, sex is disgusting.

TED: It's supposed to be disgusting. That's what it's about, being disgusting. My God, if you can't embrace the wonderful, obscene, disgustingness of sex, you might as well not bother.

SYLVIA: I've been trying!

TED: It's not a matter of trying. Either you respond to the great howl of life in death...

ANNE: Or you don't. I know what you mean, Ted. I had to learn to love words. But, boy, I always loved to fuck!

(*She laughs,* TED *laughs, looks at her.* SYLVIA *starts to speak.* STONER *bursts out.*)

STONER: I walk down the cobbled streets of Old Boston
Litter fills the gutter—
A vicious drunk accosts one—
His red face frightens with its yellow eye—
Its stained grizzle—until I see—
Oh, my Christ—it's me!

ANNE: You old monster! No one says it like you do!

STONER: Reflected in the nighttime windows of Filene's.
"On Sale" shrieks the sign.
Our souls are what's on sale
What ever happened to the City on the Hill?
The silence makes my heart bleed,
But I bear the wound as mine.

TED: Bear the wound as mine...yes!

STONER: Stinking drunk and puking in the alley, I'm—
Just like every Puritan before there was Valium!
You, Ted. Go, Sonny-Ted! Spit out your beliefs! Dare them out!

TED: A baby lemur's eyes—
Big as headlights—
They swing this way and that.

ANNE: Oh, poor thing, I bet he wants his Mama!

TED: His big lamps strain
For any sight of his vanished Mama—
Two weeks since she disappeared
He looks over his branch
And into a howling void.
In anguish bites off head of snail
Suddenly, he feels much better—
So much for milk—!

STONER: Ha! So much for milk...Annie Fannie! It's a regular happening
like asshole Thornberg's! Go! Go! Say the true thing!

ANNE: What's that noise?
Ooops, just one of my chins hitting the floor—
Let Mama sleep a little later—
She's been out all night with her little,
Blue, yellow, pink lovers again—

TED: Ha!

ANNE: Oh, a man or two still shows up when I hold up my steaming bowl
of grapes—

(The men may support her with sound, or percussive rhythm as her poem builds.)

TED: Yes! Yes!

ANNE: *(Shutting her eyes, swaying)*
But I'm no dummy, and tell truth,
The game just ain't the same...
Now, I'm starting to believe, that it just might be
You, Jesus—
Making my skin crumble,

Making my teeth get these tiny cracks—
As long as it's someone, Sweet God, Baby,
As long as it's only You,
Well, I can be gallant to the bitterest, see if I can't!

(Men laughing and applaud.)

ANNE: Sylvia, baby, share with us...can you do a little something?

SYLVIA: Oh, I, gee, there's nothing I really feel comfortable...

(EMILY appears in window. Only SYLVIA, terrified, senses her presence. The others are momentarily frozen.)

EMILY: I've got one you can have.

The *freezing* can extrapolate
Just what a glacier—
Be—
When ice skates race across your
Heart
You murmur—
That is He—

(EMILY disappears.)

STONER: What's that smell? Like wood-smoke?

TED: Come on, honey, what about the myth poem you started?

SYLVIA: Myth poem?

TED: You know, the thing, where she used to be the goddess but now she's going cheap on the docks?

SYLVIA: Oh, no, that's not ready...

TED: "Your ritual wound is a price tag now, snot-face German schoolboys suck on your serpent curls—" It's good!

SYLVIA: *(Screaming)* I've got a soufflé! It's got to come out!

(Shocked silence)

ANNE: *(Covering)* Well, damn, let's get it on the table then!

STONER: Why did we stop? We were having fun, dammit! Fun!

ANNE: Come sit at the table, honey.

TED: Sylvia? Can I help you?

SYLVIA: Look. I'm perfectly fine.

Scene Eight

(After supper)

(STONER is asleep in a chair. SYLVIA is at the table. ANNE and TED are outside in the moonlight.)

ANNE: God forgive me. But He always does.

TED: Don't talk. Don't think.

ANNE: She can't ever, ever, know. You must protect her.

TED: Don't worry.

ANNE: What about him?

TED: If a tree falls in a forest...

ANNE: I'm falling.

TED: So am I.

ANNE: This will never happen again. And I am only weak because I'm dying.

TED: We're all dying.

ANNE: Yes. Yes. Oh, yes.

(They kiss and slowly move down onto the ground. Lights up on SYLVIA at table, writing. EMILY in hovering in the window frame behind. SYLVIA does not see her.)

SYLVIA: *(Reads slowly)* The moon drags her pus-bag over the marsh.
Scabs crackle, and old wounds
Part their thighs, again...
(Begins to write. She speaks the words as she struggles to finish the poem.)
When he touches my face, he feels a fine white dust.
We bury our fear in each other,
Like dogs humping in a midnight boneyard...

I don't know. Something like that?

(SYLVIA bends her head over the page. EMILY nods, thoughtfully.)

END OF ACT TWO

ACT THREE

Scene One

(TED *and* SYLVIA'*s house*)

(TED *is hypnotizing* SYLVIA.)

TED: Breathe into my hand. Let your face soften. Heavy, soft, thick and fleshy.

SYLVIA: My face feels like an old potato. I can feel actually feel my lack of bone structure. Yuuch.

TED: Let go judgment. Let go the critic. That's your mother. That's your mirror. You are going to meet your guide. I am going to count from one to five. You are going deeper and deeper into the spirit world. The world of the ancestors. One. Two.

SYLVIA: Aaahh! Aaahhh! You're scaring me!

TED: Don't be afraid. What are you seeing? Three. Four. Close your eyes and wait. Go deeper and deeper into your blackness. Five. Where are you?

SYLVIA: I'm hearing...

TED: Mmmm...

SYLVIA: A jingling...a tramping...oh, they are carrying something—

TED: Who?

SYLVIA: It looks like...these little men. They are wearing these skirts made of skins, and bones...

TED: Yes?

SYLVIA: They are chanting and murmuring.

TED: What do you hear?

SYLVIA: I can't make out the words.

TED: Forget words. What do you here? The sound, the sound.

SYLVIA: It sounds like...tsimpapa, managuwe, tsimpapa, managuwe, awiah, awiah, awiah...tsimpapa...

TED: What do you see?

SYLVIA: They are dancing into a clearing. Tsimpapa, managuwe, tsimpapa, and then another group of them come staggering in. They are carrying something—

TED: Yes?

SYLVIA: A kind of cage...on their shoulders. It's braided with all these big flowers, like poinsettias, maybe, or hibiscus. Inside there's this big fat, huge, brown woman. Her hair is long and oily, kind of blue-black. She's naked, and her breasts are like gallon jugs, but all flattened out. Her thighs are so big that there's only a "V" down there. Just a triangle, no hair. She's smiling and smiling, and her smile is all gums! What happened to her teeth? Her mouth is bloody. Oh, Ted, they pulled out her teeth!

TED: Ritual purposes. Blow jobs or something. It's all right. Now what's happening?

SYLVIA: They're putting the cage down on the ground and opening the door. She's smiling, and she's lying down. A little man is going to her. He's getting on top of her. Oh, I can't look at this anymore. It's repulsive! All that brown greasy fat! Her feet are so little, and the soles are black with dirt! They are all chanting!

TED: What! What!

SYLVIA: Bab-weh, bab-weh, bab-weh! He's going up and down on her, and everyone is smiling. Some of the men are masturbating. I'm going to throw up!

TED: Get through it. This is your vision. What's the woman doing?

SYLVIA: Her eyes are rolling back like an idiot. She's not happy, not sad, just lying there. Her arms are around the man. Her legs are around the man.

TED: Good. Yes. Good. Now what?

SYLVIA: Oh! (Surprised. Perhaps pleasantly) Oh. Oh!

TED: What do you see?

SYLVIA: Oh, Ted! She's breaking the man's back with her legs! She's folding him!

TED: Really? Are you sure?

SYLVIA: (Intensely) Yes! She, it looks like she's inhaling him, or something, it's like a whirlpool, or a blender! He's getting broken!

TED: Are you positive? How are the other men reacting?

SYLVIA: They are dropping their musical instruments! The ones that were playing with themselves just stopped. Some of them are running out of the clearing. Some of them are on their knees. What could this mean?

TED: How about the little fellow?

SYLVIA: She's, oh my God! She's swallowing him! His head and his arms and legs are sticking out, but they are getting pulled into her! It's like watching a birth, but in reverse! This is fantastic! Oh, Ted, I wish you could see this!

TED: My God.

SYLVIA: Her face! It looks different. She's not frightened. She's big as a house, she's getting bigger! Ha ha, yes! Yes! Yes! Om balala, Mehyah!

TED: What? What's that you're saying?

SYLVIA: I didn't say anything. All the men have run off now. The little man is gone, almost. There's just one little finger sticking out from her, oops, now that's gone too. She's just lying there. She's humming.

TED: That's enough. I'm bringing you back up, now. You are swimming back to the here and now. Into your body, into this room. You are swimming into the present. I'm going to count from five. When I get to one, you will be with me. Happy, alert, and ready to fix dinner. Five, four, three, two, one.

SYLVIA: Wow! What happened?

TED: You had a vision.

SYLVIA: Oh, I did? Oh! That's wonderful. Did you tape-record it?

TED: No. But I made some notes.

SYLVIA: *(Reading them)* It's starting to come back! Was I speaking in tongues?

TED: Yes, you were. Good for you.

SYLVIA: Did I bypass my intellect?

TED: I think so. Yes. Definitely.

SYLVIA: Oh, I can use this! This is so exciting!

TED: Terrific.

SYLVIA: What's the matter? Are you sulking?

TED: No. Of course not.

SYLVIA: You are. You are sulking. Is big sulky Ted mad wif his Syvie?

TED: Don't be ridiculous.

SYLVIA: Oh, baby. I really had some kind of vision. I really did, you know. I went out!

TED: All right, all right. You needn't go on and on about it.

SYLVIA: Sweetie. You're frightened!

TED: *(Savagely)* You just had a little experience, a badly needed one, a little jaunt in the unknown, and, well, I'm delighted!

Scene Two

(TED *and* SYLVIA's *house)*

(TED, STONER, ANNE, *and* SYLVIA *are at dinner.)*

ANNE: Attention, everyone, Robert has some big news. Honey?

STONER: I've finished it. The defining Mather poem. I broke that fucker's back. Ha-ha.

TED:	ANNE:
Oh, marvelous!—	And when he read it to me
	I just started to weep!
	It is an utter masterpiece!

TED: Bravo, Bob-Father—after your long incubation in darkness—

SYLVIA: Well. Gee. Can we hear it?

STONER: Oh, well. *(Clears his throat)*
In Old Nantucket, the drugstore boys spit phlegm-slick wads
Of gin-soaked Bazooka Joe into the cobblestones.
The relentless sea flickers its withered tongue
Over the ragged rocks.
A gray drizzle coats the shabby house where Cotton Mather
died with greasy rain.

Its slick rot reflects the pink and green lights
Of the new Burrito Bell.
The corpse of a drowned Nantucket Indian bangs restless
Against the sea-bell,
Alive again with every undulation of the tide
Dead for more than a century, he'd still like to sink his
Tommy-hawk into a white bonnet.

I have a floater in my eye.
It dogs me everywhere.
It curls like a dried-out tail of a Confederate horse.
I think I'll dry out again.

(A silence. ANNE *gets up and kisses his head.*

ANNE: You magnificent man. You've made me weep. Again!

TED: Really, Dr Stoner, I don't know what one can say. It's wonderful. You've put your finger on something. On a number of things, actually.

STONER: It costs, my boy. It costs. To bear witness.

SYLVIA: I think it's Taco Bell.

STONER: What?

SYLVIA: You said Burrito Bell. I think it's Taco Bell.

ANNE: *(Whispers)* He needs a B word.

SYLVIA: But it doesn't work as a symbol of New America if it isn't the right—

ANNE: SHHHH!

STONER: What's she saying, my dear?

ANNE: Nothing, she loves—

SYLVIA: *(Loudly)* It's Taco Bell. There is no such thing as Burrito Bell.

(Pause)

STONER: Are you sure?

ANNE: Now, wait a minute. I'm sure I've seen a Burrito Bell, they have all sorts of—

SYLVIA: And Cotton Mather's house was in Boston. I'm pretty sure. But other than that, it's, gee, just a great poem. So unexpected, about the floater at the end. I can tell how you got there, it was kind of unconscious, right, you were talking about a corpse of a drowned Indian, well, a drowned corpse is a floater, and floater in your eye, floater and floater, and there you were, weren't you? And there was so much water in the poem that, naturally, you wanted to dry out! *(Pause)* Anybody ready for more coffee?

ANNE: Bob, do you want some coffee?

STONER: *(Quietly)* Is that how I got floater? I'd like a brandy, please, Ted. That *is* how I got floater. Floater and floater. Oh, God. How transparent.

ANNE: Ted, he doesn't drink—

STONER: I'd like a brandy, please.

(TED gets him one. STONER drinks it and subsides into a sort of sulking coma.)

SYLVIA: Well, my God, did I say something wrong? It just occurred to me that he might want to be accurate. Everyone just goes along with everything because of his reputation, and they just let him just be wrong, and—

ANNE: *(Aside to SYLVIA)* You've destroyed his confidence for no reason at all! It's the best new poem he's written in ten years!

STONER: It's the *only* poem I've written in ten years. And she's right. I can't stand her, but she's right. It's drivel.

TED: No, Bob-Father, no! It's free, it shimmers, it marries the great, hard New England undermyth with the shifting, slimy flicker of the new Godlessness....

STONER: Who do you think I am? Fucking Matthew Arnold?

SYLVIA: Exactly, yes, Daddy-Bob. How silly, you, posing as some kind of a college existentialist when you're really a renegade Calvinist, or more recently, a failed Catholic—

TED: It is Catholicism that has failed us—

SYLVIA: Oh, how the fuck would you know, you've never been to a church where they didn't kill a chicken.

ANNE: Now hold on a minute—I think we're forgetting that God spelled backward is Dog! Good, real, shaggy, warm Dog! Not nearly as grand, but much more fun at the beach!

TED: Ha! Brilliant!

SYLVIA: Isn't it possible, Dr Stoner, I mean this is just a thought, that God is punishing you for your sins by reducing you to free association—?

STONER: Aaaghh!

ANNE: Hey, everything I write is based on free association!

SYLVIA: I know.

TED: *(Suddenly)* Oh, why can't we all stop talking, and—and—sing! Or—fuck! Or build a barn, plant a tomato plant, anything but think our dead, tired thoughts. We need a wordless anthem for our lost time, a... koan. A new reality. Let's all...shut up and look inside ourselves.

(Pause. They all look inside themselves.)

STONER: *(Brooding, upset)* When I try to look inside myself all I find that's left is a craving for nicotine and a handful of unspeakable sexual fantasies about, you know, nurses. *(Humbly)* I'm sorry. But since we're being honest.

TED: Good for you, Bob-Father! I'd rather hear about nicotine and your strange longings than all the sacred, petrified wisdom-turds of our dying civilization. Maybe I'm mad—but some nights, when I walk in the fields, I listen to the weird star-struck language of the night-birds— *(He makes a bird-call sound.)* —and I feel that the wall of illusion is about to dissolve—the bird-speak is about to become clear, that I'm on the verge of the miraculous.

ANNE: *(Moved, quietly)* Yes. Marvelous.

STONER: Idiot! You idiot!

TED:	SYLVIA:
Daddy-Bob?	Ha-ha-ha!

STONER: Understand the language of the birds? I've woken up to hear them plotting on my life! Miracles! You fool! You don't know the utter horror of miracles! I take three thousand milligrams of lithium a day to keep me from walking on water, and sometimes I do it anyway!

TED: I'm sorry—I didn't mean...

STONER: You think all creation's some big Hindu illusion? You wing-growing bastard. Turn yourself into a goddamn bald eagle. And I hope some teenager pops you with his daddy's shotgun.

ANNE: Testy! Testy!

STONER: Think you're the first man to dream of wings? You've never experienced the horrible freedom of the winged mad. You want a miracle? Try this one! One and one make two! But you won't stop 'til they make three! Or cat!

TED: Bob-Father, you're excited. I think you misunderstand what the Zen-masters are saying.

STONER: I'm saying have the guts to call a spade a spade, recognize the cold hard law of gravity for what it is, which is the grace of God—recognize how many angels are at work each day insuring that Newton's apple continues to fall down, down, down, not up into the ozone with all your Zuni medicine men flapping around as bats and hoot owls along with *me* when I forget to take my pills! Have the guts to give glory to the truth! *(Quietly)* If only that, we should have the guts to give glory to what truths we can.

SYLVIA: *(Odd, avid)* Like what, Daddy-Bob?

STONER: Like—

SYLVIA: Go on.

STONER: Like the truth that I'm an old, washed-up has-been and ten years past being any kind of man at all.

ANNE: Oh, lover, what are you talking about?

STONER: You're very sweet, my dear, and very slick. And I've been slick, too, haven't I? I never let on that I know of your little recreations, do I?

ANNE: Oh, baby! What an idea!

STONER: You know what? I sneak around. I follow her. The Poet Laureate of the United States of America. I dog her like a spy. To doctor's offices and shabby student apartments, and once, oh, once, she betrayed me with her own husband! I know! I'm an old bastard, but I'm not a complete fool!

ANNE: Robert, we agreed to trust each other!

STONER: But that was when I thought you'd stick with me.

ANNE: Honey, I have my own way of sticking with you. We didn't make rules.

STONER: Bad enough that I'm washed up, but to be such a sorry old cuckold in the bargain, bewitched by an aging vixen!

SYLVIA: *(Delighted)* "Aging Vixen!" Now what's the point of saying things like "Aging Vixen!"

ANNE: *(Angry)* Baby, you don't get to be a cuckold if you can't stick it in.

(Pause)

STONER: *(Devastated)* Oh, Anne. Once you told me that you loved our naps and cozy lie-downs. That I delivered you from yourself! That our love was carnal in the best of all Platonic worlds!

ANNE: Well, maybe the best of all Platonic worlds doesn't make it when you need a man's warm love-stick in you, stirring away your troubles!

SYLVIA: You are disgusting!

TED: There's nothing disgusting about people trying to carve some kind of comfort out of the howling blackness that calls itself life.

SYLVIA: Oh, please. The only howling blackness around is you. What would you know about comfort.

ANNE: He comforted me pretty good, once.

SYLVIA: What?

ANNE: Gee. Me and my big mouth.

STONER: *(Anguished)* No! No! No! You did it with him? My adopted son Tedipus?

(Pause)

SYLVIA: What?

TED: I'm not quite sure...what is going on, here—

SYLVIA: What's going on is it's out and you can't stuff it back in.

TED: But it's not true!

ANNE: Baby, it's no use. Truth is out and truth will make us free, and I think we need a healing, here.

SYLVIA: Shut up. Ted, I want you to tell me. Say it!

TED: All right! All right! You asked for it. I know this sounds—try to understand this. It—allowed me to bring—more of myself to you. And I never thought you'd know. If a tree falls in the forest—

SYLVIA: It hits the ground all the same, you bastard!

TED: I won't apologize for nothing! It was *less* than nothing!

ANNE: Oh, really?

SYLVIA: Nothing, nothing, and nothing.

ANNE: I said I'm sorry, and I meant it.

SYLVIA: I said shut up.

TED: Don't make such a big fucking deal about it! One bloody time in our whole marriage!

STONER: Oh, Son, it was wrong. You should have left her to me. You had all those students and actresses already, you could have left me this withered Jezebel for my dotage!

SYLVIA & ANNE: Students! Actresses! Withered Jezebel!

TED: All right! Yes! What! I've got a hunger in me—it's who I am, see? This is my life!

ANNE: Robert!

SYLVIA: *(Swivels her head to look at* ANNE*)* You abomination!

ANNE: I'm leaving. Bob, are you coming? I said are you coming with me?

STONER: No, strumpet! I could have born the rest, but to shame me with my adopted son! I want to go back to Vera! What's her address?

TED: Bob-Father—

STONER: No!

TED: Look, Sylvia—I know you don't see it this way right now, but I think this will be very good for us, this coming forward with—Bob-Father—forgive me.

STONER: I'm not your Bob-Father! Meet the great emptiness! You and your Buddhist crap! *I'm* the great emptiness! Let's meet! I told you you would have to kill me! *(Gets up and starts swinging at* TED.*)*

TED: I said forgive me.

*(*STONER *picks up a wine bottle.)* ANNE: Stop it! Stop it! Put that down!

STONER: *(Throws it into the ceiling)* Fire storm! Rejoice!

ANNE: Help! Help me, Sylvia!

*(*STONER *throws wine glass into the ceiling.)*

STONER: Hailstorm!

SYLVIA & STONER: Rejoice!

*(*STONER *breaks out of murderous hallucination in terror.)*

STONER: Annie, Annie, come and get me! I'm so afraid!

ANNE: I'm here, lover, I'm— *(She tries to get close to him.)*

STONER: *(He swings at* ANNE, *frenzied)* Painted Harpy! *(She leaves, devastated.)*

STONER: *(To* TED*)* Bastard of a Rat-Son!

(Seizes TED *and drags him over to the window, forcing him out. Hangs him out over the drop by his arms)*

TED: Shit! You're breaking my fucking arm!

STONER: —Him the almighty power
Hurled headlong flaming from the
Ethereal sky—aha ha ha!

TED: Let me up! You old shit!

STONER: —With hideous ruin and combustion down
To bottomless perdition, there to dwell—
Now show me *yours*, pretty Boy! Do the shak shaka shaka one! Do it!

TED: *Shak shaka shak shaka—*
Sylvia!
shaka shaka shaka shak

TED:	STONER:
Call the police!	—in Adamantine Chains
Shaka shaka shaka shak!	and penal Fire—who
	durst defie th'
	Omnipotent to Arms!!

STONER: How do you like them apples! Now *that's* a piece of work! You free associating, jingle-writing wife-stealing scribbler-dibbler! And that's just off the top of my fucking head!

TED: It's off the top of Milton's fucking head!

STONER: What's that you say?

TED: It's from Paradise Lost! Everyone knows that.

STONER: *(Concerned)* They do?

TED: You can call me thin but I write my own fucking ticket. Oh, go ahead. Let go.

SYLVIA: Do it! Smash him! Kill him! Let him fall!

*(*STONER *looks at her, pulls* TED *up.)*

STONER: I'm so tired.

(He pulls TED *inside.* TED *drops to floor, holding his arm.)*

STONER: Where the hell am I? Who opened this window? I'm freezing. Anne? Anne?

SYLVIA: She's gone.

STONER: Did I say something?

SYLVIA: Dr Stoner, there's going to be a black mass in this room in about five minutes. I don't think you want to be here when the girls arrive.

STONER: *(Scuttling towards the door)* Awfully decent of you. Thanks for the tip—

SYLVIA: Out! *(She opens the grate of wood-burning stove and jabs at burning coals with a poker. Picks up a bound manuscript from a shelf. Dumps it onto the fire.)*

TED: My arm...is broken...what are you doing!

SYLVIA: Cold in here.

TED: My manuscript!

SYLVIA: Not anymore! *(Prodding the embers with poker)*

TED: *(Staring into flames)* You—

SYLVIA: Move please.

TED: You—cunt.

SYLVIA: *(Holding poker at his stomach. Screams)* Get out!

Scene Three

(Same)

(SYLVIA is sitting at the table. She has an open notebook. EMILY is with her drinking coffee.)

SYLVIA: I say three magic words—
I hate you.
The sun just rose.
My first haiku.

EMILY: I admire that. I could never say that.

SYLVIA: Would you like some more coffee?

EMILY: Oh, no. It goes right through me.

SYLVIA: Most of them are about my husband, but this one is for my mother.
Old red bladder, eyes like foreskins
I am sick to death of your love-tentacles—

EMILY: You're scaring me.

SYLVIA: It was you in the root cellar, Mommy—
With your nuzzling suction cups—

EMILY: I can't stay very long today. I have a feeling that Someone...might show up.

SYLVIA: You just don't get it, do you?

EMILY: *(Heading for the window)* I'll just slip out while you're having such a wonderful hot streak. You remind me of me in 1862. What a year I had—

(SYLVIA swivels her head to look at EMILY.)

EMILY: I won't bore you.

SYLVIA: Hey, not so fast—*I* invited *you*.

(EMILY slinks back to her seat, and sits down, miserable.)

SYLVIA: Haven't you figured out that there's no one out there? You've been wandering around in the dark for a hundred years. No one's even lit a match.

EMILY: You can be awfully mean.

SYLVIA: I'm going to be joining you soon. EMILY: Look before you leap!

SYLVIA: All roads lead to Rome. This collection is going to make my name.

EMILY: W-What are you going to call it?

SYLVIA: *(Lovingly stroking her notebook)* "The Blood Tide."

(SYLVIA puts on a pair of red gloves and crosses into Interview area with her notebook.)

Scene Four

(A radio program)

(INTERVIEWER is sitting with SYLVIA.)

INTERVIEWER: Good evening, and welcome to "Pot Shots." We're visiting with poet Sylvia Fluellen, author of the recent run-away best seller, "The Blood Tide." "I don't read poetry, but I read Fluellen" is a comment that we've heard again and again in the past few weeks. Sylvia Fluellen, reading from her extraordinary new collection.

SYLVIA: You liked to feel a flutter on your tongue
Or you complained that dinner was overdone.
I tried to please you, to keep you
In live insects, terrified prawns,
Things that would resist your teeth,

But then you wanted sucklings,
And I prayed and plucked a kitten from behind the stove,
Sleepy at its mother's dug.

My kitchen was a chamber of horrors!
Piglets shrieked as you bit their heads off.
After the sow, which you ate in fifteen minutes,
I knew that I was next.

I packed my suitcase. I could hear you on the stair.
I threw the family spaniel at you—
You bit him in two.
I jumped out the window!

I managed to distract you in the lane by pointing out the
Neighbor's cow—
The last time I saw you,
You were squatting in the moonlight,
With a leg bone in your jaws.

I've changed my name, and I move every week.
I wear a strong perfume so you can't snuff me out.
The papers are awash with your atrocities.

No one knows what's going on
There is a crime wave in this city.
And I'm unmasking you!

Scene Five

(Later)

(ANNE's bedroom)

(ANNE sits on the bed. Her nightstand holds her vodka bottle, and a multitude of prescription bottles. She's drunk, but steady.)

ANNE: Most gals would dress in their best black for the most important date of their lives. Not me. For you, honey, I'm putting on the softest blue dress with a mauve scarf. I've always known that you like the most tender colors. *(She begins to dress and make up her face.)* Just make yourself comfortable. I won't be long. The thing I like about you is, I don't have to maintain any mystery. We've been intimate for years. I've always thought you were a real softy. The one that loved a girl for what she was inside. You really want to get inside. Not just inside the way most guys want to, but you want to tear a girl apart the way other men only dream of. And I'll tell you what. I don't think it will be so bad. I think it will be all right. When I first saw lines around my eyes and mouth, when my knees first started to get a little baggy, my trim brown knees, I cried. I thought you were the enemy, the corroding tide that would carry me farther and farther away from the shores of love. Men all say I'll love you when you're old, but they only like to say it to you when you're really young. They can't do it, poor things, they'd like to but they just can't. But you. You've been gentle, you've been slow. But you've rained your constant acid kisses down on my poor flesh since the day I first bloomed. And you've never left my side. It's been you, perched jealously at the top of every bed where I groaned in joy. It's been you sucking away my beauty through a twenty-year-long straw. And now I understand that it's because you love me. You love me so truly you've been sucking me out of myself. Blasting my body so that I'll leave it finally, to be with you. You want to eat me. Well, I surrender. I don't know what it will be like. But I think maybe you know more about this than I. *(Starts swallowing pills by handful)*

Scene Six

(Later)

(SYLVIA's *kitchen*)

(SYLVIA *is alone, wiping dishes.*)

SYLVIA: It's almost over, I can feel it.

EMILY: *(Rushing in)* I've been doing some thinking. Don't throw in the towel.

SYLVIA: Throw in the towel? You misunderstand.

EMILY: You are just about to break.

SYLVIA: Oh, yes.

EMILY: The Blood Tide. Wow. I could never have written that. *(Her greatest compliment)* It was—*appalling*! And I'm a tough audience! Now, I know how upset you are about, well—

SYLVIA: Marriage is forever. He's about to find out.

EMILY: Don't get me wrong, I'd love your company. I'm just....

SYLVIA: Afraid? That I'll walk all over you? I just might.

EMILY: *(Desperate)*
I cannot think you dead—
That sunshine smile—
Those —
(EMILY *slaps herself in the face at a look from* SYLVIA.)

SYLVIA: I'll be going home, now. *(She carefully selects a frying pan and a wire whisk. Holding her implements like sacred flails, she climbs up into the window ledge and stands, the back lit image of a sacred domestic Goddess. She whistles shrilly to attract attention from the road below.)* He pushed me!!! *(She falls out of window.)*

(EMILY runs to SYLVIA's frame and bends out, watching.)

EMILY: *(Hand to her mouth. Looking out the window)* Oh, my! Now that's what I call guts.

Scene Seven

(Later)

(A classroom)

(TED is teaching.)

TED: When the poet writes, "Dead leaves to where there are no roses are..." he's talking, isn't he, about the passing of beauty into mulch, and there is the suggestion that the mulch is the bed from which beauty will evolve again.

(One of the STUDENTS puts a bloodstained veil over her head.)

VEILED STUDENT: As in, for example, the girl that was beauty turns into the mulch of the abandoned wife.

TED: Possibly, Miss...Margolis, is it? And we all know you were cast in The Bacchae and we're very happy for you, except that when we're talking about the decay of female beauty, the mulch just turns into slime, and gradually into more and more corrosive elements.

(Another STUDENT throws a plastic bag full of something slimy and green. It bursts on the wall by TED's head.)

THROWING STUDENT: Elements like truth, like the daybreak of anger, like the light of realization. Corrosive like honesty, like the power to shriek for justice!

TED: Listen. How dare you judge my life by rumor and innuendo!

(Third STUDENT stands up, wearing a pig mask.)

PIG STUDENT: No, you listen. I'm sure there are some women here who would rather hear about truth than to listen to a pedantic sadist nattering about beauty!

TED: Pedantic! I'm no pedant, young lady. I've lain eye to eye with a she-mamba, and she's the one who blinked!

THROWING STUDENT: Blinked! She jumped out a fucking window! The blood tide is rising, Mr Magus.

PIG STUDENT: It's licking your ankles, cock-sucker!

STUDENTS: *(Chanting softly)*
Shak shak shak shak shaka
Shaka shaka shak
Shak shak shak
Shak shaka shaka shaka shak

TED: What do you want!

PIG STUDENT: We want to go everywhere with you!

THROWING STUDENT: We want to be your companion!

VEILED STUDENT: Till death do us part!

PIG STUDENT: Yours!

CLASS: Shak shak shak shak!

TED: I'm going to meet my agent for lunch. And I can tell you you're not going with me. This class is fucking dismissed!

(Girls surround him. He fights his way to the door and exits. Girls follow him, chanting.)

STUDENTS: Shak shaka shaka shaka shak!

Scene Eight

(A summer evening. VERA's and STONER's cabin.)

(VERA and STONER are sitting on the porch. VERA is reading a newspaper. STONER is sunk in thought.)

VERA: *(Delicately)* I see where your young friend Ted has got some very sturdy reviews for his new book. "—Finally found his voice. Like a cloud of poisonous gas—evokes the miasma of a world gone mad. Self-aware Denial holding itself erect in shaky dignity over a cosmic abyss." Does that make any sense?

STONER: *(Sad. Quiet)* Oh, who gives a shit. There's nothing to be said anymore, and I'm not the man to say it. I'm cured of my enthusiasms, and here I am, all old and gray with my old gray wife. I'm blurred, small and soggy, ready to play model trains for the rest of my life. *(Pause)* Are you sure you want me back?

VERA: I've forgiven you.

STONER: *(Confused)* For what?

VERA: Oh, Robert! You know, I really think in many ways this was just the worst. Of your many, many spectacular betrayals. What are you looking at?

My old baby. You used to be mad for justice, like some beautiful Greek. Then you were just mad. It's really just grotesque. No, Love, not grotesque. Just, oh—God, I don't know what. Boy, I'm chilly out here. Honey, do you want me to get your sweater?

(STONER *sobs briefly.*)

VERA: What is it, Baby?

STONER: Someone just walked over my grave. I'm tired, my dear. Let's go up to bed and curl up together like sour spoons.

VERA: My old darling.

STONER: It's so quiet tonight. The girls are underground.

(They sit in silence for a moment.)

VERA: Look at that old pus-bag of a moon.

END OF PLAY

WOOLLY MAMMOTH PRODUCTION HISTORY

* denotes world premiere

1999-2000:
THE DEAD MONKEY by Nick Darke
THE DARK KALAMAZOO* by Oni Faida Lampley
BUG by Tracy Letts
STOP KISS by Diana Son
WONDER OF THE WORLD* by David Lindsay-Abaire

1998-99:
FREEDOMLAND by Amy Freed
JUNE BRIDE by Sara Felder
THE LAST ORBIT OF BILLY MARS* by Robert Alexander
THE MARRIAGE OF MR MISSISSIPPI by Friedrich Dürrenmatt
THE ART ROOM* by Billy Aronson
THE CHINESE ART OF PLACEMENT by Stanley Rutherford

1997-98:
CIVIL SEX* by Brian Freeman
BRIMSTONE AND TREACLE by Dennis Potter
THE GENE POOL* by Christi Stewart-Brown
MAN, WOMAN, DINOSAUR* by Regina Porter
PEORIA by Jon Klein
DEAD FUNNY by Terry Johnson

1996-97:
QUILLS by Doug Wright
A HUEY P NEWTON STORY by Roger G Smith
THE BIG SLAM by Bill Corbett
NEVER SWIM ALONE by Daniel MacIvor
TRIPPING THROUGH THE CAR HOUSE* by Regina Porter
RAISED IN CAPTIVITY by Nicky Silver

1995-96:
WATBANALAND by Doug Wright
RUSH LIMBAUGH IN NIGHT SCHOOL by Charlie Varon
LYNNWOOD PHARMACY* by David Bucci
THE OBITUARY BOWL* by Barbara McConagha

BIRTH AND AFTER BIRTH by Tina Howe
THE GIGLI CONCERT by Tom Murphy

1994-95:
THE ARTIFICIAL JUNGLE by Charles Ludlum
THE PITCHFORK DISNEY by Philip Ridley
THE PSYCHIC LIFE OF SAVAGES* by Amy Freed
WANTED by Al Carmines, David Epstein
NAKED BREATH by Tim Miller

1993-94:
HALF OFF* by Harry Kondoleon
GOODNIGHT DESDEMONA (GOOD MORNING JULIET) by Ann-Marie
MacDonald
Single Exposures Solo Festival:
  PORTABLES by Claire Porter
  MEN DIE SOONER by Tom Cayler
  MY QUEER BODY by Tim Miller
  RENO BESIDE MYSELF by Reno
  SALLY'S RAPE by Robbie McCauley
THE FOOD CHAIN* by Nicky Silver

1992-93:
BILLY NOBODY* by Stanley Rutherford
THE MASK* by Namu Lwanga
FREE WILL AND WANTON LUST* by Nicky Silver
THE COCKBURN RITUALS* by John Strand
STRINDBERG IN HOLLYWOOD* by Drury Pifer

1991-92:
MUD PEOPLE by Keith Huff
THE FEVER by Wallace Shawn
AFRICAN TOURIST* by Drury Pifer
LIFE DURING WARTIME by Keith Reddin
KVETCH by Steven Berkoff

1990-91:
THE ROCKY HORROR SHOW by Richard O'Brien
JON SPELMAN: ON THE BEDPOST OVERNIGHT* by Jon Spelman
FAT MEN IN SKIRTS* by Nicky Silver
DAVID'S REDHAIRED DEATH* by Sherry Kramer

1989-90:
THE DEAD MONKEY by Nick Darke
ZERO POSITIVE by Harry Kondoleon
TALES OF THE LOST FORMICANS by Constance Congdon
HURLYBURLY by David Rabe

1988-89:
CHRISTMAS ON MARS by Harry Kondoleon
THE SECOND MAN by S N Behrman
LUNA VISTA* by Douglas Gower
THE DAY ROOM by Don DeLillo

1987-88:
HARVEY by Mary Chase
SHARON AND BILLY by Alan Bowne
THE VAMPIRES by Harry Kondoleon
AUNT DAN AND LEMON by Wallace Shawn

1986-87:
TO CLOTHE THE NAKED by Luigi Pirandello
LIFE AND LIMB by Keith Reddin
NATIONAL DEFENSE* by T J Edwards
SAVAGE IN LIMBO by John Patrick Shanley

1985-86:
CHRISTMAS ON MARS by Harry Kondoleon
NEW YORK METS* by T J Edwards
AND THINGS THAT GO BUMP IN THE NIGHT by Terrence McNally

1984-85:
AMERICA HURRAH by Jean-Claude van Itallie
BLOOD MOON by Nicholas Kazan
LOOKING GLASS by Michael Sutton & Cynthia Mandelberg
THE VIENNA NOTES by Richard Nelson
METAMORPHOSIS* by Ralph Hunt

1983-84:
R U R by Karel Capek
MARIE AND BRUCE by Wallace Shawn
THE CHOIR by Errol Bray
SPACE INVADERS by Alan Spence

1982-83:
MYSTERY PLAY by Jean-Claude van Itallie
WAS HE ANYONE? by N F Simpson
SUPERIOR ATTACHMENTS* by Carroll Carlson
THE HOTHOUSE by Harold Pinter

1981-82:
THE KRAMER by Mark Medoff
VATZLAV by Slawomir Mrozek
THE EMPIRE BUILDERS by Boris Vian
LOVE MOUSE/MEYER'S ROOM by Sheldon Rosen

1980-81:
THE FROEGLE DICTUM* by the company

FITS & STARTS* by Mark Medoff
THE PLACE WHERE THE MAMMALS DIE by Jorge Diaz

CONTACT INFORMATION

Woolly Mammoth Theatre Company
1401 Church St N W
Washington DC 20005-1903
Administration: 202 234-6130
Box office: 202 393-3939
Fax: 202 667-0904
E-mail: WoollyMamm@aol.com
Web: www.woollymammoth.net

Staff
Howard Shalwitz, *Artistic Director*
Kevin Moore, *Managing Director*
Tom Prewitt, *Associate Artistic Director*
Michael Kyrioglou, *Director of Marketing & P R*
Kerri Rambow, *Director of Development*
Brian Smith, *Production Manager*
Hana Sellers, *Technical Director*
Dennis Keefe, *Audience Services Manager*
Mary Resing, *Literary Manager*
Robert Alexander, *Playwright-in-Residence*